IN HER WORDS

IN HER WORDS

Women's Writings in the
History of Christian Thought

Edited by

Amy Oden

First published in Great Britain 1995
Society for Promoting Christian Knowledge
Holy Trinity Church
Marylebone Road
London NW1 4DU

First published in the United States of America 1994
by Abingdon Press, Nashville, Tennessee

British Library Cataloguing-in-Publication Data
A catalogue record for this book is available from the British Library

ISBN 0-281-04873-8   2001 5435

Printed in the United States of America

I explained all this to you, you will recall, because I wanted to let you see the way.
Catherine of Siena

To the women whose lifework has written this book, and whose witnesses can let us see the way.

CONTENTS

CONTENTS

ACKNOWLEDGMENTS

I am blessed by communities and individuals who have provided support and challenge in this project. I thank my teacher William S. Babcock, Professor of History of Christianity and Director of the Graduate Program in Religious Studies at Southern Methodist University, for his inspiration, generosity, and tireless tutoring in Latin. I thank for all their nitty-gritty work my research assistants Kathy Bird and Barbara Bowser, and the library staff at Saint Paul School of Theology, and student assistants Bev Henson and Katie Nigh. I thank my colleagues at Saint Paul School of Theology in Kansas City, and the Wimberly School of Religion at Oklahoma City University for their kind interest in and support of my work. I thank my editor, Bob Ratcliff, for his imaginative vision of this project and for asking me to do it. I thank my family, Tal and Jane Oden, Tal and Janet Oden, Tim and Kathy Oden, and Andy and Adrienne Oden, whose spirit of inquiry and charity have shaped my work. And I thank especially my husband, Steve Lindley, and son, Walker Oden Lindley, whose lives surround me with grace.

INTRODUCTION

"Where were the women?" "What did they have to say?" "How did they shape the life and thought of the church?" For many of us, the courses we took in church history or the history of Christian theology left these questions unanswered. By implication, the impression we received was that these questions could not be answered; there was no record by women. Indeed, we have texts aplenty telling us what Christianity has thought about women, but what have women thought about Christianity?

Happily, the last quarter of the twentieth century has brought increased awareness of the status, role, and contribution of women within the history of Christianity. A wealth of research on women and religion has produced new information, new readings of existing information, new methods of interpretation, and new categories of inquiry. Still, a collection of writings of Christian women themselves has yet to be made available to a general audience. The corpus of extant women's writings within the history of Christianity is vast, rich, and diverse. This comes as a surprise to many in the light of the historical resistance within Christianity and its resident cultures to the education, speech, and writing of women. We have too easily accepted history's *dicta* against women's speech, convinced that indeed there is no record left by women.

This anthology is but a beginning in providing source documentation that represents and demonstrates the variation, range, and depth of women's written contributions to the broad spectrum of Christian thought. The purpose of this book is not so much to argue for a women's tradition that can be isolated and identified within church history, nor to focus on issues of the status of women in church and society. Rather, this collection will make available primary sources from female writers or from traditions associated with female figures and let them, as much as possible, speak for themselves on a range of issues and ideas.

The authors and excerpts included were chosen either because (1) they are representative of a class of writings; (2) they are unique in either style, form, or content; or (3) they were particularly influential at a particular point in the history of Christian thought. Nearly all of these texts emerge from Christian life explicitly grounded in some form of community, likely a primarily women's community. And nearly all found audience and application among subsequent Christian communities.

Admittedly, this anthology is limited to what women who wrote had to say about Christianity. No doubt many women who did not write, and many women who did write and whose writings were not preserved, made contributions to the range and scope of Christian thought which would substantially alter this landscape. These selections can give us only a starting place as we seek to retrieve women's contribution to the development of Christian thought.

Each writing reflects interest in and insight about doctrinal norms, theological claims, spiritual experiences, and the practical consequences of all of these for personal and ecclesial Christian life. Questions concerning the Trinity, salvation, human being, the Holy Spirit, Jesus Christ, and the mission of the Christian church are asked and answered. Many writers are gripped by the engagement of Christian thought with pressing cultural or social issues of their day. At the heart of nearly every text, however, lie basic theological claims about God and about us.

The reader will notice that in some cases, the forms in which these theological insights are expressed may not be the forms of discourse traditionally associated with theology. While Phoebe Palmer's letter to a friend on "Entire Devotion to God" and Sor Juana's *Respuesta* follow patterns of formal argument, Clare of Assisi's *Rule* and Jane de Chantal's letters of spiritual direction do not. It must be remembered, of course, that most of the theologians traditionally recognized by church historians as "great" also engaged in theological construction in the form of sermons, correspondence, "table talk," narrative, prayer, poetry, and the like.

The following reminders are offered concerning the historical nature of these texts:

1. The women in this book do not all speak in one voice, and, given the opportunity to gather together (what a wonderful thought!), would probably

find themselves in serious disagreement about many things. The different languages, nationalities, communal affiliations, races, classes, personal histories, religious experiences, and theological claims of these writers make for texts that do not all say the same thing or share the same way of speaking.

2. Just as these writers do not speak in one voice, neither do they speak with twentieth-century voices. They used the language of their day to make their claims, and seldom will it read like a feminist manifesto. In some cases, the language may sound irritatingly conventional or disappointingly stereotypical. We cannot, and should not, expect them to use categories of twentieth-century feminism. However, there is plenty of shared territory if we are careful listeners. We honor these women when we ask first what *their* questions are and what *they* see as important, when we listen carefully, and when we take each writing on its own within the historical and personal context in which it was written. Contemporary questions are urgent and valuable and must be asked. Paradoxically, we can only hear the answers in these writings when we allow their voices to speak without interruption or easy judgment. We might begin with questions such as: What did the author think was important? Why? What might have been the response of other women of her day? How might church leaders have responded?

3. In much of the writing by women in almost all periods of Christian history, self-deprecating disclaimers and phrases were used. Often self-deprecation was a literary device that would no more be left out than good grammar. This can be very jarring, or at least disconcerting, to the twentieth-century reader, but should not lead to the conclusion that these writers believed themselves lacking all authority. These writers were skillful people who, much of the time, appear to function strictly within prescribed roles. Yet the insistent and authoritative tone in these writings suggests a much broader reality. Read these writings with the presumption that the women who wrote them knew themselves to be powerful and liberating messengers of God.

4. The authorship of some texts included is not known with certainty. In some cases, such as that of Macrina, male witnesses have preserved in writing the thought and teaching of a significant female figure. In other cases, most notably Thecla and several of the martyrs, fictionalized accounts by unknown authors—perhaps male, perhaps female—have been included. In both cases, the writings warrant inclusion here because of the powerful contribution made by these women to the history of Christian

thought, even when penned by another. Nevertheless, these are exceptions and have been kept to a minimum.

5. The English translations included here are used by permission. For that reason, gender-specific language, particularly *man* or *men,* has not been made inclusive. The reader will want to be aware, however, that in many cases gender-specific language in English does not reflect gender-specific language in the original text.

In each case, introductory material is provided, although only in brief form. The focus and weight of the book is to be kept on the writers and their writings. For further study, the reader is referred to the texts from which these excerpts were taken and to the general bibliography provided. This collection is by no means exhaustive, and, as further research turns up further writings by women within the history of Christian thought, this publication anticipates the happy risk of becoming obsolete.

Amy G. Oden
Oklahoma City, Oklahoma
Feast of St. Clare 1993

SECTION I

100–600 C.E.

CHAPTER ONE

The Gospel of Mary (c. 100s)

Mary Magdalene

Mary Magdalene was a native of Magdala, a village on the western side of the sea of Galilee. Although Western tradition has mistakenly identified her with the repentant sinner spoken of yet left unnamed in Luke 7:37-50, she is only specifically identified as the one out of whom Jesus cast seven demons. We do not know what affliction she suffered, but only that her grateful response was to minister to Jesus as he traveled and preached. As his close friend, according to John 20:11-18, she was the first to see the risen Christ.

The Gospel of Mary

Supposedly authored by Mary Magdalene, this text dates from the second century and does convey a closeness between Mary and Jesus that some of the other disciples may have found enviable. In this "gospel," Mary shares her experience of Christ's coming to her in a vision to impart special knowledge and honor. While the other disciples mourn Christ's death and fear for their lives Mary claims to have a continuing experience of Christ. Peter, whom legend holds had a running rivalry with Mary Magdalene for Jesus' friendship, ridicules her vision until another disciple jumps in to defend her: "If the Savior made her worthy who are you to reject her!" *The Gospel of Mary* is among the "Gnostic gospels," accepted by some early (Gnostic) Christians as canon.

THE GOSPEL OF MARY

[The Coptic papyrus, from which the first six pages have been lost, begins in the middle of this gospel.]

" . . . will, then, matter be saved or not?"

The Saviour said, "All natures, all formed things, all creatures exist in and with one another and will again be resolved into their own roots, because the nature of matter is dissolved into the roots of its nature alone. He who has ears to hear, let him hear" [cf. Matt. 11:15, etc.].

Peter said to him, "Since you have now explained all things to us, tell us this: what is the sin of the world?" [cf. John 1:29].

The Saviour said, "Sin as such does not exist, but you make sin when you do what is of the nature of fornication, which is called 'sin.' For this reason the Good came into your midst, to the essence of each nature, to restore it to its root." He went on to say, "For this reason you come into existence and die [. . .] whoever knows may know [. . .] a suffering which has nothing like itself, which has arisen out of what is contrary to nature. Then there arises a disturbance in the whole body. For this reason I said to you, Be of good courage [cf. Matt. 28:9], and if you are discouraged, still take courage over against the various forms of nature. He who has ears to hear, let him hear." When the Blessed One had said this, he greeted all of them, saying "Peace be with you [cf. John 14:27]. Receive my peace for yourselves. Take heed lest anyone lead you astray with the words, 'Lo, here!' or 'Lo, there!' [cf. Matt. 24:5, 23; Luke 17:21] for the Son of Man is within you [cf. Luke 17:21]. Follow him; those who seek him will find him [cf. Matt. 7:7]. Go, therefore, and preach the Gospel of the Kingdom [cf. Matt. 4:23; 9:15; Mark 16:15]. I have left no commandment but what I have commanded you, and I have given you no law, as the lawgiver did, lest you be bound by it."

When he had said this, he went away. But they were grieved and mourned greatly, saying, "How shall we go to the Gentiles and preach the Gospel of the Kingdom of the Son of Man? If even he was not spared, how shall we be spared?"

Then Mary stood up and greeted all of them and said to her brethren, "Do not mourn or grieve or be irresolute, for his grace will be with you all and will defend you. Let us rather praise His greatness, for he prepared us and made us into men." When Mary said this, their hearts changed for the better, and they began to discuss the words of the [Saviour].

Peter said to Mary, "Sister, we know that the Saviour loved you more than other women [cf. John 11:5, Luke 10:38-42]. Tell us the words of the Saviour which you have in mind since you know them; and we do not, nor have we heard them."

Mary answered and said, "What is hidden from you I will impart to you."

And she began to say the following words to them. "I," she said, "I saw the Lord in a vision and I said to him, 'Lord, I saw you to-day in a vision.' He answered and said to me, 'Blessed are you, since you did not waver at the sight of me. For where the mind is, there is your countenance' [cf. Matt. 6:21]. I said to him, 'Lord, the mind which sees the vision, does it see it through the soul or through the spirit?' The Saviour answered and said, 'It sees neither through the soul nor through the spirit, but the mind, which is between the two, which sees the vision, and it is . . . ' "

[At this point pages 11-14 of the papyrus are lost.]

" . . . and Desire said, 'I did not see you descend; but now I see you rising. Why do you speak falsely, when you belong to me?' The soul answered and said, 'I saw you, but you did not see me or recognise me; I served you as a garment and you did not recognize me.' After it had said this, it went joyfully and gladly away. Again it came to the third power, Ignorance. This power questioned the soul: 'Whither are you going? You were bound in wickedness, you were bound indeed. Judge not' [cf. Matt. 7:1]. And the soul said, 'Why do you judge me, when I judged not? I was bound, though I did not bind. I was not recognised, but I recognised that all will go free, things both earthly and heavenly.' After the soul had left the third power behind, it rose upward, and saw the fourth power, which had seven forms. The first form is darkness, the second desire, the third ignorance, the fourth the arousing of death, the fifth is the kingdom of the flesh, the sixth is the wisdom of the folly of the flesh, the seventh is wrathful [?] wisdom. These are the seven participants in wrath. They ask the soul, 'Whence do you come, killer of men, or where are you going, conqueror of space?' The soul answered and said, 'What seizes me is killed; what turns me about is overcome; my desire has come to an end and ignorance is dead. In a world I was saved from a world, and in a "type," from a higher "type" and from the fetter of the impotence of knowledge, the existence of which is temporal. From this time I will reach rest in the time of the moment of the Aeon in silence.' "

When Mary had said this, she was silent, since the Saviour had spoken thus far with her. But Andrew answered and said to the brethren, "Say what you think concerning what she said. For I do not believe that the Saviour said this. For certainly these teachings are of other ideas."

Peter also opposed her in regard to these matters and asked them about the Saviour. "Did he then speak secretly with a woman [cf. John 4:27], in preference to us, and not openly? Are we to turn back and all listen to her? Did he prefer her to us?"

Then Mary grieved and said to Peter, "My brother Peter, what do you think? Do you think that I thought this up myself in my heart or that I am lying concerning the Saviour?"

Levi answered and said to Peter, "Peter, you are always irate. Now I see that you are contending against the woman like the adversaries. But if the Saviour made her worthy, who are you to reject her? Surely the Saviour knew her very well [cf. Luke 10:38-42]. For this reason he loved her more than us [cf. John 11:5]. And we should rather be ashamed and put on the Perfect Man, to form us [?] as he commanded us, and proclaim the gospel, without publishing a further commandment or a further law than the one which the Saviour spoke." When Levi had said this, they began to go out in order to proclaim him and preach him.

CHAPTER TWO

Thecla, *Acts of Paul and Thecla* (c.150–200)

Thecla

Thecla is described in this fictional account as a disciple of Paul. She was condemned to death for her powerful witness of chastity, but was miraculously saved from execution. This account reports a long and active life for Thecla. She became a patron saint of virgins in the early church with numerous shrines and a considerable following. The popularity of Thecla and this *Acts* is attested as well by the survival of these accounts in Greek, Coptic, Syriac, Armenian, Slavonic, Arabic, and five Latin versions.

Acts of Paul and Thecla

This text was written in Greek in the latter half of the second century. Tertullian reports that it was written by a presbyter in Asia Minor whose enthusiasm, rather than heretical leanings, accounts for this romantic description of the exploits of Paul and Thecla. When the true authorship was discovered, the presbyter was deprived of office and the work was considered fiction. It chronicles many of Paul's missionary endeavors and the conversion of Thecla, a virgin. Through Paul's preaching in praise of chastity at Iconium, Thecla is convinced to renounce her impending marriage and commit herself to a life of witness. Not surprisingly, her fiancé is upset, and her own mother is outraged by her recklessness, proposing that Thecla be burned as an example to other women who follow Paul! The rest of the *Acts* tell of Thecla's heroic resistance of others' plans for her, of her fierce commitment to purity and faithfulness even when faced by wild animals in the arena, and of the comfort and support offered her by other women.

THE ACTS OF PAUL AND THECLA

As Paul was going up to Iconium after the flight from Antioch, his fellow-travellers were Demas and Ermogenes, full of hypocrisy; and they were importunate with Paul, as if they loved him. But Paul, looking only to the goodness of Christ, did them no harm, but loved them exceedingly, so that he made the oracles of the Lord sweet to them in the teaching both of the birth and the resurrection of the Beloved; and he gave them an account, word for word, of the great things of Christ, how He had been revealed to him. . . .

And while Paul was thus speaking in the midst of the church in the house of Onesiphorus, a certain virgin Thecla, the daughter of Theocleia, be-trothed to a man named Thamyris, sitting at the window close by, listened night and day to the discourse of virginity and prayer, and did not look away from the window, but paid earnest heed to the faith, rejoicing exceedingly. And when she still saw many women going in beside Paul, she also had an eager desire to be deemed worthy to stand in the presence of Paul, and to hear the word of Christ; for never had she seen his figure, but heard his word only.

And as she did not stand away from the window, her mother sends to Thamyris. . . .

. . . Thamyris, as if she had been lost, was running up and down the streets, one of the gatekeeper's fellow-slaves informed him that she had gone out by night. And having gone out, they examined the gatekeeper; and he said to them: She has gone to the foreigner into the prison. And having gone, they found her, as it were, enchained by affection. And having gone forth thence, they drew the multitudes together, and informed the governor of the circumstance. And he ordered Paul to be brought to the tribunal; but Thecla was wallowing on the ground in the place where he sat and taught her in the prison; and he ordered her too to be brought to the tribunal. And she came, exulting with joy. And the crowd, when Paul had been brought, vehemently cried out: He is a magician! away with him! But the proconsul gladly heard Paul upon the holy works of Christ. And having called a council, he summoned Thecla, and said to her: Why dost thou not obey Thamyris, according to the law of the Iconians? But she stood looking earnestly at Paul. And when she gave no answer, her mother cried out, saying: Burn the wicked wretch, burn in the midst of the theatre her that will not marry, in order that all the women that have been taught by this man may be afraid.

And the governor was greatly moved; and having scourged Paul, he cast him out of the city, and condemned Thecla to be burned. And immediately the governor went away to the theatre, and all the crowd went forth to the spectacle of Thecla. But as a lamb in the wilderness looks round for the shepherd, so she kept searching for Paul. And having looked upon the crowd, she saw the Lord sitting in the likeness of Paul, and said: As I am unable to endure my lot, Paul has come to see me. And she gazed upon him with great earnestness, and he went up into heaven. But the maid-servants and virgins brought the faggots, in order that Thecla might be burned. And when she came in naked, the governor wept, and wondered at the power that was in her. And the public executioners arranged the faggots for her to go up on the pile. And she, having made the sign of the cross, went up on the faggots; and they lighted them. And though a great fire was blazing, it did not touch her; for God, having compassion upon her, made an underground rumbling, and a cloud overshadowed them from above, full of water and hail; and all that was in the cavity of it was poured out, so that many were in danger of death. And the fire was put out, and Thecla saved. . . .

And Paul sent away Onesiphorus and all his house to Iconium; and thus, having taken Thecla, he went into Antioch. And as they were going in, a certain Syriarch, Alexander by name, seeing Thecla, became enamoured of her, and tried to gain over Paul by gifts and presents. But Paul said: I know not the woman whom thou speakest of, nor is she mine. But he, being of great power, himself embraced her in the street. But she would not endure it, but looked about for Paul. And she cried out bitterly, saying: Do not force the stranger; do not force the servant of God. I am one of the chief persons of the Iconians; and because I would not have Thamyris, I have been cast out of the city. And taking hold of Alexander, she tore his cloak, and pulled off his crown, and made him a laughing-stock. And he, at the same time loving her, and at the same time ashamed of what had happened, led her before the governor; and when she had confessed that she had done these things, he condemned her to the wild beasts. And the women were struck with astonishment, and cried out beside the tribunal: Evil judgment! impious judgment! And she asked the governor, that, said she, I may remain pure until I shall fight with the wild beasts. And a certain Tryphaena, whose daughter was dead, took her into keeping, and had her for a consolation.

And when the beasts were exhibited, they bound her to a fierce lioness;

and Tryphaena accompanied her. But the lioness, with Thecla sitting upon her, licked her feet; and all the multitude was astonished. And the charge on her inscription was: Sacrilegious. And the women cried out from above: An impious sentence has been passed in this city! And after the exhibition, Tryphaena again received her. For her daughter Falconilla had died, and said to her in a dream: Mother, thou shalt have this stranger Thecla in my place, in order that she may pray concerning me, and that I may be transferred to the place of the just.

And when, after the exhibition, Tryphaena received her, at the same time indeed she grieved that she had to fight with the wild beasts on the day following. . . .

And Thecla, having been taken out of the hand of Tryphaena, was stripped, and received a girdle, and was thrown into the arena, and lions and bears and a fierce lioness were let loose upon her; and the lioness having run up to her feet, lay down; and the multitude of the women cried aloud. And a bear ran upon her; but the lioness, meeting the bear, tore her to pieces. And again a lion that had been trained against men, which belonged to Alexander, ran upon her; and she, the lioness, encountering the lion, was killed along with him. And the women made great lamentation, since also the lioness, her protector, was dead.

Then they sent in many wild beasts, she standing and stretching forth her hands, and praying. And when she had finished her prayer, she turned and saw a ditch full of water, and said: Now it is time to wash myself. And she threw herself in, saying: In the name of Jesus Christ I am baptized on my last day. And the women seeing, and the multitude, wept, saying: Do not throw thyself into the water; so that also the governor shed tears, because the seals were going to devour such beauty. She then threw herself in in the name of Jesus Christ; but the seals having seen the glare of the fire of lightning, floated about dead. And there was round her, as she was naked, a cloud of fire; so that neither could the wild beasts touch her, nor could she be seen naked.

And the women, when other wild beasts were being thrown in, wailed. And some threw sweet-smelling herbs, others nard, others cassia, others amomum, so that there was abundance of perfumes. And all the wild beasts that had been thrown in, as if they had been withheld by sleep, did not touch her; so that Alexander said to the governor: I have bulls exceedingly terrible; let us bind to them her that is to fight with the beasts. And the governor, looking gloomy, turned, and said: Do what thou wilt. And they bound her by the feet between them, and put red-hot irons under the privy parts of the bulls, so that they, being rendered more furious, might kill her. They rushed about, therefore; but the burning flame consumed the ropes, and she was as if she had not been bound. But Tryphaena fainted standing beside the arena, so that the crowd said: Queen Tryphaena is dead. And the governor put a stop to the games, and the city was in dismay. And Alexander entreated the governor, saying: Have mercy both on me and the city, and release this woman. For if Caesar hear of these things, he will speedily destroy the city also along with us, because his kinswoman Queen Tryphaena has died beside the ABACI.

And the governor summoned Thecla out of the midst of the wild beasts, and said to her: Who art thou? and what is there about thee, that not one of the wild beasts touches thee? And she said: I indeed am a servant of the living God; and as to what there is about me, I have believed in the Son of God, in whom He is well pleased; wherefore not one of the beasts has touched me. For He alone is the end of salvation, and the basis of immortal life; for He is a refuge to the tempest-tossed, a solace to the afflicted, a shelter to the despairing; and, once for all, whoever shall not believe on Him, shall not live for ever.

And the governor having heard this, ordered her garments to be brought, and to be put on. And Thecla said: He that clothed me naked among the wild beasts, will in the day of judgment clothe thee with salvation. And taking the garments, she put them on. The governor therefore immediately issued an edict, saying: I release to you the God-fearing Thecla, the servant of God. And the women shouted aloud, and with one mouth returned thanks to God, saying: There is one God, the God of Thecla; so that the foundations of the theatre were shaken by their voice. And Tryphaena having received the good news, went to meet the holy Thecla, and said: Now I believe that the dead are raised; now I believe that my child lives. Come within, and I shall assign to thee all that is mine. She therefore went in along with her, and rested eight days, having instructed her in the word of God, so that most even of the maid-servants believed. And there was great joy in the house. . . .

She was cast, then, into the fire when seventeen years old, and among the wild beasts when eighteen. And she was an ascetic in the cave, as has been said, seventy-two years, so that all the years of her life were ninety. And having accomplished many cures, she rests in the place of the saints, having fallen asleep on the twenty-fourth of the month of September in Christ Jesus our Lord, to whom be glory and strength for ever and ever. Amen.

CHAPTER THREE

Perpetua,
The Martyrdom
of Perpetua (203)

Perpetua and Felicitas

Perpetua was a young, married woman from a good family and upbringing in Carthage. Other than these generalities, we know little about her life. In 202–3 C.E., while still nursing her newborn son, Perpetua was arrested and imprisoned on charges of being a Christian. In the account of her martyrdom, we learn that she provided leadership for other Christians in Carthage, offering prayers and inspiring them to courage. Felicitas, her slave, was also arrested and imprisoned. Although pregnant, Felicitas prayed for strength to endure until after her child was born. The witness of these two women was legendary, and it represents an important pattern of Christian life in North Africa.

The Martyrdom of Perpetua and Felicitas

This text offers a firsthand account of their arrest, imprisonment, and subsequent visions. Perpetua's own authorship of the largest portion of this work is widely undisputed, even though the narrative is continued by the catechist Saturus, and certainly edited by a skilled writer (perhaps Tertullian). The story begins when Perpetua's father visits her in jail to plead with her to give up this nonsense, at least for the infant's sake. She responds with the famous words, "I cannot be called anything else than what I am, a Christian." Her visions during confinement make up a significant portion of the text, and her bravery under persecution is highlighted throughout.

She, along with Felicitas and four other catechumens, was martyred at Carthage in 202–3 C.E.

THE MARTYRDOM OF PERPETUA

1. If instances of ancient faith which both testified to the grace of God and edified persons were written expressly for God's honor and humans' encouragement, why shouldn't recent events be similarly recorded for those same purposes? For these events will likewise become part of the past and vital to posterity, in spite of the fact that contemporary esteem for antiquity tends to minimize their value. And those who maintain that there is a single manifestation of the one Holy Spirit throughout the ages ought to consider that since a fullness of grace has been decreed for the last days of the world these recent events should be considered of greater value because of their proximity to those days. For "In the last days," says the Lord, "I shall diffuse my spirit over all humanity and their sons and daughters shall prophesy; the young shall see visions, and the old shall dream dreams."

Just as we valued those prophecies so we acknowledge and reverence the new visions which were promised. And we consider the other powers of the Holy Spirit to be instruments of the Church to which that same Spirit was sent to administer all gifts to all people, just as the Lord allotted. For this reason we deem it necessary to disseminate the written accounts for the glory of God, lest anyone with a weak or despairing faith might think that supernatural grace prevailed solely among the ancients who were honored either by their experience of martyrdom or visions. For God always fulfills what he promises, either as proof to non-believers or as an added grace to believers.

And so, brothers and dear ones, we share with you those things which we have heard and touched with our hands, so that those of you who were eye-witnesses of these deeds may be reminded of the glory of the Lord, and those of you now learning of it through this narration may associate yourselves with the holy martyrs and, through them, with the Lord Jesus Christ to whom there is glory and honor forever. Amen.

2. Arrested were some young catechumens; Revocatus and Felicitas (both servants), Saturninus, Secundulus, and Vibia Perpetua, a young married woman about twenty years old, of good family and upbringing. She had a father, mother, two brothers (one was a catechumen like herself), and

an infant son at the breast. The following account of her martyrdom is her own, a record in her own words of her perceptions of the event.

3. While I was still with the police authorities (she said) my father out of love for me tried to dissuade me from my resolution. "Father," I said, "do you see here, for example, this vase, or pitcher, or whatever it is?" "I see it," he said. "Can it be named anything else than what it really is?", I asked, and he said, "No." "So I also cannot be called anything else than what I am, a Christian." Enraged by my words my father came at me as though to tear out my eyes. He only annoyed me, but he left, overpowered by his diabolical arguments.

For a few days my father stayed away. I thanked the Lord and felt relieved because of my father's absence. At this time we were baptized and the Spirit instructed me not to request anything from the baptismal waters except endurance of physical suffering.

A few days later we were imprisoned. I was terrified because never before had I experienced such darkness. What a terrible day! Because of crowded conditions and rough treatment by the soldiers the heat was unbearable. My condition was aggravated by my anxiety for my baby. Then Tertius and Pomponius, those kind deacons who were taking care of our needs, paid for us to be moved for a few hours to a better part of the prison where we might refresh ourselves. Leaving the dungeon we all went about our own business. I nursed my child, who was already weak from hunger. In my anxiety for the infant I spoke to my mother about him, tried to console my brother, and asked that they care for my son. I suffered intensely because I sensed their agony on my account. These were the trials I had to endure for many days. Then I was granted the privilege of having my son remain with me in prison. Being relieved of my anxiety and concern for the infant, I immediately regained my strength. Suddenly the prison became my palace, and I loved being there rather than any other place.

4. Then my brother said to me, "Dear sister, you already have such a great reputation that you could ask for a vision indicating whether you will be condemned or freed." Since I knew that I could speak with the Lord, whose great favors I had already experienced, I confidently promised to do so. I said I would tell my brother about it the next day. Then I made my request and this is what I saw.

There was a bronze ladder of extraordinary height reaching up to heaven, but it was so narrow that only one person could ascend at a time. Every conceivable kind of iron weapon was attached to the sides of the ladder: swords, lances, hooks, and daggers. If anyone climbed up carelessly or without looking upwards, he/she would be mangled as the flesh adhered to the weapons. Crouching directly beneath the ladder was a monstrous dragon who threatened those climbing up and tried to frighten them from ascent.

Saturus went up first. Because of his concern for us he had given himself up voluntarily after we had been arrested. He had been our source of strength but was not with us at the time of the arrest. When he reached the top of the ladder he turned to me and said, "Perpetua, I'm waiting for you, but be careful not to be bitten by the dragon." I told him that in the name of Jesus Christ the dragon could not harm me. At this the dragon slowly lowered its head as though afraid of me. Using its head as the first step, I began my ascent.

At the summit I saw an immense garden, in the center of which sat a tall, grey-haired man dressed like a shepherd, milking sheep. Standing around him were several thousand white-robed people. As he raised his head he noticed me and said, "Welcome, my child." Then he beckoned me to approach and gave me a small morsel of the cheese he was making. I accepted it with cupped hands and ate it. When all those surrounding us said "Amen," I awoke, still tasting the sweet cheese. I immediately told my brother about the vision, and we both realized that we were to experience the sufferings of martyrdom. From then on we gave up having any hope in this world.

5. A few days later there was a rumor that our case was to be heard. My father, completely exhausted from his anxiety, came from the city to see me, with the intention of weakening my faith. "Daughter," he said, "have pity on my grey head. Have pity on your father if I have the honor to be called father by you, if with these hands I have brought you to the prime of your life, and if I have always favored you above your brothers, do not abandon me to the reproach of men. Consider your brothers; consider your mother and your aunt; consider your son who cannot live without you. Give up your stubbornness before you destroy all of us. None of us will be able to speak freely if anything happens to you."

These were the things my father said out of love, kissing my hands and throwing himself at my feet. With tears he called me not daughter, but woman. I was very upset because of my father's condition. He was the only member of my family who would find no reason for joy in my suffering. I tried to comfort him saying, "Whatever God wants at this tribunal will happen, for remember that our power comes not from ourselves but from God." But utterly dejected, my father left me.

6. One day as we were eating we were suddenly rushed off for a hearing. We arrived at the forum and the news spread quickly throughout the area near the forum, and a huge crowd gathered. We went up to the prisoners' platform. All the others confessed when they were questioned. When my turn came my father appeared with my son. Dragging me from the step, he begged: "Have pity on your son!"

Hilarion, the governor, who assumed power after the death of the pro-consul Minucius Timinianus, said, "Have pity on your father's grey head; have pity on your infant son; offer sacrifice for the emperors' welfare." But I answered, "I will not." Hilarion asked, "Are you a Christian?" And I answered, "I am a Christian." And when my father persisted in his attempts to dissuade me, Hilarion ordered him thrown out, and he was beaten with a rod. My father's injury hurt me as much as if I myself had been beaten, and I grieved because of his pathetic old age. Then the sentence was passed; all of us were condemned to the beasts. We were overjoyed as we went back to the prison cell. Since I was still nursing my child who was ordinarily in the cell with me, I quickly sent the deacon Pomponius to my father's house to ask for the baby, but my father refused to give him up. Then God saw to it that my child no longer needed my nursing, nor were my breasts in-flamed. After that I was no longer tortured by anxiety about my child or by pain in my breasts.

7. A few days later while all of us were praying, in the middle of a prayer I suddenly called out the name "Dinocrates." I was astonished since I hadn't thought about him till then. When I recalled what had happened to him I was very disturbed and decided right then that I had not only the right, but the obligation, to pray for him. So I began to pray repeatedly and to make moaning sounds to the Lord in his behalf. During that same night I had this vision: I saw Dinocrates walking away from one of many very dark places. He seemed very hot and thirsty, his face grimy and colorless. The wound on his face was just as it had been when he died. This Dinocrates was my blood-brother who at the age of seven died very tragically from a cancerous disease which so disfigured his face that his death was repulsive to every-one. It was for him that I now prayed. But neither of us could reach the other because of the great distance between. In the place where Dinocrates stood was a pool filled with water, and the rim of the pool was so high that it extended far above the boy's height. Dinocrates stood on his toes as if to drink the water but in spite of the fact that the pool was full, he could not drink because the rim was so high!

I realized that my brother was in trouble, but I was confident that I could help him with his problem. I prayed for him every day until we were transferred to the arena prison where we were to fight wild animals on the birthday of Geta Caesar. And I prayed day and night for him, moaning and weeping so that my petition would be granted.

8. On the day that we were kept in chains, I had the following vision: I saw the same place as before, but Dinocrates was clean, well-dressed, looking refreshed. In place of the wound there was a scar, and the fountain which I had seen previously now had its rim lowered to the boy's waist. On the rim, over which water was flowing constantly, there was a golden bowl filled with water. Dinocrates walked up to it and began to drink; the bowl never emptied. And when he was no longer thirsty, he gladly went to play as children do. Then I awoke, knowing that he had been relieved of his suffering.

9. A few days passed. Pudens, the official in charge of the prison (the official who had gradually come to admire us for our persistence), admitted many prisoners to our cell so that we might mutually encourage each other. As the day of the games drew near, my father, overwhelmed with grief, came again to see me. He began to pluck out his beard and throw it on the ground. Falling on his face before me, he cursed his old age, repeating such things as would move all creation. And I grieved because of his old age.

10. The day before the battle in the arena, in a vision I saw Pomponius the deacon coming to the prison door and knocking very loudly. I went to open the gate for him. He was dressed in a loosely fitting white robe, wearing richly decorated sandals. He said to me, "Perpetua, come. We're waiting for you!" He took my hand and we began to walk over extremely rocky and winding paths. When we finally arrived short of breath, at the arena, he led me to the center saying, "Don't be frightened! I'll be here to help you." He left me and I stared out over a huge crowd which watched me with apprehension. Because I knew that I had to fight with the beasts, I wondered why they hadn't yet been turned loose in the arena. Coming towards me was some type of Egyptian, horrible to look at, accompanied by fighters who were to help defeat me. Some handsome young men came forward to help and encourage me. I was stripped of my clothing, and suddenly I was a man. My assistants began to rub me with oil as was the custom before a contest, while the Egyptian was on the opposite side rolling in the sand. Then a certain man appeared, so tall that he towered above the amphitheatre. He wore a loose purple robe with two parallel stripes across the chest; his sandals were richly decorated with gold and silver. He carried a rod like that of an athletic trainer, and a green branch on which were

golden apples. He motioned for silence and said, "If this Egyptian wins, he will kill her with the sword; but if she wins, she will receive this branch." Then he withdrew.

We both stepped forward and began to fight with our fists. My opponent kept trying to grab my feet but I repeatedly kicked his face with my heels. I felt myself being lifted up into the air and began to strike at him as one who was no longer earth-bound. But when I saw that we were wasting time, I put my two hands together, linked my fingers, and put his head between them. As he fell on his face I stepped on his head. Then the people began to shout and my assistants started singing victory songs. I walked up to the trainer and accepted the branch. He kissed me and said, "Peace be with you, my daughter." And I triumphantly headed towards the Sanavivarian Gate. Then I woke up realizing that I would be contending not with wild animals but with the devil himself. I knew, however, that I would win. I have recorded the events which occurred up to the day before the final contest. Let anyone who wishes to record the events of the contest itself, do so."

11. The saintly Saturus also related a vision which he had and it is recorded here in his own hand. Our suffering had ended (he said), and we were being carried towards the east by four angels whose hands never touched us. And we floated upward, not in a supine position, but as though we were climbing a gentle slope. As we left the earth's atmosphere we saw a brilliant light, and I said to Perpetua who was at my side, "This is what the Lord promised us. We have received his promise."

And while we were being carried along by those four angels we saw a large open space like a splendid garden landscaped with rose trees and every variety of flower. The trees were as tall as cypresses whose leaves rustled gently and incessantly. And there in that garden-sanctuary were four other angels, more dazzling than the rest. And when they saw us they showed us honor, saying to the other angels in admiration, "Here they are! They have arrived."

And those four angels who were carrying us began trembling in awe and set us down. And we walked through a violet-strewn field where we met Jocundus, Saturninus, and Artaxius who were burned alive in that same persecution, and Quintus, also a martyr, who had died in prison. We were asking them where they had been, when the other angels said to us, "First, come this way. Go in and greet the Lord."

12. We went up to a place where the walls seemed constructed of light. At the entrance of the place stood four angels who put white robes on those who entered. We went in and heard a unified voice chanting endlessly,

"Holy, holy, holy." We saw a white haired man sitting there who, in spite of his snowy white hair, had the features of a young man. His feet were not visible. On his right and left were four elderly gentlemen and behind them stood many more. As we entered we stood in amazement before the throne. Four angels supported us as we went up to kiss the aged man, and he gently stroked our faces with his hands. The other elderly men said to us, "Stand up." We rose and gave the kiss of peace. Then they told us to enjoy ourselves. I said to Perpetua, "You have your wish." She answered, "I thank God, for although I was happy on earth, I am much happier here right now."

13. Then we went out, and before the gates we saw Optatus the bishop on the right and Aspasius the priest and teacher on the left, both looking sad as they stood there separated from each other. They knelt before us saying, "Make peace between us, for you've gone away and left us this way." But we said to them "Aren't you our spiritual father, and our teacher? Why are you kneeling before us?" We were deeply touched and we embraced them. And Perpetua began to speak to them in Greek and we invited them into the garden beneath a rose tree. While we were talking with them, the angels said to them, "Let them refresh themselves, and if you have any dissensions among you, forgive one another." This disturbed both of them and the angels said to Optatus, "Correct your people who flock to you as though returning from the games, fighting about the different teams." It seemed to us that they wanted to close the gates, and there we began to recognize many of our friends, among whom were martyrs. We were all sustained by an indescribable fragrance which completely satisfied us. Then in my joy, I awoke.

14. The remarkable visions narrated above were those of the blessed martyrs Saturus and Perpetua, just as they put them in writing. As for Secundulus, while he was still in prison God gave him the grace of an earlier exit from this world, so that he could escape combat with the wild beasts. But his body, though not his soul, certainly felt the sword.

15. As for Felicitas, she too was touched by God's grace in the following manner. She was pregnant when arrested, and was now in her eighth month. As the day of the contest approached she became very distressed that her martyrdom might be delayed, since the law forbade the execution of a pregnant woman. Then she would later have to shed her holy and innocent blood among common criminals. Her friends in martyrdom were equally sad at the thought of abandoning such a good friend to travel alone on the same road to hope.

And so, two days before the contest, united in grief they prayed to the

33

Lord. Immediately after the prayers her labor pains began. Because of the additional pain natural for an eighth-month delivery, she suffered greatly during the birth, and one of the prison guards taunted her; "If you're complaining now, what will you do when you'll be thrown to the wild beasts? You didn't think of them when you refused to sacrifice." She answered, "Now it is I who suffer, but then another shall be in me to bear the pain for me, since I am now suffering for him." And she gave birth to a girl whom one of her sisters reared as her own daughter.

16. Since the Holy Spirit has permitted, and by permitting has willed, that the events of the contest be recorded, we have no choice but to carry out the injunction (rather, the sacred trust) of Perpetua, in spite of the fact that it will be an inferior addition to the magnificent events already described. We are adding an instance of Perpetua's perseverance and lively spirit. At one time the prisoners were being treated with unusual severity by the commanding officer because certain deceitful men had intimated to him that the prisoners might escape by some magic spells. Perpetua openly challenged him; "Why don't you at least allow us to freshen up, the most noble of the condemned, since we belong to Caesar and are about to fight on his birthday? Or isn't it to your credit that we should appear in good condition on that day?" The officer grimaced and blushed, then ordered that they be treated more humanely and that her brothers and others be allowed to visit and dine with them. By this time the prison warden was himself a believer.

17. On the day before the public games, as they were eating the last meal commonly called the free meal, they tried as much as possible to make it instead an *agape*. In the same spirit they were exhorting the people, warning them to remember the judgment of God, asking them to be witnesses to the prisoners' joy in suffering, and ridiculing the curiosity of the crowd. Saturus told them, "Won't tomorrow's view be enough for you? Why are you so eager to see something you hate? Friends today, enemies tomorrow! Take a good look so you'll recognize us on that day." Then they all left the prison amazed, and many of them began to believe.

18. The day of their victory dawned, and with joyful countenances they marched from the prison to the arena as though on their way to heaven. If there was any trembling it was from joy, not fear. Perpetua followed with quick step as a true spouse of Christ, the darling of God, her brightly flashing eyes quelling the gaze of the crowd. Felicitas too, joyful because she had safely survived child-birth and was now able to participate in the contest with the wild animals, passed from one shedding of blood to

another; from midwife to gladiator, about to be purified after child-birth by a second baptism. As they were led through the gate they were ordered to put on different clothes; the men, those priests of Saturn, the women, those of the priestesses of Ceres. But that noble woman stubbornly resisted even to the end. She said, "We've come this far voluntarily in order to protect our rights, and we've pledged our lives not to recapitulate on any such matter as this. We made this agreement with you." Injustice bowed to justice and the guard conceded that they could enter the arena in their ordinary dress. Perpetua was singing victory psalms as if already crushing the head of the Egyptian. Revocatus, Saturninus and Saturus were warning the spectators, and as they came within sight of Hilarion they informed him by nods and gestures: "You condemn us; God condemns you." This so infuriated the crowds that they demanded the scourging of these men in front of the line of gladiators. But the ones so punished rejoiced in that they had obtained yet another share in the Lord's suffering.

19. Whoever said, "Ask and you shall receive," granted to these petitioners the particular death that each one chose. For whenever the martyrs were discussing among themselves their choice of death, Saturus used to say that he wished to be thrown in with all the animals so that he might wear a more glorious crown. Accordingly, at the outset of the show he was matched against a leopard but then called back; then he was mauled by a bear on the exhibition platform. Now Saturus detested nothing as much as a bear and he had already decided to die by one bite from the leopard. Consequently, when he was tied to a wild boar the professional gladiator who had tied the two together was pierced instead and died shortly after the games ended, while Saturus was merely dragged about. And when he was tied up on the bridge in front of the bear, the bear refused to come out of his den; and so a second time Saturus was called back unharmed.

20. For the young women the devil had readied a mad cow, an animal not usually used at these games, but selected so that the women's sex would be matched with that of the animal. After being stripped and enmeshed in nets, the women were led into the arena. How horrified the people were as they saw that one was a young girl and the other, her breasts dripping with milk, had just recently given birth to a child. Consequently both were recalled and dressed in loosely fitting gowns.

Perpetua was tossed first and fell on her back. She sat up, and being more concerned with her sense of modesty than with her pain, covered her thighs with her gown which had been torn down one side. Then finding her hair-clip which had fallen out, she pinned back her loose hair thinking it not proper for a martyr to suffer with dishevelled hair; it might seem that she was mourning in her hour of triumph. Then she stood up. Noticing that Felicitas was badly bruised, she went to her, reached out her hands and helped her to her feet. As they stood there the cruelty of the crowds seemed to be appeased and they were sent to the Sanavivarian Gate. There Perpetua was taken care of by a certain catechumen, Rusticus, who stayed near her. She seemed to be waking from a deep sleep (so completely had she been entranced and imbued with the Spirit). She began to look around her and to everyone's astonishment asked, "When are we going to be led out to that cow, or whatever it is." She would not believe that it had already happened until she saw the various markings of the tossing on her body and clothing. Then calling for her brother she said to him and to the catechumen, "Remain strong in your faith and love one another. Do not let our excruciating sufferings become a stumbling block for you."

21. Meanwhile, at another gate Saturus was similarly encouraging the soldier, Pudens. "Up to the present," he said, "I've not been harmed by any of the animals, just as I've foretold and predicted. So that you will now believe completely, watch as I go back to die from a single leopard bite." And so at the end of that contest, Saturus was bitten once by the leopard that had been set loose, and bled so profusely from that one wound that as he was coming back the crowd shouted in witness to his second baptism: "Salvation by being cleansed; Salvation by being cleansed;" And that man was truly saved who was cleansed in this way.

Then Saturus said to Pudens the soldier, "Goodbye, and remember my faith. Let these happenings be a source of strength for you, rather than a cause for anxiety." Then asking Pudens for a ring from his finger, he dipped it into the wound and returned it to Pudens as a legacy, a pledge and remembrance of his death. And as he collapsed he was thrown with the rest to that place reserved for the usual throat-slitting. And when the crowd demanded that the prisoners be brought out into the open so that they might feast their eyes on death by the sword, they voluntarily arose and moved where the crowd wanted them. Before doing so they kissed each other so that their martyrdom would be completely perfected by the rite of the kiss of peace.

The others, without making any movement or sound, were killed by the sword. Saturus in particular, since he had been the first to climb the ladder and was to be Perpetua's encouragement, was the first to die. But Perpetua, in order to feel some of the pain, groaning as she was struck between the ribs, took the gladiator's trembling hand [and] guided it to her throat.

Perhaps it was that so great a woman, feared as she was by the unclean spirit, could not have been slain had she not herself willed it.

O brave and fortunate martyrs, truly called and chosen to give honor to our Lord Jesus Christ! And anyone who is elaborating upon, or who reverences or worships that honor, should read these more recent examples, along with the ancient, as sources of encouragement for the Christian community. In this way, there will be new examples of courage witnessing to the fact that even in our day the same Holy Spirit is still efficaciously present, along with the all powerful God the Father and Jesus Christ our Lord, to whom there will always be glory and endless power. Amen.

Acts of the Martyrs

Acts of the Martyrs

Written in a variety of forms and styles, these acts include at least twenty-eight different texts recounting the martyrdoms of early Christians. Some *acta* reflect strict court records of martyrs' trials. Others stand as moving narratives, written by loyal friends, of the martyrs' final struggles. Common to all of these accounts is a portrayal of the courage and faithfulness of these Christians, men and women, slave and free, in the face of heinous treatment. The selections included here are two acts devoted solely to women (*The Martyrdom of Aqapê, Irenê, and Chionê and Companions* and *The Martyrdom of Crispina*) and one act about both women and men (*The Martyrs of Lyons*).

The Martyrs of Lyons (177/78)

This emotional and dramatic account tells of an anti-Christian uprising in Gaul in 177 C.E. Largely comprised of immigrants from Asia Minor, the Christian community at Lyons was banned from public places, and "the finest were taken" and tortured to extract confessions. This excerpt narrates the trials of Blandina in particular as she stands firm in the face of mob violence. The early Christian historian Eusebius is the sole source for this text, which claims to be a letter written from the churches at Lyons and Vienne to the churches of Asia and Phrygia.

THE MARTYRS OF LYONS

1. The servants of Christ who dwell in Vienne and Lyons in Gaul, to our brothers in Asia and Phrygia who have the same faith and hope in the

redemption: peace, grace, and glory from God the Father and from Jesus Christ our Lord. (Then after other preliminary remarks in order, they begin their account as follows.)

The intensity of our afflictions here, the deep hatred of the pagans for the saints, and the magnitude of the blessed martyrs' sufferings, we are incapable of describing in detail; indeed, it would be impossible to put it down in writing. . . .

In the first place, they heroically endured all that the people *en masse* heaped on them: abuse, blows, dragging, despoiling, stoning, imprisonment, and all that an enraged mob is likely to inflict on their most hated enemies. They were dragged into the forum and interrogated before the entire populace by the tribune and the city authorities. When they confessed, they were locked up in prison to await the arrival of the governor. . . .

From then on the blessed martyrs underwent torments beyond all description; and Satan strove to have some word of blasphemy escape their lips.

All the wrath of the mob, the prefect, and the soldiers fell with overwhelming force on the deacon Sanctus of Vienne, on Maturus who was, though newly baptized, a noble athlete, on Attalus whose family came from Pergamum, who had always been *a pillar and ground* of the community there, and on Blandina, through whom Christ proved that the things that men think cheap, ugly, and contemptuous are deemed worthy of glory before God, by reason of her love for him which was not merely vaunted in appearance but demonstrated in achievement.

All of us were in terror; and Blandina's earthly mistress, who was herself among the martyrs in the conflict, was in agony lest because of her bodily weakness she would not be able to make a bold confession of her faith. Yet Blandina was filled with such power that even those who were taking turns to torture her in every way from dawn to dusk were weary and exhausted. They themselves admitted that they were beaten, that there was nothing further they could do to her, and they were surprised that she was still breathing, for her entire body was broken and torn. They testified that even one kind of torture was enough to release her soul, let alone the many they applied with such intensity. Instead, this blessed woman like a noble athlete got renewed strength with her confession of faith: her admission, 'I am a Christian; we do nothing to be ashamed of,' brought her refreshment, rest, and insensibility to her present pain. . . .

. . . From this time on the types of their martyrdoms were of every variation. For, plaiting one crown of many different flowers and colours, they offered it to the Father. Surely it behoved these noble athletes, after sustaining a brilliant contest and a glorious victory, to win the great crown of immortality.

Maturus, then, Sanctus, Blandina, and Attalus were led into the amphitheatre to be exposed to the beasts and to give a public spectacle of the pagans' inhumanity, for a day of gladiatorial games was expressly arranged for our sake. Once again in the amphitheatre Maturus and Sanctus went through the whole gamut of suffering as though they had never experienced it at all before—or rather as though they had defeated their opponent in many contests and were now fighting for the victor's crown. Once again they ran the gauntlet of whips (according to the local custom), the mauling by animals, and anything else that the mad mob from different places shouted for and demanded. And to crown all they were put in the iron seat, from which their roasted flesh filled the audience with its savour. But that was not enough for them, and they continued to rage in their desire to break down the martyrs' resistance. But from Sanctus all they would hear was what he had repeated from the beginning, his confession of faith.

Though their spirits endured much throughout the long contest, they were in the end sacrificed, after being made all the day long a spectacle to the world to replace the varied entertainment of the gladiatorial combat. Blandina was hung on a post and exposed as bait for the wild animals that were let loose on her. She seemed to hang there in the form of a cross, and by her fervent prayer she aroused intense enthusiasm in those who were undergoing their ordeal, for in their torment with their physical eyes they saw in the person of their sister him who was crucified for them, that he might convince all who believe in him that all who suffer for Christ's glory will have eternal fellowship in the living God.

But none of the animals had touched her, and so she was taken down from the post and brought back to the gaol to be preserved for another ordeal: and thus for her victory in further contests she would make irreversible the condemnation of the *crooked serpent,* and tiny, weak, and insignificant as she was she would give inspiration to her brothers, for she had put on Christ, that mighty and invincible athlete, and had overcome the Adversary in many contests, and through her conflict had won the crown of immortality. . . .

Finally, on the last day of the gladiatorial games, they brought back Blandina again, this time with a boy of fifteen named Ponticus. Every day they had been brought in to watch the torture of the others, while attempts were made to force them to swear by the pagan idols. And because they persevered and condemned their persecutors, the crowd grew angry with them, so that they had little pity for the child's age and no respect for the woman. Instead, they subjected them to every atrocity and led them through every torture in turn, constantly trying to force them to swear, but to no avail.

Ponticus, after being encouraged by his sister in Christ so that even the pagans realized that she was urging him on and strengthening him, and after nobly enduring every torment, gave up his spirit. The blessed Blandina was last of all: like a noble mother encouraging her children, she sent them before her in triumph to the King, and then, after duplicating in her own body all her children's sufferings, she hastened to rejoin them, rejoicing and glorying in her death as though she had been invited to a bridal banquet instead of being a victim of the beasts. After the scourges, the animals, and the hot griddle, she was at last tossed into a net and exposed to a bull. After being tossed a good deal by the animal, she no longer perceived what was happening because of the hope and possession of all she believed in and because of her intimacy with Christ. Thus she too was offered in sacrifice, while the pagans themselves admitted that no woman had ever suffered so much in their experience.

Martyrdom of Agapê, Irenê, and Chionê and Companions (304)

Not only these three young women, but their companions Agatho, Cassia, Philippa, and Eutychia as well were martyred in March and April of 304 C.E. at Saloniki. It is likely that they had fled to a nearby mountain in response to Diocletian's edict, promulgated early in 303, to surrender the sacred books. There they formed a group of consecrated women living on their own in the wilderness in order to evade the Diocletian persecutions. By the time the soldiers arrested them, the fourth edict, ordering sacrifice under pain of death, was in effect as well. They were tried in three hearings. This brief excerpt gives a sense of the women's testimony before the magistrate and their own theological reading of the situation.

THE MARTYRDOM OF SAINTS AGAPÊ, IRENÊ, AND CHIONÊ AT SELENIC (304)

... When the persecution was raging under the Emperor Maximian, these women, who had adorned themselves with virtue, following the precepts of the Gospel, abandoned their native city, their family, property, and possessions because of their love of God and their expectation of heavenly things. Performing deeds worthy of their father Abraham, they fled the persecutors, according to the commandment, and took refuge on a high mountain. There they gave themselves to prayer: though their bodies resided on a mountain top, their souls lived in heaven.

2. . . . . they were captured and brought to the official who was conducting the persecution. . . .

3. . . . .] 'You may read it,' said the prefect Dulcitius. And the charge was duly read: 'To you, my lord, greetings from Cassander, *beneficiarius*. This is to inform you, Sir, that Agatho, Irenê, Agapê, Chionê, Cassia, Philippa, and Eutychia refuse to eat sacrificial food, and so I have referred them to your Genius.'

'What is this insanity,' said the prefect Dulcitius, 'that you refuse to obey the order of our most religious emperors and Caesars?' And turning to Agatho, he said, 'When you came to the sacrifices, why did you not perform the cult practices like other religious people?'

'Because I am a Christian,' said Agatho.

The prefect Dulcitius said: 'Do you still remain in the same mind today?'

'Yes,' said Agatho.

The prefect Dulcitius said: 'What do you say, Agapê?'

'I believe in the living God,' replied Agapê, 'and I refuse to destroy my conscience.'

'What do you say, Irenê?' asked the prefect Dulcitius. 'Why did you disobey the command of our lords the emperors and Caesars?'

'Because of my fear of God,' said Irenê.

'What do you say, Chionê?' asked the prefect.

'I believe in the living God,' replied Chionê, 'and I refuse to do this.'

The prefect said: 'And how about you, Cassia?'

'I wish to save my soul,' said Cassia.

The prefect said: 'Are you willing to partake of the sacrificial meat?'

'I am not,' said Cassia.

The prefect said: 'And what say you, Philippa?'

'I say the same,' said Philippa.

'What do you mean, the same?' said the prefect.

Said Philippa, 'I mean, I would rather die than partake.'

'Eutychia,' said the prefect, 'what do you say?'

'I say the same,' said Eutychia; 'I would rather die.'

The prefect said: 'Do you have a husband?'

'He is dead,' said Eutychia.

'When did he die?' asked the prefect.

'About seven months ago,' said Eutychia.

The prefect said: 'How is it then that you are pregnant?'

Eutychia said: 'By the man whom God gave me.'

The prefect said: 'But how can you be pregnant when you say your husband is dead?'

Eutychia said: 'No one can know the will of almighty God. So God willed it.'

The prefect said: 'I urge Eutychia to cease this madness and to return to sound reason. What do you say? Will you obey the imperial command?'

'No, I will not,' said Eutychia. 'I am a Christian, a servant of almighty God.'

The prefect said: 'Since Eutychia is pregnant, she shall be kept meanwhile in gaol.'

4. . . . Then he added, 'What say you, Agapê? Will you perform all the actions which religious persons perform in honour of our lords the emperors and Caesars?'

Agapê replied, 'It is not at all in Satan's power. He cannot move my reason; it is invincible.'

The prefect said: 'What say you, Chionê?'

Chionê said: 'No one can change my mind.'

The prefect said: 'Do you have in your possession any writings, parchments, or books of the impious Christians?'

Chionê said: 'We do not, Sir. Our present emperors have taken these from us.'

'Who was it who gave you this idea?' asked the prefect.

'God almighty,' said Chionê.

The prefect said: 'Who was it who counselled you to commit such folly?'

'It was almighty God,' answered Chionê, 'and his only begotten Son, our Lord Jesus Christ.'

The prefect Dulcitius said: 'It is clear to all that you are all liable to the crime of treason against our lords the emperors and Caesars. But seeing that you have persisted in this folly for such a long time, in spite of strong warnings and so many decrees, sanctioned by stern threats, and have despised the command of our lords the emperors and Caesars, remaining in this impious name of Christian, and seeing that even today when you were ordered by the soldiers and officials to deny your belief and signify this in

43

writing, you refused—therefore you shall receive the punishment appropriate for you.'

Then he read the sentence written on a sheet: 'Whereas Agapê and Chionê have with malicious intent acted against the divine decree of our lords the Augusti and Caesars, and whereas they adhere to the worthless and obsolete worship of the Christians which is hateful to all religious men, I sentence them to be burned.' Then he added, 'Agatho, Irenê, Cassia, Philippa, and Eutychia, because of their youth are to be put in prison in the meanwhile.'

Martyrdom of Crispina (304)

Crispina was a prominent woman at the colony of Thacora when she was arrested and subsequently executed on December 5, 304, for violating Diocletian's edict ordering sacrifice under pain of death. The majority of this account is considered authentic, relying on legitimate documents and oral reports. This excerpt demonstrates that Crispina was capable of both moral and theological discourse with her captors and that she stood as an articulate representative for early Christianity. Her story was told by Christians for centuries to come.

THE MARTYRDOM OF CRISPINA

1. It was the fifth day of December in the ninth consulate of Diocletian Augustus and the eighth of Maximian Augustus in the colony of Tebessa. The proconsul Anullinus sat in judgement on the tribunal in his council-chamber, and the court clerk spoke: 'Crispina, a lady of Toura, is to be tried at your good pleasure: she has spurned the law of our lords the emperors.'

'Bring her in,' said the proconsul Anullinus.

When Crispina had come in, the proconsul Anullinus said: 'Are you aware of what is commanded by the sacred decree?'

'No,' said Crispina, 'I do not know what has been commanded.'

Anullinus said: 'That you should offer sacrifice to all our gods for the welfare of the emperors, in accordance with the law issued by our lords the reverend Augusti Diocletian and Maximian and the most noble Caesars Constantius and Maximus.'

'I have never sacrificed,' replied Crispina, 'and I shall not do so save to the one true God and to our Lord, Jesus Christ, his Son, who was born and died.'

'Break with this superstition,' said the proconsul Anullinus, 'and bow your head to the sacred rites of the gods of Rome.'

Crispina replied: 'Every day I worship my God almighty. I know of no other God besides him.'

'You are a stubborn and insolent woman,' said Anullinus, 'and you will soon begin to feel the force of our laws against your will.'

'Whatever happens,' said Crispina, 'I shall be glad to suffer it on behalf of the faith which I hold firm.'

Anullinus said: 'It is merely the folly of your mind that you will not put aside this superstition and worship the sacred gods.'

'I worship daily,' replied Crispina, 'but I worship the living and true God, who is my Lord, and besides him I know no other.'

Anullinus said: 'I put before you the sacred edict. You must obey it.'

'I will obey the edict,' replied Crispina, 'but the one given by my Lord Jesus Christ.'

'I will have you beheaded,' said the proconsul Anullinus, 'if you do not obey the edicts of our lords the emperors. You will be forced to yield and obey them: all the province of Africa has offered sacrifice, as you are well aware.'

'May they never find it easy,' replied Crispina, 'to make me offer sacrifice to demons: but I sacrifice to the Lord *who has made heaven and earth, the sea, and all things that are in them.*'

2. 'So our gods are not acceptable to you!' said Anullinus. 'But you shall be forced to show them respect if you want to remain alive for any worship at all!'

'That piety is worthless,' replied Crispina, 'which forces men to be crushed against their will.'

Anullinus said: 'But all we ask of your religion is that you bow your head in the sacred temples and offer incense to the gods of Rome.'

'I have never done this since I was born,' replied Crispina; 'I do not know how; nor will I ever do it so long as I live.'

'Do so now,' said Anullinus, 'if you wish to escape unharmed from the sanctions of the law.'

'I do not fear anything you say,' replied Crispina. 'That is nothing. But if I deliberately choose to commit a sacrilege, the God who is in heaven will destroy me at once, and I shall not be found in him on the last day.'

'You will not commit sacrilege,' said Anullinus, 'if you obey the sacred edicts.'

Crispina replied, 'Perish *the gods who have not made heaven and earth!*

I offer sacrifice to the eternal God who abides for ever. He is the true God who is to be feared; he has made the sea, the green grass, and the dry earth. But what can men offer me who are the creatures of his hand?'

Anullinus said: 'Revere the religion of Rome, which is observed by our lords the unconquerable Caesars as well as ourselves.'

'I have told you again and again,' replied Crispina, 'I am prepared to undergo any tortures that you wish to subject me to rather than defile my soul with idols which are stones and the creations of men's hands.' . . .

Anullinus said: 'If you despise the worship of our venerable gods, I shall order your head to be cut off.'

'I should thank my God,' replied Crispina, 'if I obtained this. I should be very happy to lose my head for the sake of my God. For I refuse to sacrifice to these ridiculous deaf and dumb statues.'

Anullinus the proconsul said: 'And so you absolutely persist in this foolish frame of mind?'

Crispina replied, 'My God who is and who abides for ever ordered me to be born; it was he who gave me salvation through the saving waters of baptism: he is at my side, helping me, strengthening his handmaid in all things so that she will not commit sacrilege.'

4. Anullinus said: 'Why should we suffer this impious Christian woman any further? Read back the minutes of the trial from the record.'

And when they were read, the proconsul Anullinus read the sentence from a tablet: 'Seeing that Crispina has persisted in infamous superstition and refuses to offer sacrifice to our gods in accordance with the heavenly decrees of the Augustan law, I have ordered her to be executed with the sword.'

Crispina replied, 'I bless God who has so deigned to free me from your hands. Thanks be to God!' And making the sign of the cross on her forehead and putting out her neck, she was beheaded for the name of the Lord Jesus Christ, to whom is honour for ever. Amen.

Macrina, *On the Soul and the Resurrection* (380)

Macrina (327–379)

Macrina is often called Macrina the Younger in relation to her paternal grandmother, Macrina the Elder (d. c.340), whose powerful Christian witness shaped both early Christianity and her family. Macrina was a young woman of determined spirit who, upon the death of her fiancé, used the family estate near the river Iris in Pontus to establish a community dedicated to a life of prayer, contemplation, and penance. She was a learned woman and continued throughout her life to develop intellectually and spiritually, exercising profound theological influence upon her brothers, St. Basil and St. Gregory of Nyssa. It was Gregory who gave us an admiring biography of Macrina in his *Vita Macrina Junioris*.

On the Soul and the Resurrection

This excerpt comes from Macrina's teaching as reported by her brother Gregory, in *On the Soul and the Resurrection* (380), a text that details a conversation between the two siblings. Gregory comes to her, anguished over the death of their brother Basil, only to find that she, too, is on her deathbed. He seeks her wisdom and comfort, and in the course of the conversation Macrina presents "the most sublime philosophy," laying out her view of the nature of the soul and a theology of resurrection. Even though the words were penned by Gregory, this work reflects Macrina's reputed grasp of both biblical and philosophical precepts as well as her sophisticated level of argument and discourse.

ON THE SOUL AND THE RESURRECTION

Basil, great amongst the saints, had departed from this life to God; and the impulse to mourn for him was shared by all the churches. But his sister the Teacher was still living; and so I journeyed to her, yearning for an interchange of sympathy over the loss of her brother. My soul was right sorrow-stricken by this grievous blow, and I sought for one who could feel it equally, to mingle my tears with. But when we were in each other's presence the sight of the Teacher awakened all my pain; for she too was lying in a state of prostration even unto death. Well, she gave in to me for a little while, like a skilful driver, in the ungovernable violence of my grief; and then she tried to check me by speaking, and to correct with the curb of her reasonings the disorder of my soul. She quoted the Apostle's words about the duty of not being "grieved for them that sleep"; because only "men without hope" have such feelings. With a heart still fermenting with my pain, I asked—

How can that ever be practised by mankind? . . .

What! is there no occasion for grieving, I replied to her, when we see one who so lately lived and spoke becoming all of a sudden lifeless and motionless, with the sense of every bodily organ extinct, with no sight or hearing in operation, or any other faculty of apprehension that sense possesses; and if you apply fire or steel to him, even if you were to plunge a sword into the body, or cast it to the beasts of prey, or if you bury it beneath a mound, that dead man is alike unmoved at any treatment? Seeing, then, that this change is observed in all these ways, and that principle of life, whatever it might be, disappears all at once out of sight, as the flame of an extinguished lamp which burnt on it the moment before neither remains upon the wick nor passes to some other place, but completely disappears, how can such a change be borne without emotion by one who has no clear ground to rest upon? We *hear* the departure of the spirit, we *see* the shell that is left; but of the part that has been separated we are ignorant, both as to its nature, and as to the place whither it has fled; for neither earth, nor air, nor water, nor any other element can show as residing within itself this force that has left the body, at whose withdrawal a corpse only remains, ready for dissolution.

Whilst I was thus enlarging on the subject, the Teacher signed to me with her hand, and said: Surely what alarms and disturbs your mind is not the thought that the soul, instead of lasting for ever, ceases with the body's dissolution!

I answered rather audaciously, and without due consideration of what I said, for my passionate grief had not yet given me back my judgment. In fact, I said that the Divine utterances seemed to me like mere commands compelling us to believe that the soul lasts for ever; not, however, that we were led by them to this belief by any reasoning. Our mind within us appears slavishly to accept the opinion enforced, but not to acquiesce with a spontaneous impulse. Hence our sorrow over the departed is all the more grievous; we do not exactly know whether this vivifying principle is anything by itself; where it is, or how it is; whether, in fact, it exists in any way at all anywhere. This uncertainty about the real state of the case balances the opinions on either side; many adopt the one view, many the other; and indeed there are certain persons, of no small philosophical reputation amongst the Greeks, who have held and maintained this which I have just said.

Away, she cried, with that pagan nonsense! . . .

. . . If it is not possible for the soul to exist *after* death, though the elements do, then, I say, according to this teaching our life as well is proved to be nothing else but death. But if on the other hand they do not make the existence of the soul now in the body a question for doubt, how can they maintain its evanishment when the body is resolved into its elements? Then, secondly, they must employ an equal audacity against the God in this Nature too. For how can they assert that the intelligible and immaterial Unseen can be dissolved and diffused into the wet and the soft, as also into the hot and the dry, and so hold together the universe in existence through being, though not of a kindred nature with the things which it penetrates, yet not thereby incapable of so penetrating them? Let them, therefore, remove from their system the very Deity Who upholds the world.

That is the very point, I said, upon which our adversaries cannot fail to have doubts; viz. that all things depend on God and are encompassed by Him, or, that there is any divinity at all transcending the physical world.

It would be more fitting, she cried, to be silent about such doubts, and not to deign to make any answer to such foolish and wicked propositions; for there is a Divine precept forbidding us to answer a fool in his folly; and he must be a fool, as the Prophet declares, who says that there is no God. But since one needs must speak, I will urge upon you an argument which is not mine nor that of any human being (for it would then be of small value, whosoever spoke it), but an argument which the whole Creation enunciates by the medium of its wonders to the audience of the eye, with a skilful and artistic utterance that reaches the heart. The Creation proclaims outright the

Creator; for the very heavens, as the Prophet says, declare the glory of God with their unutterable words. We see the universal harmony in the wondrous sky and on the wondrous earth; how elements essentially opposed to each other are all woven together in an ineffable union to serve one common end, each contributing its particular force to maintain the whole; how the unmingling and mutually repellent do not fly apart from each other by virtue of their peculiarities, any more than they are destroyed, when compounded, by such contrariety; how those elements which are naturally buoyant move downwards, the heat of the sun, for instance, descending in the rays, while the bodies which possess weight are lifted by becoming rarefied in vapour, so that water contrary to its nature ascends, being conveyed through the air to the upper regions; how too that fire of the firmament so penetrates the earth that even its abysses feel the heat; how the moisture of the rain infused into the soil generates, one though it be by nature, myriads of differing germs, and animates in due proportion each subject of its influence; how very swiftly the polar sphere revolves, how the orbits within it move the contrary way, with all the eclipses, and conjunctions, and measured intervals of the planets. We see all this with the piercing eyes of mind, nor can we fail to be taught by means of such a spectacle that a Divine power, working with skill and method, is manifesting itself in this actual world, and, penetrating each portion, combines those portions with the whole and completes the whole by the portions, and encompasses the universe with a single all-controlling force, self-centered and self-contained, never ceasing from its motion, yet never altering the position which it holds.

And pray how, I asked, does this belief in the existence of God prove along with it the existence of the human soul? For God, surely, is not the same thing as the soul, so that, if the one were believed in, the other must necessarily be believed in.

She replied: It has been said by wise men that man is a little world in himself and contains all the elements which go to complete the universe. If this view is a true one (and so it seems), we perhaps shall need no other ally than it to establish the truth of our conception of the soul. And our conception of it is this; that it exists, with a rare and peculiar nature of its own, independently of the body with its gross texture. We get our exact knowledge of this outer world from the apprehension of our senses, and these sensational operations themselves lead us on to the understanding of the super-sensual world of fact and thought, and our eye thus becomes the interpreter of that almighty wisdom which is visible in the universe, and points in itself to the Being Who encompasses it. Just so, when we look to our inner world, we find no slight grounds there also, in the known, for conjecturing the unknown; and the unknown there also is that which, being the object of thought and not of sight, eludes the grasp of sense.

I rejoined, Nay, it may be very possible to infer a wisdom transcending the universe from the skilful and artistic designs observable in this harmonized fabric of physical nature; but, as regards the soul, what knowledge is possible to those who would trace, from any indications the body has to give, the unknown through the known?

Most certainly, the Virgin replied, the soul herself, to those who wish to follow the wise proverb and know themselves, is a competent instructress; of the fact, I mean, that she is an immaterial and spiritual thing, working and moving in a way corresponding to her peculiar nature, and evincing these peculiar emotions through the organs of the body. For this bodily organization exists the same even in those who have just been reduced by death to the state of corpses, but it remains without motion or action because the force of the soul is no longer in it. It moves only when there is sensation in the organs, and not only that, but the mental force by means of that sensation penetrates with its own impulses and moves whither it will all those organs of sensation.

What then, I asked, is the soul? Perhaps there may be some possible means of delineating its nature; so that we may have some comprehension of this subject, in the way of a sketch.

Its definition, the Teacher replied, has been attempted in different ways by different writers, each according to his own bent; but the following is our opinion about it. The soul is an essence created, and living, and intellectual, transmitting from itself to an organized and sentient body the power of living and of grasping objects of sense, as long as a natural constitution capable of this holds together. . . .

. . . Rather, as the Scripture tells you, say that the one is *like* the other. For that which is "made in the image" of the Deity necessarily possesses a likeness to its prototype in every respect; it resembles it in being intellectual, immaterial, unconnected with any notion of weight, and in eluding any measurement of its dimensions; yet as regards its own peculiar nature it is something different from that other. Indeed, it would be no longer an "image," if it were altogether identical with that other; but where we have A in that uncreate prototype we have *a* in the image; just as in a minute particle of glass, when it happens to face the light, the complete disc of the sun is often to be seen, not represented thereon in proportion to its proper size, but so far as the minuteness of the particle admits of its being represented at all. Thus do the reflections of those ineffable qualities of Deity shine forth within the narrow limits of our nature; and so our reason, following the leading of these reflections, will not miss grasping the Mind in its essence by clearing away from the question all corporeal qualities; nor on the other hand will it bring the pure and infinite Existence to the level of that which is perishable and little; it will regard this essence of the Mind as an object of thought only, since it is the "image" of an Existence which is such; but it will not pronounce this image to be identical with the prototype. Just, then, as we have no doubts, owing to the display of a Divine mysterious wisdom in the universe, about a Divine Being and a Divine Power existing in it all which secures its continuance (though if you required a definition of that Being you would therein find the Deity completely sundered from every object in creation, whether of sense or thought, while in these last, too, natural distinctions are admitted), so, too, there is nothing strange in the soul's separate existence as a substance (whatever we may think that substance to be) being no hindrance to her actual existence, in spite of the elemental atoms of the world not harmonizing with her in the definition of her being. In the case of our living bodies, composed as they are from the blending of these atoms, there is no sort of communion, as has been just said, on the score of substance, between the simplicity and invisibility of the soul, and the grossness of those bodies; but, notwithstanding that, there is not a doubt that there is in them the soul's vivifying influence exerted by a law which it is beyond the human understanding to comprehend. Not even then, when those atoms have again been dissolved into themselves, has that bond of a vivifying influence vanished; but as, while the framework of the body still holds together, each individual part is possessed of a soul which penetrates equally every component member, and one could not call that soul hard and resistant though blended with the solid, nor humid, or cold, or the reverse, though it transmits life to all and each of such parts, so, when that framework is dissolved, and has returned to its kindred elements, there is nothing against probability that that simple and incomposite essence which has once for all by some inexplicable law grown with the growth of the bodily framework should continually remain beside the atoms with which it has been blended, and should in no way be sundered from a union once formed. For it does not follow that because the composite is dissolved the incomposite must be dissolved with it. . . .

When she had finished, I hesitated a moment, and then said: I am not yet satisfied about the thing which we have been inquiring into, after all that has been said my mind is still in doubt; and I beg that our discussion may be allowed to revert to the same line of reasoning as before, omitting only that upon which we are thoroughly agreed. I say this, for I think that all but the most stubborn controversialists will have been sufficiently convinced by our debate not to consign the soul after the body's dissolution to annihilation and nonentity, nor to argue that because it differs substantially from the atoms it is impossible for it to exist anywhere in the universe; for, however much a being that is intellectual and immaterial may fail to coincide with these atoms, it is in no ways hindered (so far) from existing in them; and this belief of ours rests on two facts: firstly, on the soul's existing in our bodies in this present life, though fundamentally different from them: and secondly, on the fact that the Divine being, as our argument has shown, though distinctly something other than visible and material substances, nevertheless pervades each one amongst all existences, and by this penetration of the whole keeps the world in a state of being; so that following these analogies we need not think that the soul, either, is out of existence, when she passes from the world of forms to the Unseen. But how, I insisted, after the united whole of the atoms has assumed, owing to their mixing together, a form quite different—the form in fact with which the soul has been actually domesticated—by what mark, when this form, as we should have expected, is effaced along with the resolution of the atoms, shall the soul follow along (them), now that that familiar form ceases to persist?

She waited a moment and then said: Give me leave to invent a fanciful simile in order to illustrate the matter before us: even though that which I suppose may be outside the range of possibility. Grant it possible, then, in the art of painting not only to mix opposite colours, as painters are always doing, to represent a particular tint, but also to separate again this mixture and to restore to each of the colours its natural dye. If then white, or black, or red, or golden colour, or any other colour that has been mixed to form the given tint, were to be again separated from that union with another and remain by itself, we suppose that our artist will none the less remember the actual nature of that colour, and that in no case will he show forgetfulness, either of the red, for instance, or the black, if after having become quite a different colour by composition with each other they each return to their natural dye. We suppose, I say, that our artist remembers the manner of the mutual blending of these colours, and so knows what sort of colour was mixed with a given colour and what sort of colour was the result, and how, the other colour being ejected from the composition, (the original colour) in consequence of such release resumed its own peculiar hue; and, supposing it were required to produce the same result again by composition, the process will be all the easier from having been already practised in his previous work. Now, if reason can see any analogy in this simile, we must search the matter in hand by its light. Let the soul stand for this Art of the painter; and let the natural atoms stand for the colours of his art; and let the mixture of that tint compounded of the various dyes, and the return of these to their native state (which we have been allowed to assume), represent respectively the concourse, and the separation of the atoms. Then, as we assume in the simile that the painter's Art tells him the actual dye of each colour, when it has returned after mixing to its proper hue, so that he has an exact knowledge of the red, and of the black, and of any other colour that went to form the required tint by a specific way of uniting with another kind—a knowledge which includes its appearance both in the mixture, and now when it is in its natural state, and in the future again, supposing all the colours were mixed over again in like fashion—so, we assert, does the soul know the natural peculiarities of those atoms whose concourse makes the frame of the body in which it has itself grown, even after the scattering of those atoms. However far from each other their natural propensity and their inherent forces of repulsion urge them, and debar each from mingling with its opposite, none the less will the soul be near each by its power of recognition, and will persistently cling to the familiar atoms, until their concourse after this division again takes place in the same way, for that fresh formation of the dissolved body which will properly be, and be called, resurrection.

You seem, I interrupted, in this passing remark to have made an excellent defence of the faith in the Resurrection. By it, I think, the opponents of this doctrine might be gradually led to consider it not as a thing absolutely impossible that the atoms should again coalesce and form the same man as before.

That is very true, the Teacher replied. For we may hear these opponents urging the following difficulty. "The atoms are resolved, like to like, into the universe; by what device, then, does the warmth, for instance, residing in such and such a man, after joining the universal warmth, again dissociate itself from this connection with its kindred, so as to form this man who is being 'remoulded'? For if the identical individual particle does not return and only something that is homogeneous but not identical is fetched, you will have something else in the place of that first thing, and such a process will cease to be a resurrection and will be merely the creation of a new man.

But if the same man is to return into himself, he must be the same entirely, and regain his original formation in every single atom of his elements.

Then to meet such an objection, I rejoined, the above opinion about the soul will, as I said, avail; namely, that she remains after dissolution in those very atoms in which she first grew up, and, like a guardian placed over private property, does not abandon them when they are mingled with their kindred atoms, and by the subtle ubiquity of her intelligence makes no mistake about them, with all their subtle minuteness, but diffuses herself along with those which belong to herself when they are being mingled with their kindred dust, and suffers no exhaustion in keeping up with the whole number of them when they stream back into the universe, but remains with them, no matter in what direction or in what fashion Nature may arrange them. But should the signal be given by the All-disposing Power for these scattered atoms to combine again, then, just as when every one of the various ropes that hang from one block answer at one and the same moment to the pull from that centre, so, following this force of the soul which acts upon the various atoms, all these, once so familiar with each other, rush simultaneously together and form the cable of the body by means of the soul, each single one of them being wedded to its former neighbour and embracing an old acquaintance. . . ."

. . . If, then, the soul is present with the atoms of the body when they are again mingled with the universe, it will not only be cognizant of the entire mass which once came together to form the whole body, and will be present with it, but, besides that, will not fail to know the particular materials of each one of the members, so as to remember by what divisions amongst the atoms our limbs were completely formed. There is, then, nothing improbable in supposing that what is present in the complete mass is present also in each division of the mass. If one, then, thinks of those atoms in which each detail of the body potentially inheres, and surmises that Scripture means a "finger" and a "tongue" and an "eye" and the rest as existing, after dissolution, only in the sphere of the soul, one will not miss the probable truth. Moreover, if each detail carries the mind away from a material acceptation of the story, surely the "hell" which we have just been speaking of cannot reasonably be thought a place so named; rather we are there told by Scripture about a certain unseen and immaterial situation in which the soul resides. In this story of the Rich and the Poor Man we are taught another doctrine also, which is intimately connected with our former discoveries. The story makes the sensual pleasure-loving man, when he sees that his own case is one that admits of no escape, evince forethought for his relations on earth; and when Abraham tells him that the life of those still in the flesh is not unprovided with a guidance, for they may find it at hand, if they will, in the Law and the Prophets, he still continues entreating that Just Patriarch, and asks that a sudden and convincing message, brought by some one risen from the dead, may be sent to them.

What then, I asked, is the doctrine here?

Why, seeing that Lazarus' soul is occupied with his present blessings and turns round to look at nothing that he has left, while the rich man is still attached, with a cement as it were, even after death, to the life of feeling, which he does not divest himself of even when he has ceased to live, still keeping as he does flesh and blood in his thoughts (for in his entreaty that his kindred may be exempted from his sufferings he plainly shows that he is not freed yet from fleshly feeling),—in such details of the story (she continued) I think our Lord teaches us this; that those still living in the flesh must as much as ever they can separate and free themselves in a way from its attachments by virtuous conduct, in order that after death they may not need a second death to cleanse them from the remnants that are owing to this cement of the flesh, and, when once the bonds are loosed from around the soul, her soaring up to the Good may be swift and unimpeded, with no anguish of the body to distract her. For if any one becomes wholly and thoroughly carnal in thought, such an one, with every motion and energy of the soul absorbed in fleshly desires, is not parted from such attachments, even in the disembodied state; just as those who have lingered long in noisome places do not part with the unpleasantness contracted by that lengthened stay, even when they pass into a sweet atmosphere. So it is that, when the change is made into the impalpable Unseen, not even then will it be possible for the lovers of the flesh to avoid dragging away with them under any circumstances some fleshly foulness; and thereby their torment will be intensified, their soul having been materialized by such surroundings. I think too that this view of the matter harmonizes to a certain extent with the assertion made by some persons that around their graves shadowy phantoms of the departed are often seen. If this is really so, an inordinate attachment of that particular soul to the life in the flesh is proved to have existed, causing it to be unwilling, even when expelled from the flesh, to fly clean away and to admit the complete change of its form into the impalpable; it remains near the frame even after the dissolution of the frame, and though now outside it, hovers regretfully over the place where its material is, and continues to haunt it.

Then, after a moment's reflection on the meaning of these latter words, I said: I think that a contradiction now arises between what you have said and the result of our former examination of the passions. For if, on the one hand, the activity of such movements within us is to be held as arising from our kinship with the brutes, such movements I mean as were enumerated in our previous discussion, anger, for instance, and fear, desire of pleasure, and so on, and, on the other hand, it was affirmed that virtue consists in the good employment of these movements, and vice in their bad employment, and in addition to this we discussed the actual contribution of each of the other passions to a virtuous life, and found that through desire above all we are brought nearer God, drawn up, by its chain as it were, from earth towards Him,—I think (I said) that that part of the discussion is in a way opposed to that which we are now aiming at.

How so? she asked.

Why, when every unreasoning instinct is quenched within us after our purgation, this principle of desire will not exist any more than the other principles; and this being removed, it looks as if the striving after the better way would also cease, no other emotion remaining in the soul that can stir us up to the appetence of Good.

To that objection, she replied, we answer this. The speculative and critical faculty is the property of the soul's godlike part; for it is by these that we grasp the Deity also. If, then, whether by forethought here, or by purgation hereafter, our soul becomes free from any emotional connection with the brute creation, there will be nothing to impede its contemplation of the Beautiful; for this last is essentially capable of attracting in a certain way every being that looks towards it. If, then, the soul is purified of every vice, it will most certainly be in the sphere of Beauty. The Deity is in very substance Beautiful; and to the Deity the soul will in its state of purity have affinity, and will embrace It as like itself. Whenever this happens, then, there will be no longer need of the impulse of Desire to lead the way to the Beautiful. Whoever passes his time in darkness, he it is who will be under the influence of a desire for the light; but whenever he comes into the light, then enjoyment takes the place of desire, and the power to enjoy renders desire useless and out of date. It will therefore be no detriment to our participation in the Good, that the soul should be free from such emotions, and turning back upon herself should know herself accurately what her actual nature is, and should behold the Original Beauty reflected in the mirror and in the figure of her own beauty. For truly herein consists the real assimilation to the Divine; viz. in making our own life in some degree a copy of the Supreme Being. For a Nature like that, which transcends all thought and is far removed from all that we observe within ourselves, proceeds in its existence in a very different manner to what we do in this present life. Man, possessing a constitution whose law it is to be moving, is carried in that particular direction whither the impulse of his will directs: and so his soul is not affected in the same way towards what lies before it, as one may say, as to what it has left behind; for hope leads the forward movement, but it is memory that succeeds that movement when it has advanced to the attainment of the hope; and if it is to something intrinsically good that hope thus leads on the soul, the print that this exercise of the will leaves upon the memory is a bright one; but if hope has seduced the soul with some phantom only of the Good, and the excellent way has been missed, then the memory that succeeds what has happened becomes shame, and an intestine war is thus waged in the soul between memory and hope, because the last has been such a bad leader of the will. Such in fact is the state of mind that shame gives expression to; the soul is stung as it were at the result; its remorse for its ill-considered attempt is a whip that makes it feel to the quick, and it would bring in oblivion to its aid against its tormentor. Now in our case nature, owing to its being indigent of the Good, is aiming always at this which is still wanting to it, and this aiming at a still missing thing is this very habit of Desire, which our constitution displays equally, whether it is baulked of the real Good, or wins that which it is good to win. But a nature that surpasses every idea that we can form of the Good and transcends all other power, being in no want of anything that can be regarded as good, is itself the plenitude of every good; it does not move in the sphere of the good by way of participation in it only, but it is itself the substance of the Good (whatever we imagine the Good to be); it neither gives scope for any rising hope (for hope manifests activity in the direction of something absent; but "what a man has, why doth he yet hope for?" as the Apostle asks), nor is it in want of the activity of the memory for the knowledge of things; that which is actually seen has no need of being remembered. Since, then, this Divine nature is beyond any particular good, and to the good the good is an object of love, it follows that when It looks within Itself, It wishes for what It contains and contains that which It wishes, and admits nothing external. Indeed there is nothing external to It, with the sole exception of evil, which, strange as it may seem to say, possesses an existence in not existing at all. For there is no other origin of evil except the negation of the existent, and the truly-existent forms the substance of the Good. That therefore which is not to be found in the existent must be in the non-existent. Whenever the soul, then, having divested itself of the multifarious emotions incident to its nature, gets its Divine form and, mounting above Desire, enters within that towards which it was once incited by that Desire, it offers no harbour within itself either for hope or for memory. It holds the object of the one; the other is extruded from the consciousness by the occupation in enjoying all that is good: and thus the soul copies the life that is above, and is conformed to the peculiar features of the Divine nature; none of its habits are left to it except that of love, which clings by natural affinity to the Beautiful. For this is what love is; the inherent affection towards a chosen object. When, then, the soul, having become simple and single in form and so perfectly godlike, finds that perfectly simple and immaterial good which is really worth enthusiasm and love, it attaches itself to it and blends with it by means of the movement and activity of love, fashioning itself according to that which it is continually finding and grasping. Becoming by this assimilation to the Good all that the nature of that which it participates is, the soul will consequently, owing to there being no lack of any good in that thing itself which it participates, be itself also in no lack of anything, and so will expel from within the activity and the habit of Desire; for this arises only when the thing missed is not found. For this teaching we have the authority of God's own Apostle, who announces a subduing and a ceasing of all other activities, even for the good, which are within us, and finds no limit for love alone. . . .

. . . But, she proceeded, the truth does not lie in these arguments, even though we may find it impossible to give a rhetorical answer to them, couched in equally strong language. The true explanation of all these questions is still stored up in the hidden treasure-rooms of Wisdom, and will not come to the light until that moment when we shall be taught the mystery of the Resurrection by the reality of it; and then there will be no more need of phrases to explain the things which we now hope for. Just as many questions might be started for debate amongst people sitting up at night as to the kind of thing that sunshine is, and then the simple appearing of it in all its beauty would render any verbal description superfluous, so every calculation that tries to arrive conjecturally at the future state will be reduced to nothingness by the object of our hopes, when it comes upon us. But since it is our duty not to leave the arguments brought against us in any way unexamined, we will expound the truth as to these points as follows. First let us get a clear notion as to the scope of this doctrine; in other words, what is the end that Holy Scripture has in view in promulgating it and creating the belief in it. Well, to sketch the outline of so vast a truth and to embrace it in a definition, we will say that the Resurrection is *"the recon-stitution of our nature in its original form."* But in that form of life, of which God Himself was the Creator, it is reasonable to believe that there was neither age nor infancy nor any of the sufferings arising from our present various infirmities, nor any kind of bodily affliction whatever. It is reason-able, I say, to believe that God was the Creator of none of these things, but that man was a thing divine before his humanity got within reach of the assault of evil; that then, however, with the inroad of evil, all these afflic-tions also broke in upon him. Accordingly a life that is free from evil is under no necessity whatever of being passed amidst the things that result from evil. It follows that when a man travels through ice he must get his body chilled: or when he walks in a very hot sun that he must get his skin darkened; but if he has kept clear of the one or the other, he escapes these results entirely, both the darkening and the chilling; no one, in fact, when a particular cause was removed, would be justified in looking for the effect of that particular cause. Just so our nature, becoming passional, had to encounter all the necessary results of a life of passion: but when it shall have started back to that state of passionless blessedness, it will no longer encounter the inevitable results of evil tendencies. Seeing, then, that all the infusions of the life of the brute into our nature were not in us before our humanity descended through the touch of evil into passions, most certainly, when we abandon those passions, we shall abandon all their visible results. No one, therefore, will be justified in seeking in that other life for the consequences in us of any passion. Just as if a man, who, clad in a ragged tunic, has divested himself of the garb, feels no more its disgrace upon him, so we too, when we have cast off that dead unsightly tunic made from the skins of brutes and put upon us (for I take the "coats of skins" to mean that conformation belonging to a brute nature with which we were clothed when we became familiar with passionate indulgence), shall, along with the casting off of that tunic, fling from us all the belongings that were round us of that skin of a brute; and such accretions are sexual intercourse, concep-tion, parturition, impurities, suckling, feeding, evacuation, gradual growth to full size, prime of life, old age, disease, and death. If that skin is no longer round us, how can its resulting consequences be left behind within us? It is folly, then, when we are to expect a different state of things in the life to come, to object to the doctrine of the Resurrection on the ground of something that has nothing to do with it. I mean, what has thinness or corpulence, a state of consumption or of plethora, or any other condition supervening in a nature that is ever in a flux, to do with the other life, stranger as it is to any fleeting and transitory passing such as that? One thing, and one thing only, is required for the operation of the Resurrection; viz. that a man should have lived, by being born; or, to use rather the Gospel words, that "a man should be born into the world"; the length or briefness of the life, the manner, this or that, of the death, is an irrelevant subject of inquiry in connection with that operation. Whatever instance we take, howsoever we suppose this to have been, it is all the same; from these differences in life there arises no difficulty, any more than any facility, with regard to the Resurrection. He who has once begun to live must necessarily go on having once lived, after his intervening dissolution in death has been repaired in the Resurrection. As to the *how* and the *when* of his dissolution, what do *they* matter to the Resurrection? Consideration of such points belongs to another line of inquiry altogether. For instance, a man may have lived in bodily comfort, or in affliction, virtuously or viciously, renowned or disgraced; he may have passed his days miserably, or happily. These and such-like results must be obtained from the length of his life and the manner of his living; and to be able to pass a judgment on the things done in his life, it *will* be necessary for the judge to scrutinize his indulgences, as the case may be, or his losses, or his disease, or his old age, or his prime, or his youth, or his wealth, or his poverty: how well or ill a man, placed in either of these, concluded his destined career; whether he was the recipient of many blessings, or of many ills in a length of life; or tasted neither of them at all, but ceased to live before his mental powers were formed. But whenever the time come that God shall have brought our nature back to the primal state of man, it will be useless to talk of such things then, and to imagine that objections based upon such things can prove God's power to be impeded in arriving at His end. His end is one, and one only; it is this: when the complete whole of our race shall have been perfected from the first man to the last,—some having at once in this life been cleansed from evil, others having afterwards in the necessary periods been healed by the Fire, others having in their life here been unconscious equally of good and of evil,—to offer to every one of us participation in the blessings which are in Him, which, the Scripture tells us, "eye hath not seen, nor ear heard," nor thought ever reached. But this is nothing else, as I at least understand it, but to be in God Himself; for the Good which is above hearing and eye and heart must be that Good which transcends the universe. But the difference between the virtuous and the vicious life led at the present time will be illustrated in this way; viz. in the quicker or more tardy participation of each in that promised blessedness. According to the amount of the ingrained wickedness of each will be computed the duration of his cure. This cure consists in the cleansing of his soul, and that cannot be achieved without an excruciating condition, as has been expounded in our previous discussion. But any one would more fully comprehend the futility and irrelevancy of all these objections by trying to fathom the depths of our Apostle's wisdom. When explaining this mystery to the Corinthians, who, perhaps, themselves were bringing forward the same objections to it as its impugners to-day bring forward to overthrow our faith, he proceeds on his own authority to chide the audacity of their ignorance, and speaks thus: "Thou wilt say, then, to me, How are the dead raised up, and with what body do they come? Thou fool, that which thou sowest is not quickened, except it die; And that which thou sowest, thou sowest not that body that shall be, but bare grain, it may chance of wheat or of some other grain; But God giveth it a body as it hath pleased Him." In that passage, as it seems to me, he gags the mouths of men who display their ignorance of the fitting proportions in Nature, and who measure the Divine power by their own strength, and think that only so much is possible to God as the human understanding can take in, but that what is beyond it surpasses also the Divine ability. For the man who had asked the Apostle, "how are the dead raised up?" evidently implies that it is impossible when once the body's atoms have been scattered that they should again come in concourse together; and this being impossible, and no other possible form of body, besides that arising from such a concourse, being left, he, after the fashion of clever controversialists, concludes the truth of what he wants to prove, by a species of syllogism, thus: If a body is a concourse of atoms, and a second assemblage of these is impossible, what sort of body will those get who rise again? This conclusion, involved seemingly in this artful contrivance of premisses, the Apostle calls "folly," as coming from men who failed to perceive in other parts of the creation the masterliness of the Divine power. For, omitting the sublimer miracles of God's hand, by which it would have been easy to place his hearer in a dilemma (for instance he might have asked "how or whence comes a heavenly body, that of the sun for example, or that of the moon, or that which is seen in the constellations; whence the firmament, the air, water, the earth?"), he, on the contrary, convicts the objectors of inconsiderateness by means of objects which grow alongside of us and are very familiar to all. "Does not even husbandry teach thee," he asks, "that the man who in calculating the transcendent powers of the Deity limits them by his own is a fool?" Whence do seeds get the bodies that spring up from them? What precedes this springing up? Is it not a death that precedes? At least, if the dissolution of a compacted whole is a death; for indeed it cannot be supposed that the seed would spring up into a shoot unless it had been dissolved in the soil, and so become spongy and porous to such an extent as to mingle its own qualities with the adjacent moisture of the soil, and thus become transformed into a root and shoot; not stopping even there, but changing again into the stalk with its intervening kneejoints that gird it up like so many clasps, to enable it to carry with figure erect the ear with its load of corn. Where, then, were all these things belonging to the grain before its dissolution in the soil? And yet this result sprang from that grain; if that grain had not existed first, the ear would not have arisen. Just, then, as the "body" of the ear comes to light out of the seed, God's artistic touch of power producing it all out of that single thing, and just as it is neither entirely the same thing as that seed nor something altogether different, so (she insisted) by these miracles performed on seeds you may now interpret the mystery of the Resurrection. The Divine power, in the superabundance of Omnipotence, does not only restore you that body once dissolved, but makes great and splendid additions to it, whereby the human being is furnished in a manner still more magnificent. "It is sown," he says, "in corruption; it is raised in incorruption: it is sown in weakness; it is raised in power: it is sown in dishonour; it is raised in glory: it is sown a natural body; it is raised a spiritual body." The grain of wheat, after its dissolution in the soil, leaves behind the slightness of its bulk and the peculiar quality of its shape, and yet it has not left and lost itself, but, still self-centred, grows into the ear, though in many points it has made an advance upon itself, viz. in size, in splendour, in complexity, in form. In the same fashion the human being deposits in death all those peculiar surroundings which it has acquired from passionate propensities; dishonour, I mean, and corruption and weakness and characteristics of age; and yet the human being does not lose itself. It changes into an ear of corn as it were; into incorruption, that is, and glory and honour and power and absolute perfection; into a condition in which its life is no longer carried on in the ways peculiar to mere nature, but has passed into a spiritual and passionless existence. For it is the peculiarity of the natural body to be always moving on a stream, to be always altering from its state for the moment and changing into something else; but none of these processes, which we observe not in man only but also in plants and brutes, will be found remaining in the life that shall be then. Further, it seems to me that the words of the Apostle in every respect harmonize with our own conception of what the Resurrection is. They indicate the very same thing that we have embodied in our own definition of it, wherein we said that the Resurrection is no other thing than *"the re-constitution of our nature in its original form."* For, whereas we learn from Scripture in the account of the first Creation, that first the earth brought forth "the green herb" (as the narrative says), and that then from this plant seed was yielded, from which, when it was shed on the ground, the same form of the original plant again sprang up, the Apostle, it is to be observed, declares that this very same thing happens in the Resurrection also; and so we learn from him the fact, not only that our humanity will be then changed into something nobler, but also that what we have therein to expect is nothing else than that which was at the beginning. In the beginning, we see, it was not an ear rising from a grain, but a grain coming from an ear, and, after that, the ear grows round the grain: and so the order indicated in this similitude clearly shows that all that blessed state which arises for us by means of the Resurrection is only a return to our pristine state of grace. We too, in fact, were once in a fashion a full ear; but the burning heat of sin withered us up, and then on our dissolution by death the earth received us: but in the spring of the Resurrection she will reproduce this naked grain of our body in the form of an ear, tail, well-proportioned, and erect, reaching to the heights of heaven, and, for blade and beard, resplendent in incorruption, and with all the other godlike marks. For "this corruptible must put on incorruption"; and this incorruption and glory and honour and power are those distinct and acknowledged marks of Deity which once belonged to him who was created in God's image, and which we hope for hereafter. The first man Adam, that is, was the first ear; but with the arrival of evil human nature was diminished into a mere multitude; and, as happens to the grain on the ear, each individual man was denuded of the beauty of that primal ear, and mouldered in the soil: but in the Resurrection we are born again in our original splendour; only instead of that single primitive ear we become the countless myriads of ears in the cornfields. The virtuous life as contrasted with that of vice is distinguished thus: those who while living have by virtuous conduct exercised husbandry on themselves are at once revealed in all the qualities of a perfect ear, while those whose bare grain (that is the forces of their natural soul) has become through evil habits degenerate, as it were, and hardened by the weather (as the so-called "hornstruck" seeds, according to the experts in such things, grow up), will, though they live again in the Resurrection, experience very great severity from their Judge, because they do not possess the strength to shoot up into the full proportions of an ear, and thereby become that which we were before our earthly fall. The remedy offered by the Overseer of the produce is to collect together the tares and the thorns, which have grown up with the good seed, and into whose bastard life all the secret forces that once nourished its root have passed, so that it not only has had to remain without its nutriment, but has been choked and so rendered unproductive by this unnatural growth. When from the nutritive part within them everything that is the reverse or the counterfeit of it has been picked out, and has been committed to the fire that consumes everything unnatural, and so has disappeared, then in this class also their humanity will thrive and will ripen into fruit-bearing, owing to such husbandry, and some day after long courses of ages will get back again that universal form which God stamped upon us at the beginning. Blessed are they, indeed, in whom the full beauty of those ears shall be developed directly they are born in the Resurrection. Yet we say this without implying that any merely bodily distinctions will be manifest between those who have lived virtuously and those who have lived viciously in this life, as if we ought to think that one will be imperfect as regards his material frame, while another will win perfection as regards it. The prisoner and the free, here in this present world, are just alike as regards the constitutions of their two bodies; though as regards enjoyment and suffering the gulf is wide between them. In this way, I take it, should we reckon the difference between the good and the bad in that intervening time. For the perfection of bodies that rise from that sowing of death is, as the Apostle tells us, to consist in incorruption and glory and honour and power; but any diminution in such excellences does not denote a corresponding bodily mutilation of him who has risen again, but a withdrawal and estrangement from each one of those things which are conceived of as belonging to the good. Seeing, then, that one or the other of these two diametrically opposed ideas, I mean good and evil, must any way attach to us, it is clear that to say a man is not included in the good is a necessary demonstration that he is included in the evil. But then, in connection with evil, we find no honour, no glory, no incorruption, no power; and so we are forced to dismiss all doubt that a man who has nothing to do with these last-mentioned things must be connected with their opposites, viz. with weakness, with dishonour, with corruption, with everything of that nature, such as we spoke of in the previous parts of the discussion, when we said how many were the passions, sprung from evil, which are so hard for the soul to get rid of, when they have infused themselves into the very substance of its entire nature and become one with it. When such, then, have been purged from it and utterly removed by the healing processes worked out by the Fire, then every one of the things which make up our conception of the good will come to take their place; incorruption, that is, and life, and honour, and grace, and glory, and everything else that we conjecture is to be seen in God, and in His Image, man as he was made.

CHAPTER SIX

Paula, Jerome's Letter CVIII "To Eustochium, Memorials of Her Mother, Paula"

Paula (347–404)

Paula was a Roman matron of status and wealth who provides an example of one pattern of Christian witness in early Christianity. At age thirty-three, a mother of five children, Paula denounced the world and embarked upon a penitential life of good works and hospitality. She pilgrimaged to Bethlehem, where she founded a monastery for men, a convent for women, and a hospice for travelers. Paula was a woman of vision and courage, committed to her Christian witness and to doing whatever it took to fulfill that witness, including begging to support her several ministries.

Letter CVIII to Eustochium

At Rome, Paula and Jerome (342–419), a biblical scholar and contemporary, became close friends. It is from him that our information on Paula is gained. Upon Paula's death, Jerome wrote a detailed letter to Eustochium, Paula's daughter, recounting her mother's virtues and ministries. In this excerpt from Jerome's Letter CVIII, "To Eustochium," we hear of Paula's travels and her Christ-like way in the world.

TO EUSTOCHIUM

1. If all the members of my body were to be converted into tongues, and if each of my limbs were to be gifted with a human voice, I could still do no justice to the virtues of the holy and venerable Paula. . . .

2. I call Jesus and his saints, yes and the particular angel who was the guardian and the companion of this admirable woman to bear witness that these are no words of adulation and flattery but sworn testimony every one of them borne to her character. They are, indeed, inadequate to the virtues of one whose praises are sung by the whole world, who is admired by bishops, regretted by bands of virgins, and wept for by crowds of monks and poor. . . .

5. . . . In what terms shall I speak of her distinguished, and noble, and formerly wealthy house; all the riches of which she spent upon the poor? How can I describe the great consideration she shewed to all and her far reaching kindness even to those whom she had never seen? What poor man, as he dying, was not wrapped in blankets given by her? What bedridden person was not supported with money from her purse? She would seek out such with the greatest diligence throughout the city, and would think it a misfortune were any hungry or sick person to be supported by another's food. So lavish was her charity that she robbed her children; and, when her relatives remonstrated with her for doing so, she declared that she was leaving to them a better inheritance in the mercy of Christ.

6. Nor was she long able to endure the visits and crowded receptions, which her high position in the world and her exalted family entailed upon her. She received the homage paid to her sadly, and made all the speed she could to shun and to escape those who wished to pay her compliments. It so happened that at that time the bishops of the East and West had been summoned to Rome by letter from the emperors to deal with certain dissensions between the churches, and in this way she saw two most admirable men and Christian prelates, Paulinus bishop of Antioch and Epiphanius, bishop of Salamis or, as it is now called, Constantia, in Cyprus. Epiphanius, indeed, she received as her guest; and, although Paulinus was staying in another person's house, in the warmth of her heart she treated him as if he too were lodged with her. Inflamed by their virtues she thought more and more each moment of forsaking her home. Disregarding her house, her children, her servants, her property, and in a word everything connected with the world, she was eager—alone and unaccompanied (if ever it could be said that she was so)—to go to the desert made famous by its Pauls and by its Antonies. And at last when the winter was over and the sea was open, and when the bishops were returning to their churches, she also sailed with them in her prayers and desires. Not to prolong the story, she went down to Portus accompanied by her brother, her kinsfolk and above all her own children eager by their demonstrations of affection to overcome their loving

mother. At last the sails were set and the strokes of the rowers carried the vessel into the deep. On the shore the little Toxotius stretched forth his hands in entreaty, while Rufina, now grown up, with silent sobs besought her mother to wait till she should be married. But still Paula's eyes were dry as she turned them heavenwards; and she overcame her love for her children by her love for God. She knew herself no more as a mother, that she might approve herself a handmaid of Christ. Yet her heart was rent within her, and she wrestled with her grief, as though she were being forcibly separated from parts of herself. The greatness of the affection had to overcome made all admire her victory the more. Among the cruel hardships which attend prisoners of war in the hands of their enemies, there is none severer than the separation of parents from their children. Though it is against the laws of nature, she endured this trial with unabated faith; nay more she sought it with a joyful heart: and overcoming her love for her children by her greater love for God, she concentrated herself quietly upon Eustochium alone, the partner alike of her vows and of her voyage. Meantime the vessel ploughed onwards and all her fellow-passengers looked back to the shore. But she turned away her eyes that she might not see what she could not behold without agony. No mother, it must be confessed, ever loved her children so dearly. Before setting out she gave them all that she had, disinheriting herself upon earth that she might find an inheritance in heaven. . . .

10. Then, after distributing money to the poor and her fellow-servants so far as her means allowed, she proceeded to Bethlehem stopping only on the right side of the road to visit Rachel's tomb. (Here it was that she gave birth to her son destined to be not what his dying mother called him, Benoni, that is the "Son of my pangs" but as his father in the spirit prophetically named him Benjamin, that is "the Son of the right hand"). After this she came to Bethlehem and entered into the cave where the Saviour was born. Here, when she looked upon the inn made sacred by the virgin and the stall where the ox knew his owner and the ass his master's crib, and where the words of the same prophet had been fulfilled, "Blessed is he that soweth beside the waters where the ox and the ass trample the seed under their feet:" when she looked upon these things I say, she protested in my hearing that she could behold with the eyes of faith the infant Lord wrapped in swaddling clothes and crying in the manger, the wise men worshipping Him, the star shining overhead, the virgin mother, the attentive foster-father, the shepherds coming by night to see "the word that was come to pass" and thus

even then to consecrate those opening phrases of the evangelist John "In the beginning was the word" and "the word was made flesh." . . .

15. I am now free to describe at greater length the virtue which was her peculiar charm; and in setting forth this I call God to witness that I am no flatterer. I add nothing. I exaggerate nothing. On the contrary I tone down much that I may not appear to relate incredibilities. My carping critics must not insinuate that I am drawing on my imagination or decking Paula, like Aesop's crow, with the fine feathers of other birds. Humility is the first of Christian graces, and hers was so pronounced that one who had never seen her, and who on account of her celebrity had desired to see her, would have believed that he saw not her but the lowest of her maids. When she was surrounded by companies of virgins she was always the least remarkable in dress, in speech, in gesture, and in gait. From the time that her husband died until she fell asleep herself she never sat at meat with a man, even though she might know him to stand upon the pinnacle of the episcopate. She never entered a bath except when dangerously ill. Even in the severest fever she rested not on an ordinary bed but on the hard ground covered only with a mat of goat's hair; if that can be called rest which made day and night alike a time of almost unbroken prayer. Well did she fulfil the words of the psalter: "All the night make I my bed to swim; I water my couch with my tears"! . . . No mind could be more considerate than hers, or none kinder towards the lowly. . . . Her liberality alone knew no bounds. Indeed, so anxious was she to turn no needy person away that she borrowed money at interest and often contracted new loans to pay off old ones. I was wrong, I admit; but when I saw her so profuse in giving, I reproved her . . . "My prayer is that I may die a beggar not leaving a penny to my daughter and indebted to strangers for my winding sheet." She then concluded with these words: "I, if I beg, shall find many to give to me; but if this beggar does not obtain help from me who by borrowing can give it to him, he will die; and if he dies, of whom will his soul be required?" . . . She obtained her wish at last and died leaving her daughter overwhelmed with a mass of debt. This Eustochium still owes and indeed cannot hope to pay off by her own exertions; only the mercy of Christ can free her from it. . . .

19. In her frequent sicknesses and infirmities she used to say, "when I am weak, then am I strong:" . . . When the exhaustion of her substance and the ruin of her property were announced to her she only said: "What is man profited, if he shall gain the whole world and lose his own soul? or what shall a man give in exchange for his soul?" . . . I know that when word was sent to her of the serious illnesses of her children and particularly of

Toxotius whom she dearly loved, she first by her self-control fulfilled the saying: "I was troubled and I did not speak," and then cried out in the words of scripture, "He that loveth son or daughter more than me is not worthy of me." And she prayed to the Lord and said: Lord "preserve thou the children of those that are appointed to die," that is, of those who for thy sake every day die bodily. I am aware that a talebearer—a class of persons who do a great deal of harm—once told her as a kindness that owing to her great fervour in virtue some people thought her mad and declared that something should be done for her head. She replied in the words of the apostle, "we are made a spectacle unto the world and to angels and to men," and "we are fools for Christ's sake" but "the foolishness of God is wiser than men." It is for this reason she said that even the Saviour says to the Father, "Thou knowest my foolishness," and again "I am as a wonder unto many, but thou art my strong refuge." "I was as a beast before thee; nevertheless I am continually with thee." In the gospel we read that even His kinsfolk desired to bind Him as one of weak mind. . . . But let us, she continued, listen to the exhortation of the apostle, "Our rejoicing is this, the testimony of our conscience that in simplicity and sincerity . . . armour against the assaults of wickedness, and particularly to defend herself against the furious on-slaughts of envy; and thus by patiently enduring wrongs she soothed the violence of the most savage breasts. . . .

20. I shall now describe the order of her monastery and the method by which she turned the continence of saintly souls to her own profit. She sowed carnal things that she might reap spiritual things; she gave earthly things that she might receive heavenly things; she forewent things temporal that she might in their stead obtain things eternal. Besides establishing a monastery for men, the charge of which she left to men, she divided into three companies and monasteries the numerous virgins whom she had gathered out of different provinces, some of whom are of noble birth while others belonged to the middle or lower classes. But, although they worked and had their meals separately from each other, these three companies met together for psalm-singing and prayer. After the chanting of the Alleluia— the signal by which they were summoned to the Collect—no one was permitted to remain behind. But either first or among the first Paula used to await the arrival of the rest, urging them to diligence rather by her own modest example than by motives of fear. At dawn, at the third, sixth, and ninth hours, at evening, and at midnight they recited the psalter each in turn. No sister was allowed to be ignorant of the psalms, and all had every day to learn a certain portion of the holy scriptures. On the Lord's day only they

proceeded to the church beside which they lived, each company following its own mother superior. Returning home in the same order, they then devoted themselves to their allotted tasks, and made garments either for themselves or else for others. If a virgin was of noble birth, she was not allowed to have an attendant belonging to her own household lest her maid having her mind full of the doings of old days and of the license of childhood might by constant converse open old wounds and renew former errors. All the sisters were clothed alike. Linen was not used except for drying the hands. So strictly did Paula separate them from men that she would not allow even eunuchs to approach them; lest she should give occasion to slanderous tongues (always ready to cavil at the religious) to console themselves for their own misdoing. When a sister was backward in coming to the recitation of the psalms or shewed herself remiss in her work, Paula used to approach her in different ways. Was she quick-tempered? Paula coaxed her. Was she phlegmatic? Paula chid her, copying the example of the apostle who said: "What will ye? Shall I come to you with a rod or in love and in the spirit of meekness?" Apart from food and raiment she allowed no one to have anything she could call her own, for Paul had said, "Having food and raiment let us be therewith content." She was afraid lest the custom of having more should breed covetousness in them; an appetite which no wealth can satisfy, for the more it has the more it requires, and neither opulence nor indigence is able to diminish it. When the sisters quarrelled one with another she reconciled them with soothing words. If the younger ones were troubled with fleshly desires, she broke their force by imposing redoubled fasts; for she wished her virgins to be ill in body rather than to suffer in soul. If she chanced to notice any sister too attentive to her dress, she reproved her for her error with knitted brows and severe looks, saying; "a clean body and a clean dress mean an unclean soul. A virgin's lips should never utter an improper or an impure word, for such indicate a lascivious mind and by the man the faults of the inward are made manifest." When she saw a sister verbose and talkative or forward and taking pleasure in quarrels, and when she found after frequent admonitions that the offender shewed no signs of improvement; she placed her among the lowest of the sisters and outside their society, ordering her to pray at the door of the refectory instead of with the rest, and commanding her to take her food by herself, in the hope that where rebuke had failed shame might bring about a reformation. The sin of theft she loathed as if it were sacrilege; and that which among men of the world is counted little or nothing she declared to be in a monastery a crime of the deepest dye. How shall I describe her kindness and attention towards the sick or the wonderful care and devotion with which she nursed them? Yet, although when others were sick and she freely gave them every indulgence, and even allowed them to eat meat; when she fell ill herself, she made no concessions to her own weakness, and seemed unfairly to change in her own case to harshness the kindness which she was always ready to show to others. . . .

27. . . . The holy scriptures she knew by heart, and said of the history contained in them that it was the foundation of the truth; but, though she loved even this, she still preferred to seek for the underlying spiritual meaning and made this the keystone of the spiritual building raised within her soul. She asked leave that she and her daughter might read over the old and new testaments under my guidance. Out of modesty I at first refused compliance, but as she persisted in her demand and frequently urged me to consent to it, I at last did so and taught her what I had learned not from myself—for self-confidence is the worst of teachers—but from the church's most famous writers. . . . While I myself beginning as a young man have with much toil and effort partially acquired the Hebrew tongue and study it now unceasingly lest if I leave it, it also may leave me; Paula, on making up her mind that she too would learn it, succeeded so well that she could chant the psalms in Hebrew and could speak the language without a trace of the pronunciation peculiar to Latin. . . .

32. Be not fearful, Eustochium: you are endowed with a splendid heritage. The Lord is your portion; and, to increase your joy, your mother has now after a long martyrdom won her crown. It is not only the shedding of blood that is accounted a confession: the spotless service of a devout mind is itself a daily martyrdom. Both alike are crowned; with roses and violets in the one case, with lilies in the other. . . .

35. The holy and blessed Paula fell asleep on the seventh day before the Kalends of February, on the third day of the week, after the sun had set. She was buried on the fifth day before the same Kalends, in the sixth consulship of the Emperor Honorius and the first of Aristaenetus. She lived in the vows of religion five years at Rome and twenty years at Bethlehem. The whole duration of her life was fifty-six years eight months and twenty-one days.

CHAPTER SEVEN

Egeria, *Pilgrimage* (404–417)

Egeria (late 4th century)

Although this account of her pilgrimage to Jerusalem is rich in detail, we know very little about the life of Egeria (also known as Aetheria, Etheria, and Echeria) prior to her journey. We know nothing of her place of birth, her upbringing, her family status, her education, her ecclesial status, or even the exact date of her pilgrimage. We can infer from the very fact of her extensive travels that she was a woman with considerable financial means at her disposal. She had some education, as her writing reflects a thorough knowledge of Scripture. This journal serves as correspondence with her "sisters," suggesting Egeria was a member of a community of learned and devout women in Western Europe on whose behalf she was a pilgrim. Egeria shows particular interest in biblical and liturgical detail as she reports back to her community, anticipating their questions and including them in her experience with vivid description.

The Pilgrimage of Egeria

Most likely Egeria recorded her travels between 404 and 417 C.E. In the first part, Egeria reports her experiences and encounters as she visits biblical and devotional sites throughout the Holy Land, from Mount Sinai to Constantinople. Many scholars consider the second part of the text the more valuable, because it relates in detail the practice of the Jerusalem liturgy in this period. Egeria participated in the daily and Sunday offices, as well as Epiphany, Holy Week, and Easter services.

THE PILGRIMAGE OF EGERIA

9. By chance we experienced a very pleasant event, for the day we arrived at the rest-station of Arabia was the most blessed feast of the Epiphany, and that same day they would be keeping vigil in the church. And so we were kept there two days by the holy bishop, a holy and true man of God well known to me since the time I visited the Thebaid. The holy bishop is from the monks, for from early childhood he was raised in a monastic dwelling, and thus is as learned in Scripture as he is without fault in his life, as I wrote above. At this point we sent back the Roman soldiers who had come with us through Roman authority, escorting us all this time through unsafe places. Because there was a public highway through Egypt, which goes through the city of Arabia, running from the Thebaid to Pelusium, we no longer needed to trouble the soldiers.

Thus we traveled there all through the land of Goshen, wending our way through seemingly endless vineyards which yield wine as well as balsam, and among orchards and cultivated fields and many gardens along the banks of the Nile, as well as many estates which were once the lands of the children of Israel. What more can I say? I do not think that I have ever seen a more beautiful territory than the land of Goshen. And so from the city of Arabia we made our way for two full days through the land of Goshen, arriving at Tanis, where Saint Moses was born. [Num. 13:23] This same city of Tanis at one time was Pharaoh's capital. As I said above, I already knew these places when I traveled from Alexandria to the Thebaid, but I wanted to know better the places which the children of Israel traversed going from Rameses to the holy mountain of God, Sinai, and so I had to return again from the land of Goshen and from there to Tanis. Setting out from Tanis, we went over a road I knew and arrived at Pelusium. Making our way by each of the rest-stations of Egypt along the way we had come, I reached the borders of Palestine. And from there, in the name of Christ our God, I again traveled some distance through Palestine and returned to Aelia, that is, Jerusalem. . . .

It was always our custom that when we had reached the place we wanted to go, first we said a prayer, then a selection from Scripture was read, then an appropriate psalm was sung, and we again said a prayer. We always maintained this custom, God willing, whenever we arrived at the place we desired to visit.

To complete the work we had begun, we hurried on to reach Mount Nebo. Along the way a presbyter of that place, Livias, guided us, because we had asked him to come with us from the rest-station because he knew the area better. This presbyter told us, "If you wish to see the water which flowed from the rock, which Moses gave the children of Israel when they are thirsty, turn at about the sixth mile along the road." [Ex. 17:6; Num. 20:8] When he said this, we were quite eager to go, and immediately turned off the road according to the directions of the presbyter who was guiding us. In that place is a small church at the foot of a mountain which is not Nebo, but a nearer one which is not far from Nebo. Many monks who are truly holy are there; they are called aescetics.

11. These holy monks very hospitably received us, permitting us to come in and greet them. When we entered with them, they prayed with us, and kindly gave us *eulogia,* as they customarily give to those whom they hospitably receive. There, between the church and the monks' cells, from a rock flows a great stream of water, very beautiful and limpid, and of the most delicious taste. Then we asked those holy monks who stay there why this water was of such quality and taste. Then they said: "This is the water which Moses gave the children of Israel in the desert." We prayed here according to our custom, heard a reading from the book of Moses, and said one psalm. Then we set off towards the mountain along with the holy clerics and monks, who had accompanied us. Many of the holy monks, who dwell near that water and were able to undertake the task, kindly agreed to ascend Mount Nebo with us. Going forth from this place we drew near to the foot of Mount Nebo, which was very high. The greater part could be climbed by riding a donkey, but a small part was so steep that it had to be climbed on foot. And so we did.

12. We reached Mount Nebo, where there is now a small church. Within that church, in the place where the pulpit stands, I saw a slightly elevated place, about the size of a tomb. Then I asked the holy men what it was. They replied, "Here Saint Moses was placed by the angels, because as Scripture tells us 'his tomb shall be known by no human being.' [Deut. 34:6; Jude 9] Thus it is certain that he was buried by angels. His tomb where he is buried, is shown even today, for we were shown it by the older monks who lived there, and thus we can show it to you." The older monks told us that the tradition was handed down to them by their predecessors in monastic life.

Soon we said a prayer and did everything in each holy place according to our customary order. As we were just leaving the church, those who knew the holy place, that is, the presbyters and holy monks, told us, "If you want to see the places which are written about in the books of Moses, go outside the doors of the church and from the summit where there is a view, look attentively, and we will tell you which are here and can be seen." We were pleased to hear this and immediately went outside. From the door of the church we saw the place where the Jordan enters the Dead Sea, which appeared just below the place where we stood. In the distance we saw not only Livias, which was on this side of the Jordan, but also Jericho which is across the Jordan. This is how high the place was where we stood, before the church door! From there can be seen the greater part of Palestine, which is the land of promise, and all the land of Jordan as far as the eye can see. [Deut. 9:28; Heb. 11:9] . . .

23. Departing from Tarsus, I came to a certain city on the sea-coast there in Cilicia, called Pompeiopolis. From there, passing through the borders of Isuria I stayed in the city called Corycus, and on the third day I came to the city which is called Selucia of Isauria. When I had arrived there, I called on the bishop, a truly holy man chosen from among the monks; I also saw in the same city a very beautiful church. Because it is about a mile and a half from the city to Saint Thecla's martyrium, on a flatish hill, I decided to go out there and stay overnight.

At the holy church one finds nothing except numberless monastic dwellings for men and women. I discovered there my very dear friend the holy deaconess Marthana, to whose life everyone in the East bears testimony, whom I had gotten to know in Jerusalem, where she had gone up to pray. She rules these monastic dwellings of *aputactitae* or virgins. When she saw me, how can I tell you what joy it was to her or to me? But let us return to the topic.

Many monastic dwellings are on the hill, and in the middle there is a great wall which encloses the church in which is very beautiful. The wall was erected there to protect the church from the Isaurians, who are quite evil and frequently steal, and would be likely to attempt something against the monastery which is established there. When I had come there in the name of God, prayer was made at the shrine and the reading was from the Acts of Thecla. I gave thanks to God who deigned to fulfill all my desires, though I am unworthy and undeserving.

I spent two days there, seeing the holy monks and *aputactitae,* both men and women, who live there; having prayed and made my communion. . . .

. . . From this place, ladies, my light, as I am writing this to your affection, I have proposed to go up in the name of Christ our God to Asia, to Ephesus, in order to pray at the martyrium of the blessed apostle John. But if after this I am in the body, if I have come to find out about other places, either I will speak of them in the presence of your affection, or certainly, if anything else occurs to me, I will write you. You indeed, ladies, my light, deign to remember me, whether I be in the body or out of the body. . . .

30. The next day, the Lord's Day, begins the Paschal week, which they call the Great Week. When the rites have been celebrated from cock crow until morning, according to custom in the Anastasis and the Cross, on the Lord's day the people proceed according to custom to the great church which is called the Martyrium because it is behind the Cross, where the Lord suffered, and therefore is a martyr's shrine. When all things are celebrated according to custom in the great church, before the dismissal, the archdeacon calls out and first says: "During the whole week which begins tomorrow, let us come together to the Martyrium, the great church." Then he speaks again and says: "Today at one let us all be prepared to go to the Eleona." When the dismissal is given in the great church, the Martyrium, the bishop is led with hymns to the Anastasis, and there are done all the things which it is the custom to do on the Lord's Day at the Anastasis after the dismissal at the Martyrium. Then each one goes home to eat a quick meal, so that by one o'clock all will be ready to go to the church which is in Eleona, which is on Mount Olivet, where is the cave in which the Lord taught.

31. At one o'clock all of the people go up to Mount Olivet, that is, the Eleona, into the church: the bishop is seated, they sing hymns and antiphons appropriate to the day and place, as are the readings. And when it is about three o'clock, they go down singing hymns to the Imbomon, which is in the place from which the Lord ascended into heaven, and everyone sits down there, for in the bishop's presence all the people are ordered to sit down, so that only the deacons remain standing. There hymns and antiphons appropriate to the day and place are sung; similarly readings and prayers are interspersed. When it is about one o'clock, that place in the Gospel is read where infants with palms and branches ran to the Lord, saying, "Blessed is he who comes in the name of the Lord." [Matt. 21:9] Immediately the bishop rises with all of the people and then they all walk from there to the summit of Mount Olivet. For all the people walk before the bishop singing hymns and antiphons, always responding: "Blessed is he who comes in the name of the Lord." And whatever children in this place, even those not able to walk, are carried on their parent's shoulders, all holding branches, some of palm, some of olive; thus the bishop is led in the same way that the Lord once was. And from the height of the mountain all the way to the city, And from there to the Anastasis through the whole city, all go on foot, the

matrons as well as the noble men thus lead the bishop, singing responses, going slowly so that the people may not tire. Then by evening they arrive at the Anastasis. When they have arrived there, although it is evening, they nonetheless say the Lucernare, and another prayer is said at the Cross and the people are dismissed.

32. The next day, Monday, all which is customary from cock crow until dawn, is done at the Anastasis, and at nine o'clock and at noon as during the whole of Lent. But at three o'clock everyone gathers in the Great Church, the Martyrium, and there they sing hymns and antiphons until seven in the evening; Scripture passages appropriate to the day and place are read; prayers are interspersed. The Lucernare is held there, when the time comes. Thus finally by night they give the dismissal at the Martyrium. When the dismissal is given they lead the bishop from there to the Anastasis with hymns. But when he has entered into the Anastasis, a hymn is sung, a prayer offered, the catechumens blessed, then the faithful, and the dismissal given. . . .

41. From the Pasch until the fortieth day, which is Pentecost, absolutely no one fasts here, not even those are *aputactitae*. For on those days all things are done according to custom at the Anastasis from cock crow to morning; likewise at the sixth hour and at the Lucernare. On the Lord's Day everyone proceeds as usual to the Martyrium, the great church, according to custom, and from there they go to the Anastasis with hymns. But on Wednesday and Fridays, because absolutely no one fasts here on these days, they proceed to Sion, but in the morning the service is performed according to the appointed order.

42. On the fortieth day after the Pasch, which is Thursday, the day before noon on Wednesday everyone goes to Bethlehem to celebrate the vigil. They keep the vigil in the church in Bethlehem, in the church where is the cave where the Lord was born. On the next day, Thursday, the fortieth day, the service is celebrated according to its usual order, so that presbyters and the bishop preach, saying words appropriate to the day and place. Afterwards in the evening everyone returns to Jerusalem.

43. The fiftieth day, which is the Lord's Day, provides great work for the people. All things are done from the first cock crow according to custom: vigil is kept in the Anastasis that the bishop might read that place in the Gospel which is always read on the Lord's Day, that is, the resurrection of the Lord. Afterwards everything is done in the Anastasis which is customary all year long.

When the morning has come, all the people proceed to the great church, the Martyrium, where all things are performed according to custom. The presbyters preach, afterwards the bishop, and all prescribed things are done; the service is completed as usual. But on this day the dismissal is given sooner in the Martyrium, before nine o'clock. As soon as the dismissal is given in the Martyrium, all the people, down to the last one, lead the bishop to Sion, in order to arrive at Sion exactly at the third hour. When they have arrived here, that place from the Acts of the Apostles is read where the Spirit descends, that all the tongues which were spoken might be understood. [Acts 2:1-12] Afterwards the service is performed according to its proper order. The presbyters read this particular passage because this is the place on Sion (the church is something else) where after the passion of the Lord a multitude gathered with the apostles. Because the event mentioned above occurred, they there read from the Acts of the Apostles.

Afterwards the service there is performed according to its proper order, and is offered there, and then as the people are dismissed the archdeacon cries out: "Today immediately after noon let us all be ready in Eleona at the Imbomon." All the people return home to rest, so that right after lunch they may go up Mount Olivet, which is in Eleona, each doing as much as possible, so that there is not one Christian left in the city; all have gone. As soon as they have climbed Mount Olivet, which is in the Eleona, first they go into the Imbomon, which is in the place where the Lord ascended into the heavens, and there the bishop, the presbyters, as well as all the people sit. There they read lections, sung hymns are interspersed, and antiphons appropriate to the day and place are sung, for the prayers which are interspersed are always so worded that they are fitting to the time and place. The place from the Gospel is read where it speaks of the Ascension of the Lord; there is also a reading from the Acts of the Apostles which speaks of the ascension of the Lord into the heavens after the resurrection. [Mark 16:19; Luke 24:50-51; Acts 1:4-13] When this has been done, the catechumens are blessed, then the faithful, and then at the other church on the Eleona, that is in the cave in which the Lord had sat and taught the Apostles. It is about four o'clock when they come there; they have the Lucernare, prayer is said, the catechumens are blessed and then the faithful.

Then all the people down to the last one go down from there with the bishop, singing hymns and antiphons appropriate to the day; they very slowly arrive at the Martyrium. When they have come to the gate of the city, it is already night, and hundreds of church candles are brought out for the people. Because it is quite far from the gate to the great church, the Martyrium, it is thus about eight o'clock when they arrive, because all the people walk very slowly so that they will not be tired from walking. They open the great doors which face the market place, and all the people enter with the bishop into the Martyrium, singing hymns. Having entered the church, hymns are sung, prayer is offered, the catechumens are blessed and then the faithful; and from there they go again with hymns to the Anastasis.

In the same way, when they have come into the Anastasis, they sing hymns and antiphons, prayer is offered, the catechumens are blessed then the faithful; a similar service is held at the Cross. Then from there all the Christian people down to the last one lead the bishop with hymns up to Sion. When they have arrived there, appropriate Scripture is read, psalms and antiphons are sung, prayer is offered, the catechumens are blessed and then the faithful, and the dismissal is offered. When the dismissal is given all go up to kiss the bishop's hand, and then all return home about midnight. Thus the greatest labor is borne on this day, because from the first cock crow vigil is kept at the Anastasis and from there there is no ceasing the whole day. Everything which is celebrated is drawn out, so that only by midnight after the dismissal is made at Sion, does everyone return home. . . .

45. I should also write about the way those who are to be baptized at the Pasch are taught. Who ever gives his name, does so before the first day of Lent, and all the names are noted by the presbyters; this is before the start of those eight weeks which are, as I said, kept as the forty days. When all the names are noted by the presbyter, afterwards, on the next day of Lent, that which is the beginning of the eight weeks, the bishop's chair is placed in the middle of the great church, the Martyrium, and the priests sit on chairs and all the clergy stand about. One by one the "competent" are led up; if they are men with their fathers, if women with their mothers. The bishop questions individually the neighbors of each who has come up, asking, "Is the person of good life? respectful to parents? not a drunkard or liar?" He also asks about the more serious vices in a person. If the person is proved without reproach in all of the things about which the bishop has questioned the witnesses present, he notes the person's name with his own hand. If however, someone is accused of anything, the bishop immediately orders the person to leave, saying "Change yourself, and if you do reform, come to the baptismal font." He makes such inquiries about both men and women. If however someone is a wanderer without witnesses who know the person, such a one will have a hard time being admitted to baptism.

81

46. However, ladies and sisters, I ought to write you so that you do not think that this is done without reason. It is the custom here that those who are preparing for baptism throughout those forty days are exorcised the first thing early in the morning by clerics as soon as the dismissal has been given the Anastasis in the morning. Immediately afterwards the bishop's chair is placed in the Martyrium, the great church, and all who are to be baptized sit in a circle around the bishop, men as well as women, while the fathers and the mothers stand there. All of the people who wish to hear may come in and sit down, if they are of the faithful. A catechumen, however, cannot enter when the bishop is teaching the Law.

The teaching is this way: Beginning with Genesis through those forty days he goes through the Scripture, first expounding carnally, then explaining spiritually. The resurrection and all things about the faith are taught during those days; this is called catechesis. When five weeks of teaching have been completed, then they receive the Symbol. He expounds the meaning of the whole Symbol as he did Scripture first carnally, and then spiritually. And so it is that in this place all of the faithful follow the Scriptures when they are read in church, because the catechesis is given during those hours. God knows, ladies and sisters, that the faithful who have come in to hear the catechesis which is explained by the bishop raise their voices [in questioning] more than when the bishop sits and preaches [in church] about each of the things being explained. Dismissal from the catechesis is given at about nine and from there the bishop is led with hymns to the Anastasis and the service for nine o'clock in the morning is performed. Thus they are taught each day during the seven weeks.

But in the eighth week of Lent, which is called the Great Week, they are not called to be taught, because all things must be done which were described above. When the seven weeks have passed, there remains only the Paschal Week which here is called the Great Week, then in the morning the bishop comes into the great church called the Martyrium. In the back, in the apse behind the altar, the bishop's chair is placed, and they come by one by one, each man with his father and each woman with her mother, and give back the Symbol to the bishop. After they have given back the Symbol to the bishop, the bishop speaks to all and says: "For all these seven weeks you have been taught all the Law of Scripture and you have also heard the faith. You have heard about the resurrection of the flesh, but of the whole explanation of the Symbol, you could hear only that allowed to catechumens. You are not yet able to know of a higher mystery, that of Baptism because you are still catechumens. Do not think that this is done without reason; when you have been baptized in the name of the Lord, you will hear about it through the eight Paschal days after the dismissal in the Anastasis. But as long as you are catechumens you cannot be told the more secret mysteries of God."

SECTION II

600–1500 C.E.

CHAPTER EIGHT

Leoba,
Life of Saint Leoba
(late 700s)

Leoba (700–779)

Born in Wessex, England, Leoba was sent as a child to Wimborne to study the sacred sciences under Mother Tetta. Leoba was a diligent student and became known both for her intellect and for her sanctity. She was a religious teacher of royalty, and was deeply respected in her own lifetime as a person of depth. She was a spiritual friend of Boniface (680–754), who asked her to come to Germany to help establish Christianity there. She stands as a representative of the decisive role played by women in the Christianization of Europe and of the strong tradition of female leadership in Christianity in England. This biography was based on written and oral accounts of those who knew her, especially four of her disciples.

Life of Saint Leoba

This *vita* recounts the extraordinary piety and intellect of a young girl intent upon a religious life. It describes Leoba's training under Mother Tetta and her spiritual dreams. The prophecy of the aged nun Tetta that Leoba would speak in "wise counsel" and that she would benefit many in other lands is borne out as the story progresses. We see her friendships with Boniface, a much-loved churchman, Queen Hiltigard, and the many women of her community. Striking in this text is the wholly female context of her education and formation.

THE LIFE OF SAINT LEOBA

... In the island of Britain, which is inhabited by the English nation, there is a place called Wimbourne, an ancient name which may be translated "Winestream." It received this name from the clearness and sweetness of the water there, which was better than any other in that land. In olden times the kings of that nation had built two monasteries in the place, one for men, the other for women, both surrounded by strong and lofty walls and provided with all the necessities that prudence could devise. From the beginning of the foundation the rule firmly laid down for both was that no entrance should be allowed to a person of the other sex. No woman was permitted to go into the men's community, nor was any man allowed into the women's, except in the case of priests who had to celebrate Mass in their churches; even so, immediately after the function was ended the priest had to withdraw. Any woman who wished to renounce the world and enter the cloister did so on the understanding that she would never leave it. She could only come out if there was a reasonable cause and some great advantage accrued to the monastery. Furthermore, when it was necessary to conduct the business of the monastery and to send for something outside, the superior of the community spoke through a window and only from there did she make decisions and arrange what was needed.

It was over this monastery, in succession to several other abbesses and spiritual mistresses, that a holy virgin named Tetta was placed in authority, a woman of noble family (for she was a sister of the king), but more noble in her conduct and good qualities. Over both the monasteries she ruled with consummate prudence and discretion. She gave instruction by deed rather than by words, and whenever she said that a certain course of action was harmful to the salvation of souls she showed by her own conduct that it was to be shunned. She maintained discipline with such circumspection (and the discipline there was much stricter than anywhere else) that she would never allow her nuns to approach clerics. She was so anxious that the nuns, in whose company she always remained, should be cut off from the company of men that she denied entrance into the community not merely to laymen and clerics but even to bishops. There are many instances of the virtues of this woman which the virgin Leoba, her disciple, used to recall with pleasure when she told her reminiscences. . . .

. . . We will now pursue our purpose of describing the life of her spiritual daughter, Leoba the virgin.

* * *

As we have already said, her parents were English, of noble family and full of zeal for religion and the observance of God's commandments. Her father was called Dynno, her mother Aebba. But as they were barren, they remained together for a long time without children. After many years had passed and the onset of old age had deprived them of all hope of offspring, her mother had a dream in which she saw herself bearing in her bosom a church bell, which on being drawn out with her hand rang merrily. When she woke up she called her old nurse to her and told her what she had dreamt. The nurse said to her: "We shall yet see a daughter from your womb and it is your duty to consecrate her straightway to God. And as Anna offered Samuel to serve God all the days of his life in the temple, so you must offer her, when she has been taught the Scripture from her infancy, to serve Him in holy virginity as long as she shall live." Shortly after the woman had made this vow she conceived and bore a daughter, whom she called Thrutgeba, surnamed Leoba because she was beloved, for this is what Leoba means. And when the child had grown up her mother consecrated her and handed her over to Mother Tetta to be taught the sacred sciences. And because the nurse had foretold that she should have such happiness, she gave her her freedom.

The girl, therefore, grew up and was taught with such care by the abbess and all the nuns that she had no interests other than the monastery and the pursuit of sacred knowledge. She took no pleasure in aimless jests and wasted no time on girlish romances, but, fired by the love of Christ, fixed her mind always on reading or hearing the Word of God. Whatever she heard or read she committed to memory, and put all that she learned into practice. She exercised such moderation in her use of food and drink that she eschewed dainty dishes and the allurements of sumptuous fare, and was satisfied with whatever was placed before her. She prayed continually, knowing that in the Epistles the faithful are counselled to pray without ceasing. When she was not praying she worked with her hands at whatever was commanded her, for she had learned that he who will not work should not eat. However, she spent more time in reading and listening to Sacred Scripture than she gave to manual labour. She took great care not to forget what she had heard or read, observing the commandments of the Lord and putting into practice what she remembered of them. In this way she so arranged her conduct that she was loved by all the sisters. She learned from all and obeyed them all, and by imitating the good qualities of each one she modelled herself on the continence of one, the cheerfulness of another, copying here a sister's mildness, there a sister's patience. One she tried to equal in attention to prayer, another in devotion to reading. Above all, she was intent on practising charity without which, as she knew, all other virtues are void.

When she had succeeded in fixing her attention on heavenly things by these and other practices in the pursuit of virtue she had a dream in which one night she saw a purple thread issuing from her mouth. It seemed to her that when she took hold of it with her hand and tried to draw it out there was no end to it; and as if it were coming from her very bowels, it extended little by little until was of enormous length. When her hand was full of thread and it still issued from her mouth she rolled it round and round and made a ball of it. The labour of doing this was so tiresome that eventually, through sheer fatigue, she woke from her sleep and began to wonder what the meaning of the dream might be. She understood quite clearly that there was some reason for the dream, and it seemed that there was some mystery hidden in it. Now there was in the same monastery an aged nun who was known to possess the spirit of prophecy, because other things that she had foretold had always been fulfilled. As Leoba was diffident about revealing the dream to her, she told it to one of her disciples just as it had occurred and asked her to go to the old nun and describe it to her as a personal experience and learn from her the meaning of it. When the sister had repeated the details of the dream as if it had happened to her, the nun, who could foresee the future, angrily replied: "This is indeed a true vision and presages that good will come. But why do you lie to me in saying that such things happened to you? These matters are no concern of yours: they apply to the beloved chosen by God." In giving this name, she referred to the virgin Leoba. "These things," she went on, "were revealed to the person whose holiness and wisdom make her a worthy recipient, because by her teaching and good example she will confer benefits on many people. The thread which came from her bowels and issued from her mouth, signifies the wise counsels that she will speak from the heart. The fact that it filled her hand means that she will carry out in her actions whatever she expresses in her words. Furthermore, the ball which she made by rolling it round and round signifies mystery of the divine teaching, which is set in motion by the words and deeds of those who give instruction and which turns earthwards through active works and heavenwards through contemplation, at one time swinging downwards through compassion for one's neighbour, again swinging upwards through the love of God. By these signs God shows that your mistress will profit many by her words and example, and the effect of them will be felt in other lands afar off whither she will go." That this interpretation of the dream was true later events were to prove.

At the time when the blessed virgin Leoba was pursuing her quest for perfection in the monastery the holy martyr Boniface was being ordained by Gregory, Bishop of Rome and successor to Constantine, in the Apostolic See. His mission was to preach the Word of God to the people in Germany. When Boniface found that the people were ready to receive the faith and that, though the harvest was great, the labourers who worked with him were few, he sent messengers and letters to England, his native land, summoning from different ranks of the clergy many who were learned in the divine law and fitted both by their character and good works to preach the Word of God. With their assistance he zealously carried out the mission with which he was charged, and by sound doctrine and miracles converted a large part of Germany to the faith. As the days went by, multitudes of people were instructed in the mysteries of the faith and the Gospel was preached not only in the churches but also in the towns and villages. Thus the Catholics were strengthened in their belief by constant exhortation, the wicked submitted to correction, and the heathen, enlightened by the Gospel, flocked to receive the grace of Baptism. When the blessed man saw that the Church of God was increasing and that the desire of perfection was firmly rooted he established two means by which religious progress should be ensured. He began to build monasteries, so that the people would be attracted to the church not only by the beauty of its religion but also by the communities of monks and nuns. And as he wished the observance in both cases to be kept according to the Holy Rule, he endeavoured to obtain suitable superiors for both houses. For this purpose he sent his disciple Sturm, a man of noble family and sterling character, to Monte Cassino, so that he could study the regular discipline, the observance and the monastic customs which had been established there by St. Benedict. As the future superior, he wished him to become a novice and in this way learn in humble submission how to rule over others. Likewise, he sent messengers with letters to the abbess Tetta, of whom we have already spoken, asking her to send Leoba to accompany him on this journey and to take part in this embassy: for Leoba's reputation for learning and holiness had spread far and wide and her praise was on everyone's lips. The abbess Tetta was exceedingly displeased at her departure, but because she could not gainsay the dispositions of divine providence she agreed to his request and sent Leoba to the blessed man. Thus it was that the interpretation of the dream which she had previously received was fulfilled. When she came, the man of God received her with the deepest reverence, holding her in great affection, not so much because she was related to him on his mother's side as because he knew that by her holiness and wisdom she would confer many benefits by her word and example. . . .

The blessed virgin, however, persevered unwaveringly in the work of God. She had no desire to gain earthly possessions but only those of heaven, and she spent all her energies on fulfilling her vows. Her wonderful reputation spread abroad and the fragrance of her holiness and wisdom drew to her the affections of all. She was held in veneration by all who knew her, even by kings. Pippin, King of the Franks, and his sons Charles and Carloman treated her with profound respect, particularly Charles, who, after the death of his father and brother, with whom he had shared the throne for some years, took over the reins of government. He was a man of truly Christian life, worthy of the power he wielded and by far the bravest and wisest king that the Franks had produced. His love for the Catholic faith was so sincere that, though he governed all, he treated the servants and handmaids of God with touching humility. Many times he summoned the holy virgin to his court, received her with every mark of respect and loaded her with gifts suitable to her station. Queen Hiltigard also revered her with a chaste affection and loved her as her own soul. She would have liked her to remain continually at her side so that she might progress in the spiritual life and profit by her words and example. But Leoba detested the life at court like poison. The princes loved her, the nobles received her, the bishops welcomed her with joy. And because of her wide knowledge of the Scriptures and her prudence in counsel they often discussed spiritual matters and ecclesiastical discipline with her. But her deepest concern was the work she had set on foot. She visited the various convents of nuns and, like a mistress of novices, stimulated them to vie with one another in reaching perfection.

Sometimes she came to the Monastery of Fulda to say her prayers, a privilege never granted to any woman either before or since, because from the day that monks began to dwell there entrance was always forbidden to women. Permission was only granted to her, for the simple reason that the holy martyr St. Boniface had commended her to the seniors of the monastery and because he had ordered her remains to be buried there. The following regulations, however, were observed when she came there. Her disciples and companions were left behind in a nearby cell and she entered the monastery always in daylight, with one nun older than the rest; and after she had finished her prayers and held a conversation with the brethren, she returned towards nightfall to her disciples whom she had left behind in the cell. When she was an old woman and became decrepit through age she put all the convents under her care on a sound footing and then, on Bishop Lull's advice, went to a place called Scoranesheim, four miles south of Mainz. There she took up residence with some of her nuns and served God night and day in fasting and prayer.

In the meantime, whilst King Charles was staying in the palace at Aachen, Queen Hiltigard sent a message to her begging her to come and visit her, if it were not too difficult, because she longed to see her before she passed from this life. And although Leoba was not at all pleased, she agreed to go for the sake of their longstanding friendship. Accordingly she went and was received by the queen with her usual warm welcome. But as soon as Leoba heard the reason for the invitation she asked permission to return home. And when the queen importuned her to stay a few days longer she refused; but, embracing her friend rather more affectionately than usual, she kissed her on the mouth, the forehead and the eyes and took leave of her with these words: "Farewell for evermore, my dearly beloved lady and sister; farewell, most precious half of my soul. May Christ our Creator and Redeemer grant that we shall meet again without shame on the day of judgment. Never more on this earth shall we enjoy each other's presence."

So she returned to the convent, and after a few days she was stricken down by sickness and was confined to her bed. When she saw that her ailment was growing worse and that the hour of her death was near she sent for a saintly English priest named Torhthat, who had always been at her side and ministered to her with respect and love, and received from him the viaticum of the body and blood of Christ. Then she put off this earthly garment and gave back her soul joyfully to her Creator, clean and undefiled as she had received it from Him. She died in the month of September, the fourth of the kalends of October. Her body, followed by a long cortège of noble persons, was carried by monks of Fulda to their monastery with every mark of respect. Thus the seniors there remembered what St. Boniface had said, namely, that it was his last wish that her remains should be placed next to his bones. But because they were afraid to open the tomb of the blessed martyr, they discussed the matter and decided to bury her on the north side of the altar which the martyr St. Boniface had himself erected and consecrated in honour of our Saviour and the twelve Apostles. . . .

CHAPTER NINE

Dhuoda, *Manual* (841)

Dhuoda (803–843)

Dhuoda, also called Dhuodana, was an educated laywoman of the ninth century. Unusual for her time, she left a record as a lay writer in an age of clerical domination. What we know of her comes from her *Manual,* which provides insight not only into her own heart and mind, but into the spiritual life of her age as well. In this writing, we learn that she was married on June 29, 824, to Bernhard of Septimania, and that she gave birth to a son in 826. She lived most of her married life in semi-abandonment at her husband's castle, bearing a second son in March 841. The following summer her husband sent their eldest son, William, to Charles the Bald as a hostage of sorts to serve his own political interests. Further, he ordered their second son removed from the castle before baptism so that two years later, at the end of the writing of the *Manual,* Dhuoda did not yet know her second son's name.

Dhuoda's *Manual*

The tragedies in Dhuoda's life set the stage for her writing during Advent 841. Her intention was to provide a moral handbook for her son William as she and her sons faced a Christmas apart. She understood it to be her responsibility to guide him intellectually and spiritually. In eleven books or chapters she covers such diverse topics as the Trinity, the gifts of the Holy Spirit, how to overcome bad habits, and the composition of verse. One writer has suggested that "to understand Dhuoda, read her as if it were your own mother giving you advice."

MANUAL

Here Begins the Manual of Dhuoda Which She Sent to Her Son, William

Having noticed that most women in this world are able to live with and enjoy their children, but seeing myself, Dhuoda, living far away from you, my dear son William, filled with anxiety because of this, and with the desire to be of aid to you, I am sending you this little manual, written by me, for your scrutiny and education, rejoicing in the fact that, though I am absent in body, this little book will recall to your mind, as you read it, the things you are required to do for my sake.

Moral Lesson

And what shall I say, fragile vessel that I am? I shall turn to others as a friend. To be sure, if the heavens and the earth were spread through the air like a parchment, and if all the various gulfs of the sea were transformed into ink, and if all the inhabitants of the earth born into this world from the beginning of humankind up to now were scribes, which is an impossible thing contrary to nature, they would not be able to comprehend (in writing) the greatness, the breadth, the height, the sublimity, the profundity of the Almighty or tell the divinity, wisdom, piety, and clemency of Him Who is called God. Since He is thus and so great that no one can comprehend His essence, I beg you to fear Him and to love Him with all your heart, all your mind, all your understanding, to bless Him in all your ways and deeds and to sing, "For He is good, for His mercy endureth forever!"

And believe Him to be above, below, inside, and outside, for He is superior, inferior, interior, and exterior.

Admonition

I also admonish you, O my handsome and lovable son William, that amid the mundane cares of this world you not neglect the acquisition of many books, in which you may understand and learn something greater and better than is written here concerning God, your Creator, through the teaching of the most blessed doctors. Beseech Him, cherish Him, love Him; if you do so, He will be a Keeper, a Leader, a Companion, and a Fatherland for you, the Way, the Truth, and the Life, granting you generous prosperity in the world, and He will turn your enemies to peace.

What more can I say? Your admonisher, Dhuoda, is always with you, son, and if I be absent because of death, which must come, you will have this little book of moral teaching as a memorial; and in it you will be able to see me as the reflection in a mirror, reading and praying to God in mind and body, and you will find fully set down the duties you must perform for me. Son, you will have teachers who will teach you other documents of greater utility, but not under the same conditions, not with a soul burning in their breasts as I, your mother, have, O firstborn son.

On Reverence in Prayer

Prayer is called *oratio*, 'prayer,' sort of *oris ratio*, 'reason of the mouth.'

But I, Dhuoda, lukewarm and lazy, weak and always tending toward that which is low, neither a long nor a short prayer pleases me. But I place my hope in Him, Who offers to His faithful the freedom to pray. And you, son William, keep watch, ask of Him and pray in a short, firm, and pure speech. Say, not only in the church, but wherever the opportunity presents itself, pray and say, "Mercy-giving and Merciful, Just and Pious, Clement and True, have pity on Your creation, whom You created and redeemed with Your blood; have pity on me, and grant that I may walk in Your paths and Your justice; give me memory and sense that I may understand, believe, love, fear, praise, and thank You and be perfect in every good work through proper faith and goodwill, O Lord, my God. Amen." . . .

That You Must Be Kind to Great and Small

It is not necessary for me to tell you this, that the example of the greatest, oldest, and best leaders must be followed in dealing with inferiors, for, though far from me, you will have noticed it yourself; also do not doubt that the lesser ones may rise to the heights of offering models for prelates. Therefore, I urge you not to be slow in joining yourself to them, in greater and lesser services.

God is the shaper of the good and the bad in heaven and on earth. For the sake of His lesser ones, He deigned to reveal His presence here below, for, as the Fathers say, although He was the Supreme Creator of all, He was willing to take on the form of a slave. He raises the powerful in order to plunge them into the depths, and He exalts the humble, that they may rise to the heights. . . . And if He, great as He is, comports Himself thus toward the lesser ones, what should we, small as we are, do toward those who are worse off? Those who are able ought to help them, and, according to the urgings and words of the Apostle Paul, bear one another's burdens.

Love all that you may be loved by all, cherish that you be cherished; if you love all, all will love you; if you individually, they plurally. It is written in the *Grammar* of the poet Donatus, "I love you and I am loved by you, I kiss you and am kissed by you . . . "

You, therefore, my son William, cherish and befriend those by whom you wish to be befriended; love, venerate, frequent, and honor all, so that you may be worthy to receive of all reciprocal retribution and due honor. For example, a certain learned man, making a comparison with a dumb animal for our edification, offered a great and clear sermon in a few words. He said in elucidating Psalm 41, "As the hart . . .": "Harts have this custom: when several of them wish to cross a sea or a large river of swirling waters, one after the other they place their horned heads on the back of their companions and hold up each other's necks, so that, by taking a little rest, they can make a more rapid crossing. There is in them such intelligence and such wisdom that, when they perceive the first to be tiring, they change places one after the other, and they let the second be first, now upholding and comforting the others. Thus, changing one by one, they each have pass through them the compassion of brotherly love, always taking care that the head with the horns be shown and held up, lest they be submerged in the waters."

What meaning is hidden here is not hidden from the learned. Everything is immediately clear to their eyes. In this upholding, you see, and in this changing of place is shown the love which is to be kept by all in the human race, both to the great and to the small through brotherly love.

In the upholding or the erection of the heads and the horns is shown that the faithful in Christ must always keep their hearts and minds on Him. . . .

On the Reconciliation of Sin

If it should happen, my son, that you do something bad, or even if you perceive that your soul is afflicted, hasten as soon as you can to make amends in all things. Turn to Him Who sees everything; always bear witness, externally as well as internally, of your guilt and worthlessness until you have given complete satisfaction, saying, "The sins of my youth and my ignorances, do not remember. I beg You, Lord, do not destroy me with my iniquities, and do not keep my faults to the end in Thy wrath. But, in accord with Thy ancient clemency and Thy great goodness, come to my aid, for Thou art merciful."

Remember, my son, the words of the publican: "O God, be merciful to me, a sinner, for I am not worthy, miserable and unclean as I am, to raise my worthless eyes to Thee, the perfect pure One."

How You Can Be Perfect with the Aid of God

For He has said: "1. He who walketh without blemish, 2. who worketh justice, 3. who speaketh the truth, 4. who doth not use deceit in his tongue, 5. who doeth not evil to his neighbor, 6. who sweareth not to his neighbor to deceive him, 7. who putteth not out his money to usury, 8. who taketh not up a reproach against his neighbor, 9. who taketh not bribes against the innocent, 10. who patiently tolerates injuries, 11. who is pure in heart and chaste in body, 12. who is innocent in hands, 13. who is able to transgress and transgresseth not, 14. who can do evil things and doeth them not, 15. who reacheth out his hand to the poor as often as he can." . . .

Finis

Have frequent recourse to this little book. Always be, noble child, strong and brave in Christ!

This book was begun during the second year after the death of the former emperor, Louis, the 30th of November, Saint Andrew's Day, at the beginning of Advent. It was finished, by the aid of God, on the second of February, the Feast of the Purification of the blessed ever-virgin Mary, under the propitious reign of Christ, awaiting the king whom God will designate.

Reader, pray for Dhuoda, if you wish to have the merit of seeing Christ in eternal happiness.

Here ends, thanks be to God, the Manual of William, according to the word of the Gospel: "It is finished."

Hrotsvit of Gandersheim, *Dulcitius* (mid 900s)

Hrotsvit of Gandersheim (c. 900s)

Hrotsvit was a German Christian, born to a noble Saxon family early in the tenth century. She entered the abbey at Gandersheim (where only daughters of aristocracy were admitted) probably at a young age, if she followed the custom of her time. Gandersheim was a prestigous abbey, known as a center for education and religious life. Under strong leadership of religious women, the abbey had its own court of law, kept its own army, coined its own money, and the abbess had a seat in the imperial diet. Hrotsvit became a canoness—a female religious who lived in community and took the vows of celibacy and obedience, but not the vow of poverty— at Gandersheim under the Benedictine rule. She felt God had given her a gift for writing and that she should use it toward edifying Christian readers so that they would not resort to the classical works, which were beautiful, but lacked moral content. She wrote eight legends, six plays, two epics, and a short poem. Apparently, her writing was appreciated during her lifetime, but little read after her death. In recent centuries, Hrotsvit has been widely recognized for her intellect; for her familiarity with Scripture, patristic, and classical literature; and for her style.

Dulcitius

The second of her plays, *Dulcitius* is a dramatization of the martyrdom of Agapê, Irenê, and Chionê at Saloniki during the Diocletian persecution of 304 C.E.. She recounts the story, depicting the three women as sisters who hold fast to their faith and their chastity in the face of demonic seductions by the pagan Dulcitius, their would-be judge and executioner. Imprisoned, the virgins pray steadfastly and find God's hand at work when Dulcitius arrives at their pantry cell that evening. Through some enchantment, he believes the pots and pans are the sisters, smearing himself with soot as he kisses the kitchen utensils. This play was intended to remind and inspire the Christian faithful of the triumph of good over evil, and of Christianity over paganism.

DULCITIUS

The martyrdom of the holy virgins Agapes, Chionia, and Hirena whom, in the silence of night, Governor Dulcitius secretly visited, desiring that in their embrace he might delight; but as soon as he entered, he became demented and kissed and hugged the pots and the pans, mistaking them for the girls until his face and his clothes were soiled with disgusting black dirt. Afterward the Count Sissinus, acting on orders, was given the girls so he may put them to tortures. He, too, was deluded by a miraculous bane but finally ordered that Agapes and Chionia be burned and Hirena by an arrow be slain.

DIOCLETIAN: The renown of your free and noble descent and the brightness of your beauty demand that to the foremost men of my court you be wed. According to our command this will be met if Christ you deny and comply in bringing offerings to our gods.
AGAPES: Be free of care, don't trouble yourself our wedding to prepare because we cannot be compelled under any duress to betray Christ's name, which we must confess, or to stain our virginity.
DIOCLETIAN: What madness possesses you? What does this mean?
AGAPES: What signs of our madness do you see?
DIOCLETIAN: An obvious and great display.
AGAPES: In what way?
DIOCLETIAN: Chiefly in that renouncing the practices of ancient religion you follow the useless newfangled ways of Christian superstition.
AGAPES: Heedlessly you offend the majesty of God omnipotent. That is dangerous . . .
DIOCLETIAN: Dangerous to whom?
AGAPES: To you and to the state which you rule.
DIOCLETIAN: She is mad; remove her!

CHIONIA: My sister is not mad, justly did she your folly reprehend.

DIOCLETIAN: Her rage is even more absurd. Remove her from our sight and arraign the third.

HIRENA: You will find the third, too, a rebel and resisting you forever.

DIOCLETIAN: Hirena, although you are younger in birth, be greater in worth!

HIRENA: Show me, I pray you, how?

DIOCLETIAN: To the gods bow your neck and an example for your sisters so set and be the cause for their freedom!

HIRENA: Let those worship idols, sire, who wish to incur God's ire. But I won't defile my head, anointed with royal unguent sweet, by debasing myself at the idols' feet.

DIOCLETIAN: The worship of gods brings no dishonor but great honor.

HIRENA: And what dishonor is more disgraceful, what disgrace is any more shameful, than when a slave is venerated as a master?

DIOCLETIAN: I don't ask you to worship slaves but the lord gods of princes and greats.

HIRENA: Is he not anyone's slave who, for a price, is up for sale?

DIOCLETIAN: For her speech so brazen, to the tortures she must be taken.

HIRENA: That is just what we hope for, that is what we desire, that for the love of Christ through tortures we may expire.

DIOCLETIAN: Let these insolent girls who defy our decrees and words be put in chains and kept in the squalor of prison until Governor Dulcitius conducts the interrogation.

DULCITIUS: Bring forth, soldiers, the girls you hold sequestered.

SOLDIERS: Here they are whom you requested.

DULCITIUS: Wonderful, indeed, how beautiful, how graceful, how admirable these little girls are!

SOLDIERS: Yes, they are perfectly lovely.

DULCITIUS: I am captivated by their beauty.

SOLDIERS: That is understandable.

DULCITIUS: To draw them to my love, I am eager.

SOLDIERS: Your success will be meager.

DULCITIUS: Why?

SOLDIERS: Because they are firm in faith.

DULCITIUS: What if I sway them by flattery?

SOLDIERS: They will despise it utterly.

DULCITIUS: What if with tortures I frighten them?

SOLDIERS: Little will it matter to them.

DULCITIUS: Then what should be done?

SOLDIERS: Consider carefully.

DULCITIUS: Under guard they must be held in the inner room of the workshop in whose vestibule the servants' pots are kept.

SOLDIERS: Why there?

DULCITIUS: So that I may visit them often at my leisure.

SOLDIERS: At your pleasure.

DULCITIUS: What do the captives do at this time of night?

SOLDIERS: Hymns they recite.

DULCITIUS: Let us go near.

SOLDIERS: From afar we hear their tinkling voices clear.

DULCITIUS: Stand guard before the door with your lantern but I will enter and satisfy myself in their longed-for embrace.

SOLDIERS: Enter. We will guard this place.

AGAPES: What is that noise outside the door?

HIRENA: That wretched Dulcitius is coming to the fore.

CHIONIA: May God protect us!

AGAPES: Amen.

CHIONIA: What is the meaning of this clash of pots, utensils, and pans?

HIRENA: I will check. Come here, please, and look through the crack!

AGAPES: What is going on?

HIRENA: Look, the fool, the madman so base, he thinks he is enjoying our embrace.

AGAPES: What is he doing?

HIRENA: Unto his lap he pulls the utensils, he embraces the pots and the pans, giving them tender kisses.

CHIONIA: Ridiculous!

HIRENA: His face, his hands, his clothes are so soiled, so filthy, and so loath, that with all the soot that clings to him, he looks like an Ethiopian.

AGAPES: It is only right, that he should appear in sight as he is in his mind: possessed by the fiend.

HIRENA: Wait! He prepares to leave. Let us watch how he is greeted, and how he is treated by the soldiers who wait for him.

SOLDIERS: Who is coming out? A demon without doubt. Or rather, the devil himself is he, let us flee!

DULCITIUS: Soldiers, where are you taking in flight? Stay! Wait! Escort me home with your light!

SOLDIERS: The voice is our master's tone but the look the devil's own. Let us not stay! Let us run away, the apparition will slay us!

DULCITIUS: I will go to the palace and complain, and reveal to the whole court the insults I had to sustain.

DULCITIUS: Guards, let me into the palace, I must have a private audience.

GUARDS: Who is this monster vile and detestable? Covered in rags torn and despicable? Let us beat him, from the steps let us sweep him; he must not be allowed to enter.

DULCITIUS: Alas, alas, what has happened? Am I not dressed in splendid garments? Don't I look neat and clean? Yet anyone who looks at my mien loathes me as a foul monster. To my wife I shall return, and from her learn what has happened. But there is my spouse, with disheveled hair she leaves the house, and the whole household follows her in tears!

WIFE: Alas, alas, Dulcitius, my lord, what has happened to you? You are not sane; the Christians have made a laughingstock out of you.

DULCITIUS: At last now I know— this mockery to their witchcraft I owe.

WIFE: What upsets me, what makes me sad, is that you were ignorant of all that passed.

DULCITIUS: I command that those insolent girls be led forth, and that they be stripped from all their clothes publicly, so that in retaliation for ours, they experience similar mockery.

SOLDIERS: We labor in vain; we sweat without gain. Behold, their garments remain on their virginal bodies, sticking to them like skin. But he who ordered us to strip them snores in his seat, and cannot be woken from his sleep. Let us go to the emperor's court and make a report.

DIOCLETIAN: It grieves me greatly to hear how Governor Dulcitius fared, that he has been greatly deluded, so greatly insulted, so utterly humiliated. But these vile young women shall not boast with impunity of having made a mockery of our gods and those who worship them. I shall direct Count Sissinus to take due vengeance.

SISSINUS: Soldiers, where are those insolent girls that are to be tortured?

SOLDIERS: They are kept in prison.

SISSINUS: Leave Hirena there, bring the others here.

SOLDIERS: Why do you except the one?

SISSINUS: Sparing her youth. Forsooth, she may be converted easier, if she is not intimidated by her sisters' presence.

SOLDIERS: It makes sense.

SOLDIERS: Here are they whose presence you requested.

SISSINUS: Agapes and Chionia, give heed, and to my counsel accede!

AGAPES: We will not give heed.

SISSINUS: Bring offerings to the gods.

AGAPES: We bring offerings of praise forever to the true Father eternal, and to His Son coeternal, and also to the Holy Spirit.

SISSINUS: This is not what I bid, but on pain of penalty prohibit.

AGAPES: You cannot prohibit that ever, never shall we bring sacrifices to demons.

SISSINUS: Cease this hardness of heart, and make your offerings. But if you persist then I shall insist that you be killed according to the emperor's orders.

CHIONIA: It is proper—that you shouldn't delay, and the orders of your emperor obey, whose decrees you know we disdain. But if you spare us then—you, too, deserve to be slain.

SISSINUS: Soldiers, don't delay, but lead these blaspheming girls away, and throw them alive to the flames.

SOLDIERS: We shall instantly build the pyre you ask, and into the raging fire these girls we will cast, thus we will end their insults at last.

AGAPES: O Lord, nothing is impossible for You, not even that the fire forget its nature and obey You; but we are weary of delay, therefore, solve the earthly bonds that hold our souls, we pray, so that as our earthly bodies perish, our souls in heaven Your glory may cherish.

SOLDIERS: Oh, marvel, oh, stupendous miracle! Behold their souls no longer to their bodies are bound, yet no traces of injury can be found; neither their hair nor their clothes are burned by the fire, and their bodies are not at all harmed by the pyre.

SISSINUS: Bring forth Hirena.

SOLDIERS: Here she is.

SISSINUS: Hirena, at the deaths of your sisters tremble, and fear to perish according to their example.

HIRENA: I hope to follow their example and expire, so with them in heaven eternal joy I may acquire.

SISSINUS: Give in, give in to my persuasion.

HIRENA: I will never give in to evil persuasion.

SISSINUS: If you don't give in, I shall not give you a death quick and easy, but multiply your sufferings daily.

HIRENA: The more cruelly I'll be tortured, the more gloriously I'll be exalted.

SISSINUS: You fear no tortures, no pain? What you abhor, I shall ordain.

HIRENA: Whatever punishment you'll design, I will escape it with help divine.

SISSINUS: To a brothel you'll be conducted, where your body'll be shamefully polluted.

HIRENA: Better that the body be dirtied with any stain, than that the soul be polluted with idolatry vain.

SISSINUS: If you be in the company of harlots—so polluted, among the virginal choir you no longer could be counted.

HIRENA: Lust deserves punishment, but forced compliance the crown; neither is one considered guilty, unless the soul consented freely.

SISSINUS: I pitied her youth in vain; I spared her without gain!

SOLDIERS: We knew this before; she could not be moved our gods to adore, nor can she be broken by terror.

SISSINUS: I spare her no longer.

SOLDIERS: Rightly you ponder.

SISSINUS: Seize her mercilessly, drag her with cruelty, take her in dishonor to the brothel.

HIRENA: They will not succeed!

SISSINUS: Who will intercede?

HIRENA: He Whose foresight rules the world.

SISSINUS: I shall see . . .

HIRENA: Sooner than you wish, it will be.

SISSINUS: Soldiers, be not frightened by the false prophecies of this blaspheming girl.

SOLDIERS: We are not afraid, but are eager to do what you bade.

SISSINUS: Who are those approaching? How similar they are to the men, to whom we gave Hirena just then. They are the same. Why are you returning so fast? Why so out of breath, I ask?

SOLDIERS: You are the one for whom we look.

SISSINUS: Where is she whom you just took?

SOLDIERS: On the peak of mountain high.

SISSINUS: Which one?

SOLDIERS: The one close by.

SISSINUS: O you idiots, dull and blind. You have completely lost your mind!

SOLDIERS: Why do you accuse us, why do you threaten us with voice and face and abuse us?

SISSINUS: May the gods destroy you!

SOLDIERS: What have we committed; what harm have we done; how have we transgressed against your orders?

105

SISSINUS: Have I not given orders resolute that you take that rebel against the gods to a place of ill repute?

SOLDIERS: Yes, so you did command, and we were eager to fulfill your demand, but two strangers intercepted us, saying that you sent them to us to lead Hirena to the mountain's peak.

SISSINUS: That's new to me.

SOLDIERS: We can see.

SISSINUS: What were they like?

SOLDIERS: Splendidly dressed and an awe-inspiring sight.

SISSINUS: Did you follow?

SOLDIERS: We did so.

SISSINUS: What did they do?

SOLDIERS: They placed themselves on Hirena's left and right, and told us to be forthright and not to hide from you what happened.

SISSINUS: I find a sole recourse, that I mount my horse and seek out those who so freely made sport with us.

SISSINUS: Hm, I don't know what to do. I am bewildered by the witchcraft of these Christians. I keep going around the mountain and keep finding this track, but neither do I know how to proceed or how to find my way back.

SOLDIERS: We are all deluded by some intrigue; we are afflicted with a great fatigue; if you allow this insane person to stay alive, then neither you nor we shall survive.

SISSINUS: Anyone among you, I don't care which, string a bow, and shoot an arrow, and kill that witch!

SOLDIERS: Rightly so.

HIRENA: Wretched Sissinus, blush for shame, and your miserable defeat proclaim, because without the force of arms, you cannot overcome a tender young virgin.

SISSINUS: Whatever shame may come to me, I will bear it more easily, because without a doubt I know that you will die now.

HIRENA: For me this is the greatest joy I can conceive, but for you this is a cause to grieve, because you shall be damned in Tartarus for your cruelty, while I shall receive the martyr's palm and the crown of virginity; thus I will enter the heavenly bridal chamber of the eternal King, Whose is all honor and glory in all eternity.

CHAPTER ELEVEN

Hildegard of Bingen, *The Visions of St. Hildegard* (1141)

Hildegard of Bingen (1098–1179)

From an early age, Hildegard was known to have exhibited spiritual gifts of prophecy and clairvoyance. The tenth child of German parents, she was dedicated to the religious life, entering a small nearby Benedictine monastery at age eight. She was a quick learner and a natural leader. She gained influence among her sisters, who made her abbess in 1136. Later she moved her community to Rupertsberg near Bingen and built a much larger convent. Meanwhile, she had gained a solid reputation as a religious counselor to the powerful and to the troubled. She had also written in diverse fields, including saints' lives, sermons, medicine, and natural history.

The Visions of St. Hildegard

Although Hildegard had experienced mystical visions since childhood, she refused to record them. However, God's command in 1141 to "write what you see and hear!" and a painful illness that subsided only when she began to write down her visions convinced her that she must. She recorded twenty-six visions in all, comprising three books. Pope Eugenius III acknowledged Hildegard's prophetic gifts and found in her visions a source of counsel and inspiration. This excerpt from Book II is "Of the Blessed Trinity," wherein Hildegard describes her vision of God.

VISION II (FROM BOOK II)

Of the Blessed Trinity

Then I saw a most splendid light, and in that light, the whole of which burnt in a most beautiful, shining fire, was the figure of a man of a sapphire colour, and that most splendid light poured over the whole of that shining fire, and the shining fire over all that splendid light, and that most splendid light and shining fire over the whole figure of the man, appearing one light in one virtue and power. And again I heard that living Light saying to me: This is the meaning of the mysteries of God, that it may be discerned and understood discreetly what that fulness may be, which is without beginning and to which nothing is wanting, who by the most powerful strength planted all the rivers of the strong (places). For if the Lord is wanting in His own strength, what then would His work be?

Certainly vain, and so in a perfect work is seen who was its maker. On which account thou seest this most splendid Light, which is without beginning and to Whom nothing can be wanting: this means the Father, and in that figure of a man of a sapphire colour, without any spot of the imperfection of envy and iniquity, is declared the Son, born of the Father, according to the Divinity before all time, but afterwards incarnate according to the humanity, in the world, in time. The whole of which burns in a most beautiful, shining fire, which fire without a touch of any dark mortality shows the Holy Spirit, by Whom the same only-begotten Son of God was conceived according to the flesh, and born in time of the Virgin, and poured forth the light of true brightness upon the world.

But that splendid Light pours forth all that shining fire, and that shining fire all that splendid Light, and the splendid shining light of the fire, the whole of the figure of the man, making one Light existing in one strength and power: this is because the Father, Who is the highest equity, but not without the Son nor the Holy Spirit, and the Holy Spirit who is the kindler of the hearts of the faithful, but not without the Father and the Son, and the Son who is the fullness of virtue, but not without the Father and the Holy Spirit, are inseparable in the majesty of the Divinity; because the Father is not without the Son, neither the Son without the Father, nor the Father and the Son without the Holy Spirit, neither the Holy Spirit without them, and these three Persons exist one God in one whole divinity of majesty: and the unity of the Divinity lives inseparable in the three Persons, because the Trinity is not able to be divided, but remains always inviolable without any change, for the Father is declared through the Son, and the Son through the birth of creatures, and the Holy Spirit through the same Son, Incarnate.

How? It is the Father Who before all ages begat the Son, the Son, through Whom all things were made in the beginning of creatures, by the Father, and the Holy Spirit appeared in the form of a dove, in the baptism of the Son of God in the end of the ages.

Whence never let man forget to invoke Me as One God in three Persons, because these things are shown to man, that he may burn more ardently in My love, when for love of him I sent My own Son into the world, as My beloved John testified, saying: "In this appeared the Love of God to us, because He sent His only begotten Son into the world that we might live through Him. In this is love, not as if we had loved God, but because He first loved us, and sent His Son as a propitiation for our sins" *(I John iv.).*

Why so? Because in this way GOD loved us; another salvation has sprung up, than that which we had in the creation, when we were heirs of innocence and of sanctity, because the Father above showed His love, when we in our peril were placed in punishment, sending His Word, Who alone among the sons of men was perfect in holiness, into the darkness of this world, where that same Word, doing all good works, led them back to life through His meekness, who were cast out by the malice of transgression, nor were they able to return to that holiness which they had lost.

Why so? Because through that fountain of life came the paternal love of the embrace of God, which educated us to life, and in our dangers was our help, and is the most deep and beautiful light teaching us repentance.

In what way? God mercifully remembered His great work and His most precious pearl, man, I say, whom He formed from the dust of the earth, and into whom He breathed the breath of life. In what manner? He taught (us) how to live in repentance whose efficacy will never perish, because the crafty serpent deceived man by tempting him through pride, but God cast him down into repentance which brings forth humility, which the devil neither knew nor made, because he was ignorant of how to rise to a just life.

Thence this salvation of love did not spring from us, because we did not know, neither were we able to love God unto salvation, but because He the Creator and Lord of all so loved the world, that He sent His Son for its salvation, the Prince and Saviour of the faithful, Who washed and dried our wounds, and from Him also came that most sweet medicine, from which all the good things of salvation flow.

Wherefore, O man, do thou understand that no shadow *(instabilitas)* of change touches God. For the Father is the Father, the Son is the Son, and the Holy Spirit is the Holy Spirit, three Persons living inseparably in the unity of the Divinity.

In what manner? There are three virtues in a stone, three in a flame and three in a word. How? In the stone is the virtue of moisture, the virtue of palpability, and the power of fire, for it has the virtue of moisture lest it should be dissolved and broken in pieces, but it shows its palpable comprehension when used as a habitation and a defence, and it has the virtue of fire so that it may be heated and consolidated to its hardness. And this virtue of moisture signifies the Father, Whose power is never dried up nor finished; and the palpable comprehension means the Son, Who being born of the Virgin is able to be touched and comprehended, and the fiery power signifies the Holy Spirit Who is the kindler and the illuminator of the hearts of faithful men.

How is this? As man frequently attracts into his body the damp power of the stone, and falling ill is weakened, so man who through the instability of his thoughts will fear to look up to the Father, loses his faith: and in the palpable comprehension of the stone is shown that men make a habitation with it for themselves, as a defence against their enemies, thus the Son of God, Who is the true Corner-stone, is the habitation of the faithful, protecting them from evil spirits.

But as the shining fire illuminates darkness, burning those things upon which it had been lying, thus the Holy Spirit drives away infidelity, taking away all the foulness of iniquity. And in the same way that these three powers are in one stone, so the true Trinity is in one Deity.

Again, as the flame in one fire has three powers, so the One God is in Three Persons. In what manner? For in the flame abides splendid light, innate vigour, and fiery heat, but it has splendid light that it may shine, innate vigour that it may flourish, and fiery heat that it may burn. Thence consider in the splendid light, the Father Who in His paternal love sheds His light upon the faithful, and in that innate vigour of the splendid flame in which that same flame shows its power, understand the Son, Who took flesh from the Virgin, in which the Divinity declared His wonders, and in the fiery heat, behold the Holy Spirit, Who gently kindles the hearts and minds of the faithful.

But where there is neither a splendid light, nor innate vigour, nor fiery heat, there no flame is discerned: thus where neither the Father, nor the Son, nor the Holy Spirit is worshipped, there neither is He worthily venerated.

Therefore as in one flame these three powers are discerned; thus in the unity of the Divinity, three Persons are to be understood.

So also as three powers are to be noted in a word, thus the Trinity in the Unity of the Divinity is to be considered. In what way? In a word there is sound, power and breath. For it has sound that it may be heard, power that it may be understood, breath that it may be perfected.

In the sound, note the Father, Who with unerring power makes manifest all things. In the power, note the Son, Who is wonderfully begotten of the Father; and in the breath, note the Holy Spirit, Who breathes where He will and all things are accomplished.

But where no sound is heard, there neither power, works, nor breath is raised, thence neither there is the Word to be understood; so also the Father, the Son, and the Holy Spirit are not to be divided from themselves, but their work is performed unanimously.

Then as these three things are in one word, so also the supernal Trinity is in the supernal Unity: and as in a stone there is neither the virtue of moisture, without palpable comprehension, nor fiery power, nor palpable comprehension without the power of moisture, and the fiery vigour of a shining fire; neither the vigour of the shining fire, without the power of moisture and palpable comprehension; and as in a flame there is not, neither can there be caused, a splendid light without innate vigour and fiery heat, neither innate vigour without splendid light and fiery heat, neither fiery heat without splendid light and innate vigour, so in a word there neither is nor can be made a sound without power and breath, neither power without sound and breath, neither breath without sound and power, but these in their work are indivisibly inherent in each other, so also these three Persons of the supernal Trinity exist inseparably in the majesty of Divinity, neither are they divided from each other.

Thus understand, O man, One God in three Persons. But thou in the foolishness of thy mind thinkest God to be so impotent, that it is not possible to Him to subsist truly in three Persons, but to be able only to consist of One, when neither dost thou see a voice to consist without three. Why so? God is certainly in three Persons, one true God first and last.

But the Father is not without the Son, neither the Son without the Father, nor the Father nor the Son without the Holy Spirit, nor the Holy Spirit without them, because these three Persons are inseparable in Unity of the Divinity. As a word sounds from the mouth of a man, but not the mouth without the word, nor the word without life. And where remains the word? In the man. Whence does it go out? From the man. In what way? From the living man.

Thus is the Son in the Father, Whom the Father for the salvation of men sitting in darkness, sent to earth, conceived in the Virgin by the Holy Spirit. Which Son as He was only begotten in His divinity, so He was only begotten in virginity, and as He is the only Son of the Father, so He is the only Son of His mother, because as the Father begat Him before all time, so His Virgin Mother bore Him only in time, because she remained Virgin after His birth.

Thence, O man, understand in these three Persons Thy God, Who created thee in the power of His divinity, and Who redeemed thee from perdition. Be unwilling therefore to forget thy Creator as Solomon says, "Remember thy Creator in the days thy youth, before the time of thy affliction shall come, and the years draw nigh of which thou sayest: They do not please me" *(Eccles. xii.)*. What does this mean? To remember in thy intellect Him Who made thee, when, for example, in the days of thy foolish confidence, thou thoughtest it possible that thou shouldst ascend on high, casting thyself into the depths, and when standing in prosperity falling into extreme afflictions.

For the life which is in thee strives always that it may be perfected, until that time when it shall appear perfect.

In what way? An infant advances from its first birth until (it attains) its perfect stature, forsaking the petulancy of manners of foolish youth only when providing solicitously with great care, that which may be used for himself in his business, which he never did when swayed by the inconstancy of foolish youth.

Thus does the faithful man, he leaves the manners of infancy, and he mounts up to the height of the virtues, persevering in their strength, forsaking the exaltation of his covetousness, which in the madness of vices increased, and he meditates carefully in poverty what may be useful to him after he has forsaken the manners of youth.

Thence, O man! thus embrace thy God in the courage of thy strength, before the Judge of thy works shall come, when all things shall be manifested, lest anything hidden should be left, when those times come which in their duration shall not fail.

Concerning which things, but murmuring thou sayest in thy human thought: "They do not please me, neither do I understand whether they are meritorious or not, because in this my human mind is always doubtful, for when a man does good works he is anxious whether they please God or not. And when he does evil he fears concerning the remission which is of salvation." But he who sees with watchful eyes, and hears with attentive ears, offers an embrace to these mystic words of mine which emanate from me, living.

CHAPTER TWELVE

Hadewijch of Brabant, *Letters* and *Visions* (c. 1200s)

Hadewijch of Brabant (c. 1200s)

Along with Beatrice of Nazareth, Hadewijch gives us the earliest extant writing in the vernacular of Dutch prose and a look at women's religious life in the thirteenth century. Although we know little about Hadewijch, we have three complete manuscripts of her works, which include thirty-one letters, forty-five stanzaic poems, fourteen visions, and twenty-nine poems in rhyming couplets. Hadewijch lived in the first half of the thirteenth century, most likely residing in either Antwerp or Brussels. Her writing indicates she was an educated woman who spoke both French and Latin, and was at home with a number of patristic and ecclesial writers. Though such an education indicates she was of a higher class, she became a Beguine at some point, devoting herself to a life of service, probably caring for the sick, a common Beguine practice. Hadewijch rose within this community to become spiritual adviser to some of the younger Beguines.

Letters and *Visions*

Her writing indicates that she encountered opposition from both outside and inside the Beguines. In her letters, Hadewijch advises other Beguines on conduct, spiritual direction, and virtue. These often have the directness of a pastoral letter and provide a picture of what might be expected spiritually and behaviorally among Beguines. Many of her recorded visions are occasioned by a liturgical event, such as Easter, Pentecost, or the Eucharist. Her visions, as do Beatrice's, address the theme of the immediate relationship of the human soul to God, always in the context of human weakness and divine love.

VISION 7: ONENESS IN THE EUCHARIST

On a certain Pentecost Sunday I had a vision at dawn. Matins were being sung in the church, and I was present. My heart and my veins and all my limbs trembled and quivered with eager desire and, as often occurred with me, such madness and fear beset my mind that it seemed to me I did not content my Beloved, and that my Beloved did not fulfill my desire, so that dying I must go mad, and going mad I must die. On that day my mind was beset so fearfully and so painfully by desirous love that all my separate limbs threatened to break, and all my separate veins were in travail. The longing in which I then was cannot be expressed by any language or any person I know; and everything I could say about it would be unheard-of to all those who never apprehended Love as something to work for with desire, and whom Love had never acknowledged as hers. I can say this about it: I desired to have full fruition of my Beloved, and to understand and taste him to the full. I desired that his Humanity should to the fullest extent be one in fruition with my humanity, and that mine then should hold its stand and be strong enough to enter into perfection until I content him, who is perfection itself, by purity and unity, and in all things to content him fully in every virtue. To that end I wished he might content me interiorly with his Godhead, in one spirit, and that for me he should be all that he is, without withholding anything from me. For above all the gifts that I ever longed for, I chose this gift: that I should give satisfaction in all great sufferings. For that is the most perfect satisfaction: to grow up in order to be God with God. For this demands suffering, pain, and misery, and living in great new grief of soul: but to let everything come and go without grief, and in this way to experience nothing else but sweet love, embraces, and kisses. In this sense I desired that God give himself to me, so that I might content him.

As my mind was thus beset with fear, I saw a great eagle flying toward me from the altar, and he said to me: "If you wish to attain oneness, make yourself ready!"

I fell on my knees and my heart beat fearfully, to worship the Beloved with oneness, according to his true dignity; that indeed was impossible for me, as I know well, and as God knows, always to my woe and to my grief.

But the eagle turned back and spoke: "Just and mighty Lord, now show your great power to unite your oneness in the manner of union with full possession!"

Then the eagle turned round again and said to me: "He who has come, comes again; and to whatever place he never came, he comes not."

Then he came from the altar, showing himself as a Child; and that Child was in the same form as he was in his first three years. He turned toward me, in his right hand took from the ciborium his Body, and in his left hand took a chalice, which seemed to come from the altar, but I do not know where it came from.

With that he came in the form and clothing of a Man, as he was on the day when he gave us his Body for the first time; looking like a Human Being and a Man, wonderful, and beautiful, and with glorious face, he came to me as humbly as anyone who wholly belongs to another. Then he gave himself to me in the shape of the Sacrament, in its outward form, as the custom is; and then he gave me to drink from the chalice, in form and taste, as the custom is. After that he came himself to me, took me entirely in his arms, and pressed me to him; and all my members felt his in full felicity, in accordance with the desire of my heart and my humanity. So I was outwardly satisfied and fully transported. Also then, for a short while, I had the strength to bear this; but soon, after a short time, I lost that manly beauty outwardly in the sight of his form. I saw him completely come to nought and so fade and all at once dissolve that I could no longer recognize or perceive him outside me, and I could no longer distinguish him within me. Then it was to me as if we were one without difference. It was thus: outwardly, to see, taste, and feel, as one can outwardly taste, see, and feel in the reception of the outward Sacrament. So can the Beloved, with the loved one, each wholly receive the other in all full satisfaction of the sight, the hearing, and the passing away of the one in the other.

After that I remained in a passing away in my Beloved, so that I wholly melted away in him and nothing any longer remained to me of myself; and I was changed and taken up in the spirit, and there it was shown me concerning such hours.

LETTER 6

Now I want to warn you about one thing from which great harm can come. I assure you that this is one of the worst sicknesses which prevail today, and sicknesses there are in plenty. Nowadays everyone is constantly questioning the good faith of his friends, putting them to the test and complaining of their faithlessness; and people spend their time in this way who ought to be filled with an exalted love for our great God.

What does it matter to us, if our intention is good and we want to exalt our lives to God, who is so great and so exalted whether people are faithful or unfaithful to us, kind or unkind, treat us ill or well? If we cannot show good faith and kindness to them, we are harming ourselves, and the worst of the harm is that we are ruining for ourselves the sweetness of true love.

If anyone keeps good faith with you and consoles you in your need with his help, you must show your gratitude and help him in his turn, but, more than this, we must serve and love God the more fervently because of this, and leave it to Him to reward others or not as He wills. For He in His being is just, and when He gives or takes away it is always justly done; for He is exalted in the delight of His own being, and we are here, infinitely beneath Him in all our shortcomings. And especially you and I, who have not yet attained what we are, not yet acquired what we have, fall so far short of what is ours, we must forgo everything if we are to be and to have everything, we must learn, in the unity and boldness of the spirit learn the perfect life of that love which has moved us both to its works.

Ah, dear child, above all I beg you to be on your guard against instability. For there is nothing so able and so quick to separate you from our Lord as instability. Whatever troubles may come to you, do not commit the folly of believing that you are set for any other goal than the great God Himself, in the fullness of His being and of His love; do not let folly or doubt deflect you from any good practice which can lead you to this goal. If you will confide yourself to His love, you will soon grow to your full stature, but if you persist in doubting, you will become sluggish and grudging, and everything which you ought to do will be a burden to you. Let nothing trouble you, do not believe that anything which you must do for Him whom you seek will be beyond your strength, that you cannot surmount it, that it will be beyond you. This is the fervour, this is the zeal which you must have, and all the time your strength must grow. . . .

When Christ lived here as man, there was a time for all His works. When the proper time came, He did the proper work: His words and His deeds, His preaching and teaching, His admonitions, consolations, miracles, absolutions, His toils, His reproofs, His humiliations, His griefs, His sorrows until His Passion and death: in all these He waited patiently for the right time. And when the hour came for Him to work, He perfected it, valiant and mighty, and in these great and honest labours He paid the debt which every human being owes to the Father, who is God and who is truth. 'Mercy and truth met one another, justice and peace embraced one another.'

In union with God's humanity, you should live here in labour and exile; and in union with God's eternal omnipotence you should in your heart love and rejoice, gently laying all your trust in Him. In the truth which that humanity and that omnipotence share, God finds a single delight; and just as His humanity here on earth submitted to the will of His majesty, you too must submit in love to the will of Them both together. Humbly serve Them, in Their united might, and stand before Them as one standing ready to do all Their will. And let Them then do with you what They will. . . .

Therefore you must not avoid contempt or blame. For everything which we can endure or perform is welcome to God's love, which can never be sated, for that love is the consuming fire which devours all things, and which never will be quenched in all eternity.

And because you are still young, and untried in all these things, you must strive greatly to grow up, as it were out of nothing, as one who has nothing and can become nothing but who yet labours to climb out of the depths. And you must always cast yourself deep into the abyss of humility, denying everything which you have to sacrifice to God. He asks this of you, that in all your dealings with all men you use a perfect humility. Raise yourself above everything which is inferior to God Himself, if you want to be what He wants of you: and in doing this you will find peace in your whole being.

If you would act according to the being in which God has created you, your nature would be so noble that there would be no pains which you would shun, it would be so valiant that you could not bear to leave anything undone, but you would reach out for that which is best of all, for that great oneness which is God, knowing that to be your only riches. And then in mercy you must give your riches to others, and make rich those who are poor; for those who love truly will never fail in their free gifts to those others who with all their heart and all their will have surrendered themselves to God's love. True love has always given what it had to give, always conquered what it had to conquer, always withheld what it had to withhold. . . .

That is why you must choose and love God's will alone in all things. His will for you, for your friends, for Himself, even though your own wish might be for Him to give you consolation, so that you might live your life here in peace and rest.

But today, instead of loving God's will, everyone loves himself: it is everyone's will to have peace and rest, to live with God in riches and might, and to be one with Him in His joy and glory. We all want to be God along with God; but God knows that there are few of us who want to be man with Him in His humanity, to carry His Cross with Him, to hang upon it with Him, to pay with Him the debt of human kind. If we look at ourselves we can see that this is true: we will not suffer anything, we will not endure. Just let our hearts be stabbed by the slightest grief, just let someone say a scornful or slanderous word about us, let anyone act against our reputation or our peace or our will, and at once we are mortally injured: we know exactly what we want and what we do not want, there are so many different things which give us pleasure or pain, now we want this and now we want that, our joy today is our sorrow tomorrow, we would like to be here, we would like to be there, we do not want something and then we want it, and in everything all we are thinking of is our own satisfaction and how we can best seek it.

This is why we are still unenlightened in our thinking, unstable in all our being, uncertain in our reasoning and understanding. This is why we suffer so, poor wretched exiled beggars, painfully travelling through a foreign land, and there would be no need for this, were it not that all our thinking is false; and how false it is we show plainly when we do not live with Christ as He lived, do not abandon all as He did, are not abandoned by all as He was. If we look at what we do, we can see that this is true: whenever we can, we strive for our own ease, where we can gain it we fight for advancement, we fight to get our own way, we know exactly what is going to please us, we seek our own advantage in everything, in spiritual matters as well as worldly, and whatever we achieve in these ways, that is our joy and our delight, and when we have it we think that now we are something. And just as we say that, we are in truth nothing. This is how we destroy ourselves in our whole way of life, and we do not live with Christ and we do not carry the Cross with the Son of God. We only carry it with Simon, who was hired to carry the Cross of our Lord. . . .

The mark of grace is holy living. The mark of predestination in an inward and confident lifting-up of the heart, with a living trustfulness, and with an unspeakable longing to honour and to satisfy Him in His glory, which is majestic and incomprehensible and divine.

The cross which we must carry with the living Son of God is that sweet exile which men suffer for their true love, when in a longing trustfulness we await that great day on which Love shall reveal itself and manifest its noble powers and its great might on earth and in heaven. Then Love shall show itself so mighty to those who love that it will draw them out of themselves, it will rob them of heart and mind, it will make them die and make them live in the loving service of true Love.

But before Love shall show itself so greatly, before it calls men so utterly to come out of themselves to it, before it so touches them that they become one spirit and one life with Love in Love, men must pay to Love the tribute of honourable service and a life of longing exile: honourable service in all the works of virtue, and a life of longing exile in perfect obedience, always standing ready with fresh zeal and willing hands for every deed in which virtue is exercised, with a will submissive to every virtue which can pay honour to Love. And in all this there must be no other intention than that Love should be enthroned, as it should be, in men and in all creatures, according to Love's pleasure. This is to hang upon the Cross with Christ, this is to die with Him and with Him to rise again. May He help us always to do this; and for this help I entreat Him in whom is every perfect virtue.

For we are obliged to perform virtuous works not to gain admiration or happiness, not for wealth or power, nor for any pleasure in heaven or on earth, but only so that we may be pleasing to God's greatest honour, who created human nature for this, making it to His honour and His praise, and for our joy in eternal glory.

CHAPTER   THIRTEEN

Beatrice of Nazareth, *The Seven Manners of Love* (1237–68)

Beatrice of Nazareth (1200–1268)

Beatrice was a Flemish Christian who chose a religious life at age seventeen. This was not surprising, given her reputation at an early age for learning and seriousness, as evidenced by her committing the book of Psalms to heart when she was five. Her parents were devout, and, upon her mother's death when Beatrice was seven, her father had her enter a school of the Beguines, laywomen committed to a life of simplicity and poverty based on the ideal of the apostles. There she received a cultured education, including grammar, rhetoric, geometry, arithmetic, astronomy, and music. She entered a Cistercian convent in 1210, where the demanding spiritual discipline weakened her health but, she was convinced, strengthened her spirit. Throughout these years, Beatrice kept a diary, which included both her spiritual experiences and essays of theological interest.

The Seven Manners of Love

Written in her native dialect, this treatise gives an account in mystical language of the dynamic movement of holy love. For Beatrice, *minne,* or love, begins at what is highest and, through seven forms, returns to this summit. It is not clear whether this summit is God or the summit of the soul in love with God. In any case, Beatrice's own love for God encounters God's transcending love, so that she may "render love to Love." Finally, then, Beatrice can claim, "In this union in which she became 'one single spirit with God' she realized that she had reached that purity, freedom of spirit and glory for which she had been created from the very beginning."

THE SEVEN MANNERS OF LOVE

Vision of the World as a Wheel—How She Saw the Whole World Placed Beneath Her Feet, Like a Wheel

Par. 234: "After she had spent a long time in the accomplishment of her duties as prioress, it happened one day that she heard a nun reading those words of St. Bernard in which he says that 'Many are those who suffer torments for Christ but few are those who love themselves perfectly for Christ's sake.' She kept in her memory the words of this holy man and for two days she often pondered over them. But by herself she was not at all able to discover their correct meaning, wondering how man's love applied to himself could in some way be more important than bearing the sufferings of the Passion for Christ. As man, whether he be good or evil, naturally loves himself for 'no man hates his own flesh' (Eph. 5:29), this brief addition 'for Christ's sake' seemed to her to give special significance to these words, because experience alone, and not the subtlety of the human intelligence can discover the meaning of this addition.

Par. 235: Realizing that, through the efforts of meditation, she did not succeed in finding the deepest sense of these words, God's servant then turned to prayer, ardently beseeching the Lord to illuminate her on this matter. In His goodness, what could He refuse His chosen handmaid, in her arduous search and fruitful zeal? The grace of divine love not only gave her what she asked for, that is, the meaning of the words quoted above, but it also enlightened her, revealing to her the manifold secrets of the divine mysteries.

Par. 236: As soon as she was raised aloft into ecstasy, she saw placed beneath her feet the whole machine of the world as if it were a wheel. She saw herself placed above it, her eyes of contemplation magnetized towards the incomprehensible Essence of the Divinity, while the innermost point of her intelligence, in an admirable manner, considered the eternal and true God, the uncreated Most High, the Lord, in the majesty of His substance. She was so adequately positioned between God and man that, below God, but higher than the whole world, she trampled upon terrestrial things, remaining inseparably united to the Divine Essence by the embraces of charity.

In this union in which she became 'one single spirit with God' (I Cor. 6:17) she realized that she had reached that purity, freedom of spirit and glory for which she had been created from the very beginning. And as if her spirit had been transferred entirely within the Divine Spirit, she thus understood that, for a short while, she was united to the Most High Deity and rendered entirely celestial.

Par. 237: Coming back to herself, she retained in her memory the sweetness of this contemplation, delighting in it, without, however, experiencing it again. And remembering what she had seen and understood, comforted by the indescribable divine sweetness, she reposed peacefully in the arms of the Beloved, burning with the fire of love. Then she understood the sense of the words cited above, but less by intelligence than by experience, with the purified eye of the spirit, and she became aware that she loved herself perfectly for Christ's sake, but that there are few who reach this summit of perfect love."

The Seventh Manner of Holy Love

There are seven manners of holy love: They come from the Most-High and return to the summit.

The Betrothed knows still one more manner of sublime Love which submits her to a hard inward toil: attracted by a Love which is above her humanity, above human reason and intelligence, above all the heart's operations, drawn exclusively by Eternal Love in the eternity of love, in the incomprehensibility, in the inaccessible breadth and height, in the profound abyss of the Divinity Who is "all in all things" and Who remains unknowable above all things, unchangeable, the plenitude of Being Who embraces all in His power, intelligence and sovereign work. The blessed soul is so tenderly engulfed in love, so strongly drawn by desire, that her tormented heart is gnawed with impatience and her infatuated mind is overwhelmed by the strength of these desires. All in her is strained towards the fruition of Love in which she wishes to settle (wesen). This is what she demands insistently of God, what she begs ardently of Him, in the strength of her desire. For Love leaves her neither peace, nor respite, nor rest. Love raises her up and casts her down, suddenly draws her close only to torment her later, makes her die to bring her back to life again, wounds her and heals her, drives her to madness and then makes her wise again. It is in this way that love draws her to a higher state (in hoger wesen).

In spirit, she is raised above time into eternity, above the gifts of love, which is outside time, above human modes of loving, above her very nature in her desire to overpass it. Such is her being *(wesen)* and her will, her desire, and her love: to enter the certitude of truth, the pure light, the high nobleness, the exquisite beauty—to enter the sweet company of the higher spirits who are engulfed in overflowing Love and who know clearly their Love and possess Her in fruition.

Her wish is to be up there; in her desire she goes there, she comes amidst these spirits, particularly the burning Seraphim; but it is within the Great Divinity, the Most-High Trinity that she hopes to find sweet repose and lasting fruition.

She seeks [the Lord] in His majesty, she follows Him up above, contemplating Him with her heart and her mind. She knows Him, she loves Him, she desires Him so strongly that she can consider neither saint, nor man, nor angel, nor creature, unless it is in that common love in which she loves everything with Him. It is He alone Whom she has chosen in love, above all else, at the heart of everything and in everything, with all the aspirations of her heart, all the strength of her spirit, it is He Whom she desires to see and to possess in fruition.

That is why her life on the earth is henceforth a complete exile, a narrow prison and excruciating suffering. She despises the world and the earth disgusts her; all that is terrestrial can neither satisfy nor appease her and it brings her great torments to be a stranger in a distant land. She cannot forget her exile and she cannot satisfy her desire, while her nostalgia distresses her. Hers is merciless passion and torment, beyond all measure.

Thus she feels a great desire and a great longing to be liberated from this exile, to be freed from this body and, with bleeding heart, she ceaselessly repeats the words of the Apostle: *Cupio dissolvi et esse cum Christo,* that is, "I desire to be dissolved and to be with Christ." (Phil. 1:23). And in her violent desire and excruciating impatience, she wishes to be delivered in order to be with Christ, not because she is weary of the present, nor on account of future sufferings, but it is by reason of a holy love, an eternal love, that she ardently and vehemently longs to reach the land of eternity and the glory of fruition. Her nostalgia is strong and immense, her impatience pressing and painful, her suffering overwhelming beyond words, so violently does her desire torment her. However, she must live in hope and this very hope makes her sigh and languish. Ah, holy desires of love, what force you have in a loving soul! It is a blessed passion, a raging torment, a lasting suffering, a brutal death, a dying life. Up above, the soul cannot arrive; here below, she cannot feel at peace. She cannot bear to think of the

Beloved, so great is her longing for Him; not to think of Him fills her with pain on account of her desire; this is why she must live tortured and torn apart.

And so she cannot be, nor wishes to be, consoled, as the prophet says: *Renuit consolari anima mea,* that is, 'My soul refuses to be comforted' (Ps. 76:3). She refuses all consolation from God Himself and from creatures, for all the joys which she might thus obtain stimulate her love and draw her towards a higher state *(in een hoger wesen),* increasing her yearning to be united to Love and to reach fruition, thus making this exile unbearable. In spite of all God's gifts, she remains unsatisfied, unappeased, far from the presence of her Love. It is a hard, painful life, for she does not wish to be consoled as long as she has not received what she is seeking for relentlessly.

Love has drawn her and guided her, has taught her Her ways; the soul has followed Love faithfully, in great toils and countless works, in noble aspirations and violent desires, in great patience and great impatience, in suffering and in happiness, in numerous torments, in quest and supplication, loss and possession, in ascent and in suspense, in pursual and in embrace, in anguish and cares, in distress and in troubles; in immense trust and in doubt, in love and in affliction, she is ready to endure everything. In death or in life, she wishes to devote herself to Love; in her heart she endures endless sufferings and it is for Love alone that she wishes to reach her Fatherland.

When she has tried everything, in vain, in this exile, she finds her only refuge is in celestial glory. For love's work is this: to desire the most intimate union *(dat naeste wesen),* the closest adhesion to that state in which the soul abandons herself to Love. She wishes to follow Love, to know Love, to reach the fruition of Love—an impossibility in exile; so she wishes to migrate to the land where she has established her home and where she rests with Love. This she knows: every obstacle will be removed and she will be tenderly welcomed by the Beloved. She will contemplate the One she has loved so ardently and Whom she will possess for all eternity, for her eternal happiness, the One she has so faithfully served. In all plenitude she will enjoy her Beloved Whom her soul has so strongly embraced in love. Thus she will enter into the joy of her Master, as St. Augustine says: *(Qui in te intrat, in gaudium domini)* etc., that is to say, "He who enters into you, enters into the joy of his Master," and he will no longer fear but will enjoy beatitude in the Sovereign God.

It is then that the soul will be united to her spouse and will be "one single spirit with Him" (I Cor. 6:17) in an indissoluble fidelity and an eternal Love. And those who have devoted themselves to Love in the time of grace will enjoy her in eternal glory where there will be nothing other than praise and love.

May God deign to lead us all thither! Amen.

CHAPTER FOURTEEN

Clare of Assisi,
The Rule of Saint Clare
(c.1250)

Clare of Assisi (1194–1253)

Of noble birth, Clare heard Francis of Assisi preach powerfully when she was eighteen. In 1212 she left behind her life of wealth and dedicated herself to "Lady Poverty," organizing the nucleus of what would be the first convent of Poor Ladies, or Poor Clares. She was joined by her mother and two sisters, as well as other women committed to the ideal of poverty, and was made abbess of the community. In conjunction with St. Francis, Clare established a simple rule of life based on the gospel. She came to exemplify the charity and joyfulness of life that was at the heart of the Franciscan movement, and was canonized in 1255.

The Rule of Saint Clare

The Poor Clares were the most severe and radical of women's convents, requiring a life of rigorous contemplation, prayer, penance, and manual labor. Austere fasts and strict enclosure were central to their religious life. Initially, the Poor Clares were given a Rule by their bishop, but it failed to meet Clare's commitment to intense poverty. Eventually, she wrote her own *Rule,* officially approved in 1252 by Raynaldus, bishop of Ostia and Velletri. When, two days before her death, she received word of Pope Innocent IV's final approval of her *Rule,* it is reported that she kissed the document several times. This *Rule,* included here in its entirety, reflects the theological claims of this community of women led by Clare, claims about the very nature of spiritual life and of Christian relationship. It opens with the endorsement of the pope and the bishop.

THE RULE OF SAINT CLARE

1. INNOCENT, BISHOP, SERVANT OF THE SERVANTS OF GOD, TO THE BELOVED DAUGHTERS IN CHRIST THE ABBESS CLARE AND THE OTHER SISTERS OF THE MONASTERY OF SAN DAMIANO IN ASSISI: OUR BEST WISHES AND APOSTOLIC BLESSING.

The Apostolic See is accustomed to accede to the pious requests and to be favorably disposed to grant the praiseworthy desires of its petitioners. Thus, we have before Us your humble request that We confirm by [our] Apostolic authority the form of life which Blessed Francis gave you and which you have freely accepted. According to [this form of life] you are to live together in unity of mind and heart and in the profession of highest poverty. Our venerable Brother, the Bishop of Ostia and Velletri, has seen fit to approve this way of life, as the Bishop's own letters on this matter define more fully, and We have taken care to strengthen it with our Apostolic protection. Attentive, therefore, to your devout prayers, We approve and ratify what the Bishop has done in this matter and confirm it by Apostolic authority and support it by this document. To this end We include herein the text of the Bishop, which is the following:

2. RAYNALDUS, BY DIVINE MERCY BISHOP OF OSTIA AND VELLETRI, TO HIS MOST DEAR MOTHER AND DAUGHTER IN CHRIST, THE LADY CLARE, ABBESS OF SAN DAMIANO IN AS-SISI, AND TO HER SISTERS, BOTH PRESENT AND TO COME, GREETINGS AND FATHERLY BLESSINGS.

Beloved daughters in Christ, because you have rejected the splendors and pleasures of the world and, *following the footprints* (1 Pt 2:21) of Christ Himself and His most holy Mother, you have chosen to live in the cloister and to serve the Lord in highest poverty so that, in freedom of soul, you may be the Lord's servants, We approve your holy way of life in the Lord and with fatherly affection we desire freely to impart our benign favor to your wishes and holy desires. Therefore, moved by your pious prayers and by the authority of the Lord Pope as well as our own, to all of you who are now in your monastery and to all those who will succeed you we confirm forever this form of life and the manner of holy unity and highest poverty which your blessed Father Saint Francis gave you for your observance in word and writing. Furthermore, by the protection of this writing, we fortify this way of life which is the following:

CHAPTER I: IN THE NAME OF THE LORD BEGINS THE FORM OF LIFE OF THE POOR SISTERS

1. The form of life of the Order of the Poor Sisters which the Blessed Francis established, is this: 2. to observe the holy Gospel of our Lord Jesus Christ, by living in obedience, without anything of one's own, and in chastity.

3. Clare, the unworthy handmaid of Christ and the little plant of the most blessed Father Francis, promises obedience and reverence to the Lord Pope Innocent and to his canonically elected successors, and to the Roman Church. 4. And, just as at the beginning of her conversion, together with her sisters she promised obedience to the Blessed Francis, so now she promises his successors to observe the same [obedience] inviolably. 5. And the other sisters shall always be obliged to obey the successors of the blessed Francis and [to obey] Sister Clare and the other canonically elected Abbesses who shall succeed her.

CHAPTER II: THOSE WHO WISH TO ACCEPT THIS LIFE AND HOW THEY ARE TO BE RECEIVED

1. If, by divine inspiration, anyone should come to us with the desire to embrace this life, the Abbess is required to seek the consent of all the sisters; and if the majority shall have agreed, having had the permission of our Lord Cardinal Protector, she can receive her. 2. And if she judges [the candidate] acceptable, let [the Abbess] carefully examine her, or have her examined, concerning the Catholic faith and the sacraments of the Church. 3. And if she believes all these things and is willing to profess them faithfully and to observe them steadfastly to the end; and if she has no husband, or if she has [a husband] who has already entered religious life with the authority of the Bishop of the diocese and has already made a vow of continence; and if there is no impediment to the observance of this life, such as advanced age or some mental or physical weakness, let the tenor of our life be clearly explained to her.

4. And if she is suitable, let the words of the holy Gospel be addressed to her: that she should *go and sell* all that she has and take care to distribute the proceeds *to the poor* (cf. Mt 19:21). If she cannot do this, her good will suffices. 5. And let the Abbess and her sisters take care not to be concerned

about her temporal affairs, so that she may freely dispose of her possessions as the Lord may inspire her. If, however, some counsel is required, let them send her to some prudent and God-fearing men, according to whose advice her goods may be distributed to the poor.

6. Afterward, once her hair has been cut off round her head and her secular dress set aside, she is to be allowed three tunics and a mantle. 7. Thereafter, she may not go outside the monastery except for some useful, reasonable, evident, and approved purpose. 8. When the year of probation is ended, let her be received into obedience, promising to observe always our life and form of poverty.

9. During the period of probation no one is to receive the veil. 10. The sisters may also have small cloaks for convenience and propriety in serving and working. 11. Indeed, the Abbess should provide them with clothing prudently, according to the needs of each person and place, and seasons and cold climates, as it shall seem expedient to her by necessity.

12. Young girls who are received into the monastery before the age established by law should have their hair cut round [their heads]; and, laying aside their secular dress, should be clothed in religious garb as the Abbess has seen [fit]. 13. When, however, they reach the age required by law, in the same way as the others, they may make their profession. 14. The Abbess shall carefully provide a Mistress from among the more prudent sisters of the monastery both for these and the other novices. She shall form them diligently in a holy manner of living and proper behavior according to the form of our profession.

15. In the examination and reception of the sisters who serve outside the monastery, the same form as above is to be observed. 16. These sisters may wear shoes. 17. No one is to live with us in the monastery unless she has been received according to the form of our profession.

18. And for the love of the most holy and beloved Child Who *was wrapped in* the poorest of *swaddling clothes and laid in a manger* (cf. Lk 2:7–12), and of His most holy Mother, I admonish, entreat, and exhort my sisters that they always wear the poorest of garments.

CHAPTER III: THE DIVINE OFFICE AND FASTING, CONFESSION AND COMMUNION

1. The Sisters who can read shall celebrate the Divine Office according to the custom of the Friars Minor; for this they may have breviaries, but they are to read it without singing. 2. And those who, for some reasonable cause,

sometimes are not able to read and pray the Hours, may, like the other sisters, say the Our Father's.

3. Those who do not know how to read shall say twenty-four Our Father's for Matins; five for Lauds; for each of the hours of Prime, Terce, Sext, and None, seven; for Vespers, however, twelve; for Compline, seven. 4. For the dead, let them also say seven Our Father's with the *Requiem aeternam* in Vespers; for Matins, twelve: 5. because the sisters who can read are obliged to recite the Office of the Dead. 6. However, when a sister of our monastery shall have departed this life, they are to say fifty Our Father's.

7. The sisters are to fast at all times. 8. On Christmas, however, no matter on what day it happens to fall, they may eat twice. 9. The younger sisters, those who are weak, and those who are serving outside the monastery may be dispensed mercifully as the Abbess sees fit. 10. But in a time of evident necessity the sisters are not bound to corporal fasting.

11. At least twelve times a year they shall go to confession, with the permission of the Abbess. 12. And they shall take care not to introduce other talk unless it pertains to confession and the salvation of souls. 13. They should receive Communion seven times [a year], namely, on Christmas, and Thursday of Holy Week, Easter, Pentecost, the Assumption of the Blessed Virgin, the Feast of Saint Francis, and the Feast of All Saints. 14. [In order] to give Communion to the sisters who are in good health or to those who are ill, the Chaplain may celebrate inside [the enclosure].

CHAPTER IV: THE ELECTION AND OFFICE OF THE ABBESS; THE CHAPTER. THOSE WHO HOLD OFFICE AND THE DISCREETS

1. In the election of the Abbess the sisters are bound to observe the canonical form. 2. However, they should arrange with haste to have present the Minister General or the Minister Provincial of the Order of Friars Minor. Through the Word of God he will dispose them to perfect harmony and to the common good in the choice they are to make. 3. And no one is to be elected who is not professed. And if a nonprofessed should be elected or otherwise given them, she is not to be obeyed unless she first professes our form of poverty.

4. At her death the election of another Abbess is to take place. 5. Likewise, if at any time it should appear to the entire body of the sisters that she is not competent for their service and common welfare, the sisters are

bound to elect another as Abbess and mother as soon as possible according to the form given above.

6. The one who is elected should reflect upon the kind of burden she has undertaken, and to Whom she is *to render an account* (Mt 12:36) of the flock committed to her. 7. She should strive as well to preside over the others more by her virtues and holy behavior than by her office, so that, moved by her example, the sisters might obey her more out of love than out of fear. 8. She should avoid particular friendships, lest by loving some more than others she cause scandal among all. 9. She should console those who are afflicted, and be, likewise, the last refuge for those who are disturbed; for, if they fail to find in her the means of health, the sickness of despair might overcome the weak.

10. She should preserve the common life in everything, especially regarding all in the church, dormitory, refectory, infirmary, and in clothing. Her vicar is bound to do likewise.

11. At least once a week the Abbess is required to call her sisters together in Chapter. 12. There both she and her sisters must confess their common and public offenses and negligences humbly. 13. There, too, she should consult with all her sisters on whatever concerns the welfare and good of the monastery; for the Lord often reveals what is best to the lesser [among us].

14. No heavy debt is to be incurred except with the common consent of the sisters and by reason of an evident need. This should be done through a procurator. 15. The Abbess and her sisters, however, should be careful that nothing is deposited in the monastery for safekeeping; often such practices give rise to troubles and scandals.

16. To preserve the unity of mutual love and peace, all who hold offices in the monastery should be chosen by the common consent of all the sisters. 17. And in the same way at least eight sisters are to be elected from among the more prudent, whose counsel the Abbess is always bound to heed in those things which our form of life requires. 18. Moreover, if it seems useful and expedient, the sisters can and must sometimes depose the officials and discreets, and elect others in their place.

CHAPTER V: SILENCE, THE PARLOR, AND THE GRILLE

1. The sisters are to keep silence from the hour of Compline until Terce, except those who are serving outside the monastery. 2. They should also keep silence continually in the church, in the dormitory, and, only while

they are eating, in the refectory. 3. In the infirmary, however, they may speak discreetly at all times for the recreation and service of those who are sick. 4. However, they may briefly and quietly communicate what is really necessary always and everywhere.

5. The sisters may not speak in the parlor or at the grille without the permission of the Abbess or her Vicar. 6. And those who have permission should not dare to speak in the parlor unless they are in the presence and hearing of two sisters. 7. Moreover, they should not presume to go to the grille unless there are at least three sisters present [who have been] appointed by the Abbess or her Vicar from the eight discreets who were elected by all the sisters as the council of the Abbess. 8. The Abbess and her vicar are themselves bound to observe this custom in speaking. 9. [The sisters should speak] very rarely at the grille and, by all means, never at the door.

10. At the grille a curtain is to be hung inside which is not to be removed except when the Word of God is being preached, or when a sister is speaking to someone. 11. The grille should also have a wooden door which is well provided with two distinct iron locks, bolts, and bars, so that, especially at night, it can be locked by two keys, one of which the Abbess is to keep and the other the sacristan; it is to be locked always except when the Divine Office is being celebrated and for reasons given above. 12. Under no circumstances whatever is any sister to speak to any one at the grille before sunrise or after sunset. 13. Moreover, in the parlor there is always to be a curtain on the inside, which is never to be removed.

14. During the Lent of Saint Martin and the Greater Lent, no one is to speak in the parlor, except to the priest for Confession or for some other evident necessity; judgment on this is left to the prudence of the Abbess or her vicar.

CHAPTER VI: NOT HAVING POSSESSIONS

1. After the Most High Celestial Father saw fit to enlighten my heart by His grace to do penance according to the example and teaching of our most blessed Father Saint Francis, shortly after his own conversion, I, together with my sisters, voluntarily promised him obedience.

2. When the Blessed Father saw that we had no fear of poverty, hard work, suffering, shame, or the contempt of the world, but that, instead, we regarded such things as great delights, moved by compassion he wrote for us a form of life as follows: "Since by divine inspiration you have made

yourselves daughters and servants of the most high King, the heavenly Father, and have taken the Holy Spirit as your spouse, choosing to live according to the perfection of the holy Gospel, I resolve and promise for myself and for my brothers always to have that same loving care and special solicitude for you as [I have] for them."

3. And that we might never turn aside from the most holy poverty we had embraced [nor those, either, who would come after us], shortly before his death he wrote his last will for us once more, saying: "I, brother Francis, the little one, wish to follow the life and poverty of our most high Lord Jesus Christ and of His most holy mother and to persevere in this until the end; and I ask and counsel you, my ladies, to live always in this most holy life and in poverty. And keep most careful watch that you never depart from this by reason of the teaching or advice of anyone."

4. And just as I, together with my sisters, have been ever solicitous to safeguard the holy poverty which we have promised the Lord God and the Blessed Francis, so, too, the Abbesses who shall succeed me in office and all the sisters are bound to observe it inviolably to the end: 5. that is to say, they are not to receive or hold onto any possessions or property [acquired] through an intermediary, or even anything that might reasonably be called property, 6. except as much land as necessity requires for the integrity and the proper seclusion of the monastery; and this land is not to be cultivated except as a garden for the needs of the sisters.

CHAPTER VII: THE MANNER OF WORKING

1. The sisters to whom the Lord has given the grace of working are to work faithfully and devotedly, [beginning] after the Hour of Terce, at work which pertains to a virtuous life and to the common good. 2. They must do this in such a way that, while they banish idleness, the enemy of the soul, they do not extinguish the Spirit of holy prayer and devotion to which all other things of our earthly existence must contribute.

3. And the Abbess or her vicar is bound to assign at the Chapter, in the presence of all, the manual work each is to perform. 4. The same is to be done if alms have been sent by anyone for the needs of the sisters, so that the donors may be remembered by all in prayer together. 5. And all such things are to be distributed for the common good by the Abbess or her vicar with the advice of the discreets.

CHAPTER VIII: THE SISTERS SHALL NOT ACQUIRE ANYTHING AS THEIR OWN; BEGGING ALMS; THE SICK SISTERS

1. The sisters shall not acquire anything as their own, neither a house nor a place nor anything at all; instead, as pilgrims and strangers in this world who serve the Lord in poverty and humility, let them send confidently for alms. 2. Nor should they feel ashamed, since the Lord made Himself poor for us in this world. This is that summit of highest poverty which has established you, my dearest sisters, as heirs and queens of the kingdom of heaven; it has made you poor in the things [of this world] but has exalted you in virtue. Let this be your portion, which leads into the land of the living (cf. Ps 141:6). Dedicating yourselves totally to this, my most beloved sisters, do not wish to have anything else forever under heaven for the name of Our Lord Jesus Christ and His most holy Mother.

3. No sister is permitted to send letters or to receive anything or give away anything outside the monastery without the permission of the Abbess. 4. Nor is it allowed to have anything which the Abbess has not given or permitted. 5. Should anything be sent to a sister by her relatives or others, the Abbess should have it given to the sister. 6. If she needs it, the sister may use it; otherwise, let her in all charity give it to a sister who does need it. If, however, money is sent to her, the Abbess, with the advice of the discreets, may provide for the sister what she needs.

7. Regarding the sisters who are ill, the Abbess is strictly bound to inquire with all solicitude by herself and through other sisters what [these sick sisters] may need both by way of counsel and of food and other necessities and, according to the resources of the place, she is to provide for them charitably and kindly. 8. [This is to be done] because all are obliged to serve and provide for their sisters who are ill just as they would wish to be served themselves if they were suffering from any infirmity. 9. Each should make known her needs to the other with confidence. For if a mother loves and nourishes her daughter according to the flesh, how much more lovingly must a sister love and nourish her sister according to the Spirit!

10. Those who are ill may lie on sackcloth filled with straw and may use feather pillows for their head; and those who need woolen stockings and quilts may use them.

11. When the sick sisters are visited by those who enter the monastery, they may answer them briefly, each responding with some good words to those who speak to them. 12. But the other sisters who have permission [to speak] may not dare to speak to those who enter the monastery unless [they

are] in the presence and hearing of two sister-discreets assigned by the Abbess or her vicar. 13. The Abbess and her vicar, too, are obliged themselves to observe this manner of speaking.

CHAPTER IX: THE PENANCE TO BE IMPOSED ON THE SISTERS WHO SIN; THE SISTERS WHO SERVE OUTSIDE THE MONASTERY

1. If any sister, at the instigation of the enemy, shall have sinned mortally against the form of our profession, and if, after having been admonished two or three times by the Abbess or other sisters, she will not amend, she shall eat bread and water on the floor before all the sisters in the refectory for as many days as she has been obstinate; and if it seems advisable to the Abbess she shall undergo even greater punishment. 2. Meanwhile, as long as she remains obstinate, let her pray that the Lord will enlighten her heart to do penance. 3. The Abbess and her sisters, however, must beware not to become angry or disturbed on account of anyone's sin: for anger and disturbance prevent charity in oneself and in others.

4. If it should happen—God forbid—that through [some] word or gesture an occasion of trouble or scandal should ever arise between sister and sister, let she who was the cause of the trouble, at once, before offering the gift of her prayer to the Lord, not only prostrate herself humbly at the feet of the other and ask pardon, but also beg her earnestly to intercede for her to the Lord that He might forgive her. 5. The other sister, mindful of that word of the Lord: *If you do not forgive from the heart, neither will your* heavenly *Father forgive you* (Mt 6:15; 18:35), should generously pardon her sister every wrong she has done her.

6. The sisters who serve outside the monastery should not delay long outside unless some evident necessity demands it. 7. They should conduct themselves virtuously and speak little, so that those who see them may always be edified. 8. And let them zealously avoid all meetings or dealings that could be called into question. 9. They may not be godmothers of men or women lest gossip or trouble arise because of this. 10. They may not dare to repeat the rumors of the world inside the monastery. 11. And they are strictly bound not to repeat outside the monastery anything that was said or done within which could cause scandal.

12. If any one should on occasion openly offend in these two things, it shall be left to the prudence of the Abbess to impose a penance on her with mercy. But if a sister does this through vicious habit, the Abbess, with the

advice of the discreets, should impose a penance on her according to the seriousness of her guilt.

CHAPTER X: THE ADMONITION AND CORRECTION OF THE SISTERS

1. The Abbess should admonish and visit her sisters, and humbly and charitably correct them, not commanding them anything which would be against their soul and the form of our profession. 2. The sisters, however, who are subjects, should remember that for God's sake they have renounced their own wills. Hence, they are firmly bound to obey their Abbess in all things which they promised the Lord to observe and which are not against their soul and our profession.

3. On her part, the Abbess is to be so familiar with them that they can speak and act toward her as ladies do with their servant. For that is the way it should be, that the Abbess be the servant of all the sisters.

4. Indeed, I admonish and exhort in the Lord Jesus Christ that the sisters be on their guard against all pride, vainglory, envy, greed, worldly care and anxiety, detraction and murmuring, dissension and division. 5. Let them be ever zealous to preserve among themselves the unity of mutual love, which is the bond of perfection.

6. And those who do not know how to read should not be eager to learn. 7. Rather, let them devote themselves to what they must desire to have above all else: the Spirit of the Lord and His holy manner of working, to pray always to Him with a pure heart, and to have humility, patience in difficulty and weakness, and to love those who persecute, blame, and accuse us; for the Lord says: *Blessed are they who suffer persecution for justice's sake, for theirs is the kingdom of heaven* (Mt 5:10). But *he who shall have persevered to the end will be saved* (Mt 10:22).

CHAPTER XI: THE CUSTODY OF THE ENCLOSURE

1. The portress is to be mature in her manners and prudent, and of suitable age. During the day she should remain in an open cell without a door. 2. A suitable companion should be assigned to her who may, whenever necessary, take her place in all things.

3. The door is to be well secured by two different iron locks, with bars and bolts, 4. so that, especially at night, it may be locked with two keys, one of which the portress is to have, the other the Abbess. 5. And during the day

the door must not be left unguarded on any account, but should be firmly locked with one key.

6. They should take utmost care to make sure that the door is never left open, except when this can hardly be avoided gracefully. 7. And by no means shall it be opened to anyone who wishes to enter, except to those who have been granted permission by the Supreme Pontiff or by our Lord Cardinal. 8. The sisters shall not allow anyone to enter the monastery before sunrise or to remain within after sunset, unless an evident, reasonable, and unavoidable cause demands otherwise.

9. If a bishop has permission to offer mass within the enclosure, either for the blessing of an Abbess or for the consecration of one of the sisters as a nun or for any other reason, he should be satisfied with as few and virtuous companions and assistants as possible.

10. Whenever it is necessary for other men to enter the monastery to do some work, the Abbess shall carefully post a suitable person at the door who is to open it only to those assigned for the work, and to no one else. 11. At such times all the sisters should be extremely careful not to be seen by those who enter.

CHAPTER XII: THE VISITATOR, THE CHAPLAIN, AND THE CARDINAL PROTECTOR

1. Our Visitator, according to the will and command of our Cardinal, should always be taken from the Order of Friars Minor. 2. He should be the kind of person who is well known for his virtue and good life. 3. It shall be his duty to correct any excesses against the form of our profession, whether these be in the leadership or among the members. 4. Taking his stand in a public place, so that he can be seen by others, he may speak with several in a group and with individuals about the things that pertain to the duty of visitation, as it may seem best to him.

5. With respect for the love of God and of Blessed Francis we ask as a favor from the Order of Friars Minor a chaplain and a clerical companion of good character and reputation and prudent discretion, and two lay brothers who are lovers of holiness of life and virtue, to support us in our [life of] poverty, just as we have always had [them] through the kindness of the Order.

6. The chaplain may not be permitted to enter the monastery without his companion. 7. And when they enter, they are to remain in an open place, in such a way that they can see each other always and be seen by others. 8. For

the confession of the sick who cannot go to the parlor, for their Communion, for the Last Anointing and the Prayers for the Dying, they are allowed to enter the enclosure.

9. Moreover, for funeral services and on the solemnity of Masses for the Dead, for digging or opening a grave, or also for making arrangements for it, suitable and sufficient outsiders may enter according to the prudence of the Abbess.

10. To see to all these things above, the sisters are firmly obliged to have always that Cardinal of the Holy Church of Rome as our Governor, Protector, and Corrector, who has been delegated by the Lord Pope for the Friars Minor, 11. so that, always submissive and subject at the feet of that holy Church, and steadfast in the Catholic Faith, we may observe forever the poverty and humility of our Lord Jesus Christ and of His most holy Mother and the holy Gospel which we have firmly promised. Amen.

Given at Perugia, the sixteenth day of September, in the tenth year of the Pontificate of the Lord Pope Innocent IV.

Therefore, no one is permitted to destroy this page of our confirmation or to oppose it recklessly. If anyone shall have presumed to attempt this, let him know that he will incur the wrath of Almighty God and of His holy Apostles Peter and Paul.

Given at Assisi, the ninth day of August, in the eleventh year of our Pontificate.

CHAPTER FIFTEEN

Mechthild of Magdeburg,
The Flowing Light of the Godhead
(1250–70)

Mechthild of Magdeburg (1210–97)

Although she came from a noble German family, Mechthild chose to join the Beguines at Magdeburg as a young woman (c.1230) in order to follow a life of prayer and poverty. She tells us she received a "greeting" from the Holy Spirit at age twelve, and her subsequent spiritual life was active. She ably described her spiritual experiences in her sole written work, *The Flowing Light of the Godhead,* composed sometime between 1250 and 1270. Her sharp criticism in this text of abuses and corruption within the clergy brought her disfavorable attention, including talk of burning her work. In 1270 she left Magdeburg for Helfta, seeking refuge in the Cistercian convent among contemplative sisters.

The Flowing Light of the Godhead

During about a fifteen-year period starting in 1250, Mechthild wrote down her spiritual experiences, reflections, allegories, and judgments in her dialect of Low German. She handed these over to a "Heinrich," a well-known Dominican of the day who was also probably her confessor. He became a compiler of this material, organizing bits and pieces into a book, although it appears Mechthild herself was simply recording what came to her, not writing a book as such. In this work, she lays theological claim to love as the very nature of the relation of the soul to the triune God. Using the language of the court and of the natural world, Mechthild lays out a way of life and love. Soon after her death, the *Flowing Light* was translated into Latin, offering this text to a much wider audience.

THE FLOWING LIGHT OF THE GODHEAD

Of the Revelations to a loving soul

In the year of our Lord, A.D. 1250, and for fifteen years thereafter, this book was revealed in German by God to a Sister who was holy both in body and spirit. She served God devoutly in humble simplicity, abject poverty and heavenly contemplation, suffering oppression and scorn for more than forty years. She followed the light and teaching of the Preaching Order steadfastly and absolutely, advancing steadily and improving herself from day to day.

But this book was copied and put together by a Brother of the same Order. Much good is in this book on many things, as is seen in the Table of its contents.

Thou shalt read it nine times, faithfully, humbly and devoutly.

THIS IS THE FIRST PART OF THE BOOK

This book is to be joyfully welcomed for God Himself speaks in it

This book I now send forth as a messenger to all spiritual people both good and bad—for if the pillars fall, the building cannot stand. The book proclaims Me alone and shows forth My holiness with praise. All who would understand this book should read it nine times.

This Book is called The Flowing Light of the Godhead

Ah! Lord God! Who has written this book? I in my weakness have written it, because I dared not hide the gift that is in it. Ah! Lord! What shall this book be called to Thy Glory! It shall be called *The Flowing Light of My Godhead* into all hearts which dwell therein without falseness. . . .

2. Of three persons and three gifts

The true greeting of God, which comes from the heavenly flood out of the spring of the flowing Trinity, has such power that it takes all strength from the body and lays the soul bare to itself. Thus it sees itself as one of the blessed and receives in itself divine glory. The soul is thus separated from the body with its power and love and longing. Only the smallest part of life remains to the body which is as it were in a sweet sleep. The soul sees God as One and Undivided in Three Persons, and the Three Persons as one Undivided God. God greets the soul in the language of the Court of Heaven not understood in this kitchen (earthly world). And He clothes it with such garments as are worn in His Palace and girds it with strength. Then it may ask for what it will, it will be granted to it.

Should it not be granted, it is because the soul is taken further by God to a secret place where it must not ask nor pray for anyone, for God alone will play with it in a game of which the body knows nothing, any more than the peasant at the plough or the knight in the tourney; not even His loving mother Mary; she can do nothing here. Thus God and the soul soar further to a blissful place of which I neither can nor will say much. It is too great and I dare not speak of it for I am a sinful creature.

Moreover, when the Infinite God brings the unmoored soul up into the heights of contemplation, it loses touch with the earth in face of that wonder and forgets that it ever was upon the earth. When this flight is at its highest, the soul must leave it.

Then the All-Glorious God speaks: "Maiden! thou must humble thyself and descend again!"

She is affrighted and says: "Lord! Thou hast drawn me up so high, that I am out of myself and cannot praise Thee with any order in my body, for I suffer grievously and strive against my body!"

Then He speaks: "Ah! my dove! Thy voice is as music to my ears, thy words as savour to my mouth, thy longings as the gentleness of My gifts!"

And she replies: "Dear Lord! all must be as the Master ordains!"

And she sighs so deeply that her body is awakened and asks, "Lady! where hast thou been? Thou comest so lovingly back, so beautiful and strong, so free and full of spirit! But thy wanderings have taken from me all my zest, my peace, my colour, all my powers."

The soul exclaims, "Silence! Destroyer! Cease thy complaints! I will ever guard myself against thee. That my enemy should be wounded does not trouble me, I am glad of it!"

Such an encounter surges from the Flowing Godhead by many channels into the arid soul ever bringing fresh knowledge and holier revelation.

O loving God, fiery within, radiant without, now that Thou has given this even to me, so undeserving, hunger wakes in me for that life Thou has given to Thy chosen ones. To that end I would gladly suffer longer here. For no soul can or may receive this greeting till it has utterly conquered self: but in this greeting will I, yet living, die. . . .

21. Of Knowledge and Revelation

Love without Knowledge
Is darkness to the wise soul.
Knowledge without revelation
Is as the pain of Hell.
Revelation without death,
Cannot be endured.

22. Of the mission of the Virgin Mary; how the soul was made in honour of the Trinity

The sweet dew of the uncreated Trinity distilled from the spring of the eternal Godhead in the flower of the chosen Maid. And the fruit of the flower is an immortal God and a mortal man and a living comfort of everlasting love; our Redeemer is become our Bridegroom!

The bride is intoxicated by the sight of His glorious countenance. In her greatest strength she is overcome, in her blindness, she sees most clearly; in her greatest clearness, she is both dead and alive. The richer she becomes, the purer she is. . . . The more she storms, the more loving God is to her. The higher she soars, the more brightly she shines from the reflection of the Godhead the nearer she comes to Him. The more she labours, the more sweetly she rests. The more she understands, the less she speaks. The louder she calls, the greater wonders she works with His power and her might. The more God loves her, the more glorious the course of love, the nearer the resting-place, the closer the embrace. The closer the embrace, the sweeter the kiss. The more lovingly they gaze at each other, the more difficult it is to part. The more He gives her, the more she spends, the more she has. The more humbly she takes leave, the sooner she returns. The more the fire burns, the more her light increases. The more love consumes her, the brighter she shines. The vaster God's praise, the vaster her desire for Him.

Ah! whither fares our Bridegroom and Redeemer in the Jubilation of the Holy Trinity? As God willed no longer to remain in Himself, alone, therefore created He the soul and gave Himself in great love to her alone. Whereof art thou made, O Soul, that thou soarest so high over all creatures and whilst mingling in the Holy Trinity, yet remainest complete in thyself?

SOUL.— Thou hast spoken of my beginning, I was created in love, therefore nothing can express or liberate my nobleness save Love alone. Blessed Mary! Thou art the mother of this Wonder. When did that happen to thee?

THE VIRGIN MARY.— When our Father's joy was darkened by Adam's fall, so that He was an-angered, the everlasting wisdom of Almighty God was provoked. Then the Father chose me as bride that He might have something to love, because His noble bride, the soul, was dead. Then the Son chose me as mother and the Holy Spirit received me as friend. Then was I alone the bride of the Holy Trinity and the mother of orphans whom I bore before the sight of God (that they might not quite disappear as some did). As I thus became the mother of many noble children, I was so full of the milk of compassion that I nurtured the wise men and prophets before the birth of the Son of God. After that, in my youth, I nurtured Jesus; later, as the bride of God, I nurtured holy Church at the foot of the Cross; but from that I became dry and wretched, for the sword of the human agony of Jesus spiritually pierced my soul. . . . But it was reborn of His life-giving wounds and lived again, young and child-like. But were it fully to recover, God's mother must be its mother and its nurse. Ah! God! it was so and it was just! God is the soul's rightful Father and the soul His rightful bride who resembles Him in all her sorrows.

Ah! blessed Mary! In thine old age thou didst nurture the holy Apostles with thy maternal wisdom and thy powerful prayer, so that God's honour and will should be fulfilled in them. Likewise didst thou then, as now, nurture the martyrs with strong faith in their hearts; the confessors by thy protection of their ears, the maidens by thy purity, the widows with constancy, the perfect with gentleness, sinners through thy intercession. Ah! Lady! thou must still nurture us . . . till the Last Day. Then shalt thou see how God's children and thy children are weaned and grown up into everlasting life. Then shall see and know in unspeakable joy, the milk and e'en the self-same breast, which Jesus oft as infant kissed. . . .

27. How thou art to become worthy of the Way, to walk in it and be perfected

Three things make the soul worthy of this way so that it recognizes it and walks in it. Firstly, that it wills to come to God, renouncing all self-will, joyfully welcoming God's grace and willingly accepting all its demands against human desires. The second thing which keeps the soul in the way is that all things are welcome to it save sin alone. The third thing makes the creature perfect in the way, namely, that it does all things to the glory of God, so that even its smallest desire will be as highly prized by God as if it were in the highest state of contemplation possible to humanity.

For all is done in love to the glory of God. Therefore all is one.

But if I sin, then I am no longer in this way! . . .

38. *God rejoices that the soul has overcome four sins*

Our Lord delights in Heaven
Because of the loving soul He has on earth,
And says, "Look how she who has wounded Me has risen!
She has cast from her the apes of worldliness;
Overcome the bear of impurity,
Trodden the lion of pride underfoot,
Torn the wolf of desire from his revenge,
And comes racing like a hunted deer
To the spring which is Myself.
She comes soaring like an eagle
Swinging herself from the depths
Up into the heights."

39-43. *God asks the soul what it brings*

GOD:

Thou huntest sore for thy love,
What bring'st thou Me, my Queen?

SOUL.—

Lord! I bring Thee my treasure;
It is greater than the mountains,
Wider than the world,
Deeper than the sea,
Higher than the clouds,
More glorious than the sun,
More manifold than the stars,
It outweighs the whole earth!

GOD:

O thou! image of My Divine Godhead,
Enobled by My humanity,
Adorned by My Holy Spirit,—
What is thy treasure called?

SOUL:

Lord! it is called my heart's desire!
I have withdrawn it from the world,

Denied it to myself and all creatures.
Now I can bear it no longer.
Where, O Lord, shall I lay it?

GOD:

Thy heart's desire shalt thou lay nowhere
But in mine own Divine Heart
And on My human breast.
There alone wilt thou find comfort
And be embraced by My Spirit.

. . . .

SOUL:

Fish cannot drown in the water,
Birds cannot sink in the air,
Gold cannot perish
In the refiner's fire.
This has God given to all creatures
To foster and seek their own nature,
How then can I withstand mine?
    I must to God—
My Father through nature,
My Brother through humanity,
My Bridegroom through love,
His am I for ever!
    Think ye that fire must utterly slay my soul?
Nay! Love can both fiercely scorch
And tenderly love and console.
Therefore be not troubled!
Ye shall still teach me.
When I return
I will need your teaching
For the earth is full of snares.

Then the beloved goes into the Lover, into the secret hiding place of the
sinless Godhead. . . . And there, the soul being fashioned in the very nature
of God, no hindrance can come between it and God.

Then our Lord said—

    Stand, O Soul!

SOUL:

What wilt thou Lord?

THE LORD:

Thy SELF must go!

SOUL:

But Lord, what shall happen to me then?

THE LORD:

Thou art by nature already mine!
Nothing can come between Me and thee!
There is no angel so sublime
As to be granted for one hour
What is given thee for ever.
Therefore must thou put from thee
Fear and shame and all outward things.
Only of that of which thou art sensible by nature
Shalt thou wish to be sensible in Eternity.
That shall be thy noble longing,
Thine endless desire,
And that in My infinite mercy
I will evermore fulfil.

SOUL:

Lord! now am I a naked soul
And Thou a God most Glorious!
Our two-fold intercourse is Love Eternal
Which can never die.
   Now comes a blessed stillness
   Welcome to both. He gives Himself to her
   And she to Him.
   What shall now befall her, the soul knows:
      Therefore am I comforted.
   Where two lovers come secretly together
   They must often part, without parting.
Dear friend of God! I have written down this, my way of love, for thee.
May God give it to thee in thy heart. AMEN.

147

CHAPTER SIXTEEN

Angela de Foligno, *The Book of Divine Consolation* (late 1200s)

Angela de Foligno (1248–1309)

Angela came from a well-to-do family in Foligno and was married at an early age. She enjoyed an extravagant and worldly life until 1285, when she experienced a conversion. Yet it was not until the death of her husband that she embraced a new life of poverty and prayer by becoming a tertiary, or third order, Franciscan. Tertiaries were groups of laypeople who did not take vows but did form into chapters under the direction of priests of the order with which they were associated. As a tertiary, Angela sold her property, gave her wealth to the poor, and joined other women in a community of devotion. Her powerful spiritual life attracted many men and women to her, including her confessor, Arnold, a Franciscan who recorded her experiences and teachings.

The Book of Divine Consolation

Angela gives the reader a clear picture of the nature of the human soul both as it seeks God and as God calls it. This picture includes both the confessional state of the soul and, in her final visions, its triumph. She discusses the salvific role of Christ and the central place of the Eucharist in the redemptive process.

THE BOOK OF DIVINE CONSOLATION

TREATISE I: OF THE CONVERSION AND PENITENCE OF THE BLESSED ANGELA OF FOLIGNO AND OF HER MANY AND DIVERS TEMPTATIONS

As I walked (said the Blessed Angela) by the way of penitence, I did take eighteen spiritual steps before I came to know the imperfection of my life.

The first step was that I did begin to reflect upon my sins, the knowledge of which did fill my soul with so great a dread that, fearing to be condemned unto hell, I wept bitterly.

The second was, that I did begin to be so exceeding ashamed of those my sins that for shame I could not fully confess them; wherefore many times did I communicate whilst yet unconfessed and with all my sins did I receive the Body of our Lord. Being day and night reproached by my conscience because of this thing, I did pray the Blessed Francis that he would grant me to discover a confessor meet for my needs, who should be well acquainted with my sins and unto whom I could fully confess myself. In that same night did the Blessed Francis appear unto me and say: "Sister, if thou hadst prayed unto me sooner thy prayer would have been sooner granted; that which thou hast asked hath been done." Upon the next morning, therefore, I went into the church of Saint Francis and found there a friar preaching in Saint Feliciano, which friar was chaplain unto the bishop and did hold his authority; and to him I did determine to make my confession immediately that the sermon should be ended. Wherefore I did confess myself most fully and was absolved of all my sins. And in this confession I did feel no love, but only bitterness, shame, and pain. . . .

Ninthly, there was given unto me the desire to seek out and know the way of the Cross, that I might stand at its foot and find refuge there where all sinners find refuge. Unto which end I was enlightened and instructed after this manner: that if I did desire to find the way and come unto the Cross, I must first pardon all those who had offended me, and must then put away from me all earthly things, not only out of mine affections but likewise in very deed, and all men and women, friends and kindred and every other thing, but more especially my possessions must I put away, and even mine own self. And I must give my heart unto Christ (who hath done me such great good), electing to walk upon the thorny path, which is the path of tribulation. So then I did begin to put aside the best clothing and garments which I had and the most delicate food, likewise the covering for my head.

But as yet it was a shameful and a hard thing for me to do, seeing that I did not feel much love for God and was living with mine husband. Wherefore was it a bitter thing for me when any offence was said or done unto me, but I did bear it as patiently as I was able. In that time and by God's will there died my mother, who was a great hindrance unto me in following the way of God; my husband died likewise, and in a short time there also died all my children. And because I had commenced to follow the aforesaid way and had prayed God that He would rid me of them, I had great consolation of their deaths, albeit I did also feel some grief. Wherefore, because that God had shown this grace unto me, I did imagine that my heart was in the heart of God and that His will and His heart were in my heart.

Tenthly, seeking to know from God what thing I could do, the which would be most acceptable unto Him, He did of His mercy many times appear unto me, both sleeping and waking, and appearing fastened upon the Cross He did bid me gaze upon His wounds, and in a marvellous manner He did make me to know how that He had borne all things for me; and this happened many times. And when He had showed unto me one by one all the things which He had borne for me, He said, "What canst thou do for Me that will suffice?" . . .

The sixteenth was, that I did come again into the church to ask of God that He would bestow some mercy upon me. And whilst that I was praying and saying the Paternoster, God did implant that Paternoster in mine heart with so clear an understanding of the Divine goodness and mine own unworthiness that I could in no way describe it. Each word was written upon mine heart and I did speak it with great and enduring contrition and compunction. So that, although I wept because of my sins and mine unworthiness (the which I did here perceive), I did nevertheless have great consolation and did begin to taste somewhat of the Divine sweetness, because in the Paternoster I did see the Divine goodness better than in any other thing, and here likewise did I find it best. But because my sins and mine unworthiness were showed unto me in the aforesaid prayer, I did begin to be so greatly ashamed that I did not presume to raise mine eyes either to heaven or to the Crucifix, or any other thing, but did commend myself unto the Blessed Virgin, that she should implore and obtain mercy for me and forgiveness of my sins, seeing that I was yet sunk in the bitter of sin. . . .

TREATISE II: OF THE EVANGELICAL DOCTRINE SET FORTH BY THE BLESSED ANGELA

CHAPTER I: HOW IT MAY BE KNOWN THAT GOD HATH ENTERED INTO THE SOUL

It must be known that God cometh sometimes unto the soul when it hath neither called, nor prayed unto, nor summoned Him. And He doth instil into the soul a fire and a love and a sweetness not customary, wherein it doth greatly delight and rejoice; and it doth believe that this hath been wrought by God Himself there present, but this is not certain. Presently the soul doth perceive that God is inwardly within itself, because—albeit it cannot behold Him within—it doth nevertheless perceive that His grace is present with it, wherein it doth greatly delight. Yet is not even this certain. Presently it doth further perceive that God cometh unto it with most sweet words, wherein it delighteth yet more, and with much rejoicing doth it feel God within it; yet do some doubts still remain, albeit but few. For the soul possesseth as yet no perfect certainty, neither is it assured that God is truly within it, because such converse and such feelings can be produced likewise by other spirits. Wherefore is it still in doubt. And it seemeth unto me that this cometh either of its own malice and sinfulness, or else truly by the will of God, who desireth not that the soul should feel certain and secure. But when the soul doth feel the presence of God more deeply than is customary, then doth it certify unto itself that He is within it. It doth feel it, I say, with an understanding so marvellous and so profound, and with such great love and divine fire, that it loseth all love for itself and for the body, and it speaketh and knoweth and understandeth those things of the which it hath never heard from any mortal whatsoever. And it understandeth with great illumination, and with much difficulty doth it hold its peace; and if it doth hold its peace, it holdeth it out of the abundance of its zeal, that it may not be displeasing unto God its Lover nor cause offence, and likewise by reason of its humility; for it desireth not to speak of things so exceeding high that it may not draw attention unto itself. Thus hath it happened divers times unto me, that, out of my burning desire to work the salvation of my neighbour, I did speak things for the which I was reproved, and it was said unto me, "Sister, turn thee again unto the Holy Scriptures, for they say not thus, and therefore do we not understand thee." But with that feeling whereby it is certified unto the soul that God dwelleth within it, there is given unto it a disposition so perfect that it doth most entirely and verily agree with the soul in all things, and in every way do all the members of the

151

body agree with the soul and do truly form one cause together with it; neither do they rebel against the will of the soul, but do perfectly desire those things which are of God, but which, nevertheless, they had not heretofore in any way desired. And this disposition is granted unto the soul through grace—whereby it doth perceive that the Divine Being hath entered into it, and hath granted it the assurance and the desire of God and of those things which are of God, after the manner of the true love wherewith God hath loved us. Thus doth the soul feel that God is mingled with it and hath made companionship with it. . . .

. . . Then hath it the assurance and certitude that Christ dwelleth within it; but all that we can say is as nothing in comparison with that which it really is. . . .

. . . when I do reflect within myself, I do sometimes perceive most clearly that those persons who do best know God (Who is infinite and unspeakable) are those who do the least presume to speak of Him, considering that all which they do say of Him, or can possibly say, is as nothing compared with what He truly is. Wherefore, if any preacher did verily understand divine things (as I have sometimes heard them declare they do) they would not be able to speak of them, neither would they presume to say aught whatsoever of God, but would remain silent and dumb. And because God is so much greater than the mind and all other things, we are not able by any means whatsoever to measure, nor speak, nor think of Him, seeing that His goodness cannot perfectly be explained. . . .

CHAPTER XI: HOW CHRIST LAID ASIDE HIS WISDOM AND HIS OWN NATURE

Secondly, He did lay aside His own nature, making Himself poor in wisdom because He desired to appear as a simple man, one senseless and vain in the sight of men. He appeared not as a philosopher or a doctor of many words, or as one who disputeth noisily, nor yet as a scribe renowned for wisdom and learning; but in the utmost simplicity did He talk with men, showing unto them the way of truth in His life, His virtues, and His miracles. Seeing how that He is the Wisdom of the Father, the Creator and Inspirer of all learning, He might have used all the subtilty of knowledge and of argument, and, had He desired, He might have shown forth His wit and obtained glory; but with such simplicity did He declare the truth that He was esteemed of almost all people to be not only simple and foolish, but even ignorant and vain. Herein did He show unto us the way of truth, that is to say, that neither in learning nor in wisdom should we take glory unto ourselves, for being puffed up with this pride we seek to obtain the name of master before men and to cover ourselves with vainglory. . . .

Such, then, was the supreme, constant, and perfect poverty of Jesus Christ our Saviour, who, albeit He was Lord of all riches, did nevertheless choose to be poor amongst us, that He might teach us the love of poverty. And verily He was poor in possessions, in will and in spirit, beyond man's comprehension, and all for the deep love wherewith He loved us. He was poor in riches and needy of all worldly things; He was poor in friends and power, poor in worldly wisdom, in the fame of holiness and in all dignities. And finally, being poor in all things, He preached poverty and said that the poor were blessed and should judge the world. Upon the other hand He did condemn the wealthy and their riches and abundance, saying that they did deserve condemnation. He did preach this in deed and by word of mouth and by example, with all His might. . . .

CHAPTER XX: OF PRAYER, OF THE WHICH THERE ARE THREE KINDS, CORPORAL, MENTAL, AND SUPERNATURAL, OUTSIDE OF WHICH IT IS NOT POSSIBLE TO FIND GOD

Forasmuch, therefore, as the knowledge of God uncreate and of Christ crucified is needful, and seeing that without it we cannot transform our minds in His love, it behoveth us to read diligently in that aforesaid Book of Life, that is to say, the life and death of Jesus Christ. And whereas this reading, or rather knowledge, cannot possibly be acquired without devout, pure, humble, fervent, attentive, and constant prayer (not with the lips alone, but with the heart and mind and all the strength), something must be said of prayer, as well as of the Book of Life.

It is through prayer and in prayer that we find God. There are divers kinds of prayer, but in these three kinds alone is God to be found. The first is corporal, the second mental, and the third supernatural.

Corporal prayer is that which is always accompanied by the sound of words and by bodily exercises, such as kneeling down, asking pardon, and bowing oneself. This kind do I continually perform; and the reason thereof is, that, desiring to exercise myself in mental prayer, I was sometimes deceived and hindered therefrom by idleness and sleep, and did thus lose time. For this reason do I exercise myself in corporal prayer, and this corporal prayer leadeth me unto the mental. But this must be done very attentively. Therefore when thou sayest the Paternoster, thou must consider well that which thou sayest, and not repeat it in haste in order to say it a certain number of times, as do those vain women who perform good deeds for a reward.

Mental prayer is when the meditation of God filleth the mind so entirely that it thinketh on naught else save on God. But when some other reflection entereth into the mind it asketh not that it should be mental prayer because that prayer doth hinder the tongue from performing its office and it cannot speak. So completely is the mind filled with God that it can concern itself with naught else, neither think of anything save of God. Hence from this mental prayer proceedeth the supernatural.

Supernatural prayer is that during which the soul is so exalted by this knowledge, or meditation, or fulness of God that it is uplifted above its own nature and understandeth more of God than it otherwise could naturally. And understanding, it knoweth; but that which it knoweth it cannot explain, because all that it perceiveth and feeleth is above its own nature.

In these three degrees of prayer, therefore, man learneth to know God and himself. And knowing Him, he loveth Him, and loving Him he desireth to possess Him; and this is the sign of love, for he who loveth not only a part of himself, but the whole, transformeth himself in the thing beloved. . . .

CHAPTER XXVIII: THE SOUL IS UNITED WITH GOD IN THREE SEVERAL WAYS, WHEREBY IT IS FURNISHED WITH A WEAPON TO CONTROL THE LOVE OF GOD AND OF ITS NEIGHBOUR

If the love of God be not directed with discretion and protected by its weapons, it turneth unto evil. The weapons wherewith the good love of God and one's neighbour may be controlled are given unto man in the transformation of the soul.

Now this transformation is a threefold one: sometimes the soul is transformed in the will of God, sometimes with God, and sometimes within God and God within it.

The first transformation is when the soul useth all its endeavour to imitate the life of Christ crucified, for herein is made manifest the will of God Himself.

The second is when the soul is united unto God and loveth God; not only because it so willeth, but because it hath great knowledge and joy of God, the which, however, it is able to explain and set forth in words.

The third is when the soul is so entirely made one with God and God with it, that it knoweth and enjoyeth with God the most high things, the which cannot possibly be set forth in words, nor imagined save by him who feeleth them. . . .

CHAPTER XXXI: HOW THAT LOVE CREATED AND EXCITED BY THE VISION OF THE SUPREME BEING DOTH MAKE US TO LOVE GOD AND HIS CREATURES ACCORDING UNTO THEIR CONDITIONS

Thus the love created and excited by the vision of the Supreme Being maketh us to know and love Him, to know and love His creatures according unto their conditions, and more or less according unto the inclination of the Supreme Being, for in no wise may it overstep the bounds of His will. Yet everything that is love is to be feared unless this love is given unto the soul by the Supreme God; but when God sendeth the vision of the Supreme Being, together with love due and sufficient unto Him, then is it safe, and even though it have other visions and revelations it doth not change. . . .

CHAPTER XXXIX: OF THE MANY SIGNS AND EFFECTS OF LOVE WHICH ARE CAUSED BY THE SACRAMENT OF THE EUCHARIST

I come now unto the Sacrament of love and grace which is called the Eucharist, and hereof will I say something more than what hath already been said. . . .

Verily, it seemeth unto me that this Sacrament, this holy Mystery, must be considered with great diligence by those who desire to celebrate and receive this sacrifice; the soul must not pass hastily over this meditation, but must dwell upon it carefully and earnestly. And albeit the things which may be said of this Sacrament cannot be expounded or set forth, methinketh they can be reduced unto seven points, or meditations, the which should be considered one by one.

Firstly, this holy Mystery is new and above all things marvellous, and far beyond our understanding. Albeit this Mystery was shown of old, as is set down in the Holy Scriptures, and is ancient as regardeth its form, it is nevertheless new as regardeth the exhibition of the Sacrament whereby the creature receiveth grace and new strength. . . .

Secondly, this Sacrament is above all things gracious and kindleth love. For that which moveth Him who ordained this most holy Sacrament was the greatest of all things, and not less was the profit which should proceed therefrom. I know not what name I should give it, save that of immeasurable love, because of His boundless love did He institute this Sacrament.

Because of His great love towards us did He enter into the Sacrament and will abide therein until the end of the world. This He did not only in memory of His death, which is our salvation, but that He might ever and always remain nigh unto us. . . .

Thirdly, this Sacrament is above all things compassionate and induceth unto compassion and suffering, because He endured mortal and unspeakable suffering. . . .

Fourthly, this Sacrament is above all things worthy and venerable, to be regarded with the utmost reverence and humility, because He who ordained this sacrifice was Jesus Christ, God supreme and uncreate.

The soul who considereth this sacrifice hath not only to consider Him who ordained it, but likewise that which is contained in that Sacrament. For herein is contained God uncreate, invisible, and omnipotent, He who doeth all things, who is most merciful and just, Creator of the heavens and the earth, of all things visible and invisible; and this is the chief thing upon which we need here reflect. . . .

Fifthly, this Sacrament is above all things profitable, and above all things high and spiritual, and it upraiseth unto heavenly things.

This Sacrament was ordained by the most holy Trinity in order that It might bind unto Itself that which It most greatly loved, that It might draw the soul unto Itself, unto God, and away from all created things joining it together with God uncreate. . . .

Sixthly, this Sacrament is above all things profitable, and giveth us all good things and all grace.

. . . Hereby He granteth remission of sins, strength against temptation, it restraineth our opposers, augmenteth grace, and heapeth up merit; wherefore should it be received often and with great reverence. . . .

Seventhly, this Sacrament is above all things to be extolled, and is supremely worthy of all grace and praise.

All that is good, all that is holy, all that is beautiful is found in this Sacrament. . . .

We should, therefore, approach that table and that great and good thing with the utmost reverence, fear, and trembling, but above all, with exceeding great love. And the soul should approach unto this Sacrament humbly, exalted, and adorned, for it goeth unto that which is the height of all beauty and perfect glory, supreme holiness, happiness, blessedness, exaltedness, and nobility, all sweetness and all love, and which hath the sweetness of love without end.

Thus should the soul go to receive the Sacrament, in order that it may itself be received. It should be pure, that it may be purified; alive, that it may be quickened; just, that it may be justified; ready, that it may be incorporated with God uncreate who was made man, and that it may be one with Him unto all eternity. Amen.

CHAPTER SEVENTEEN

Marguerite Porete,
The Mirror of Simple Souls
(late 1200s)

Marguerite Porete (d. 1310)

Marguerite, also known as Margarita de Hannonia, came from Hainaut, an area south of Flanders, part of France and Belgium today. While we have no biographical details of her life, we do know that she was burned at the stake as a relapsed heretic in Paris in 1310. Her judges, canon lawyers who examined her work *The Mirror of Simple Souls,* referred to her by the Latin term *beguina.* Her first run-in with church authorities, sometime between 1296 and 1306, resulted in the declaration of her book as heretical and its public burning, while Marguerite was censured from further writing or speaking to spread her dangerous doctrines. She was again brought before papal authorities in 1306 or 1307 for heresy and leading people astray. It is clear she had not stopped her activities, even sending her book to some churchmen for approval. She was imprisoned in Paris for eighteen months, during which time she refused to recant; as a result, the papal inquisitor submitted articles from her book to canon lawyers to examine for doctrinal error. From her writings and trial records it is apparent that her error was shared by many extra-ecclesial groups of her day—an unwillingness to take vows, recognize a common order, or proclaim the true authority of the church in theological and spiritual matters.

The Mirror of Simple Souls

In all likelihood, Marguerite wrote this work toward the end of the thirteenth century as her own theology was shaped by her experiences as a

Beguine. She was certainly an educated woman, and as a religious she came to have a critical view of church hierarchy. Combined with this was a theological position concerning the ultimate end of the path of the human soul to God, which traditional doctrine declared heretical. At the heart of her theology stands the notion that the soul could be "annihilated" in a state of such complete union with God that it no longer had a separate existence. This stance entirely circumvented the authority of the church, rendering much of the church's role in salvation obsolete, and so, was an intolerable doctrine. Further, the suggestion that humans, or the annihilated soul, could attain a sinless state and thereby no longer have need for acts of virtue or penance threatened the very fabric of religious life. Marguerite, however, seems unapologetic, as this treatise was dictated to her by Love, the central speaker throughout. Love is questioned by Reason and is the teacher of the soul's path to perfect love.

THE MIRROR OF SIMPLE SOULS

You who will read in this book,
If you want to understand it well
Think about what you will say,
For it is difficult to understand;
You must assume Humility,
Who is the treasurer of Science
And the mother of the other virtues.
Theologians or other clerics,
You will not have any understanding of it,
So learnèd are your minds,
If you do not proceed humbly
And Love and Faith together,
The mistresses of the house,
Do not cause you to surmount Reason.
Reason herself witnesses to us
In the thirteenth chapter of this book,
And is not ashamed
That Love and Faith give her life
And she cannot free herself from them,
For they have dominion over her,
This is why she must humble herself.
Humble, therefore, your sciences
Which are founded in Reason,

And place all your trust
In those which are given
By Love and illuminated by Faith.
And thus you will understand this book
Which through Love gives life to the Soul.

Prologue

The Soul touched by God, and stripped of sin in the first state of grace, has risen by divine graces to the seventh state of grace, in which the Soul has the plentitude of her perfection through divine fruition in the land of life.

HERE SPEAKS LOVE: Among you actives and contemplatives and you who are perhaps annihilated by true love, who will hear some of the powers of the pure love, the noble love, the high love of the Free Soul, and how the Holy Spirit put His sail in the Soul, as if in His ship, I beg of you out of love, says Love, to listen carefully with the subtle understanding within you and with great diligence, for otherwise all those if they be not so who will hear this will understand badly.

Now listen with humility to a little example of worldly love, and understand it likewise with regard to divine love.

EXAMPLE: There was once a lady, a king's daughter, of great heart and nobility and of noble courage as well, who lived in a foreign land. It happened that this lady heard tell of the great courtliness and nobility of King Alexander and at once her will loved him for the great fame of his courage. But this lady was so far from this great lord in whom she had placed her love—for she could neither see nor have him—that she was often disheartened within herself, for no love except this one could content her. And when she saw that this far love, which to her was so near or within her, was so far outside of her, she thought to herself that she might ease her pain by imagining what her friend, on whose account she was so often heartbroken, looked like. So she had an image painted in the likeness of the beloved king, which resembled as nearly as possible the imagined representation that she loved with the affection of the Love which had seized her; and by means of this image and in other ways she reflected upon the King himself.

THE SOUL: Truly, in like manner, says the Soul who caused this book to be written, I say the same to you: I heard tell of a king of great power, who in his courtliness, his very great courtliness of nobility and generosity, was a noble Alexander; but he was so far from me, and I from him, that I could

160

not take comfort in myself alone, and so that I might remember him he gave me this book which represents his love in several ways. But although I have his image, it is not that I am not in a foreign land and far from the palace where the very noble friends of this lord dwell, who are all pure, perfect, and freed by the gifts of the king with whom they dwell.

THE AUTHOR: And therefore we shall tell you how our Lord is not at all freed from Love, but rather Love is freed from Him for our sake, in order that the little ones may hear Him through your intercession, for Love can do everything without doing harm.

AND THUS LOVE SPEAKS FOR YOU: There are seven beings of noble being, from which the creature receives her being, if the creature embraces all these beings, before she comes into perfect being; and we shall tell you how before this book ends.

2. Of the Enterprise of Love and Why She Had This Book Written

LOVE: Children of the holy Church, says Love, I have made this book for you, so that you will hearken in order to better merit the perfection of life and the being of peace to which the creature can come by the virtue of perfect charity, to whom this gift is given by the whole Trinity, this gift you shall hear explained in this book by the understanding of Love at the request of Reason.

3. Here Love Speaks of the Commandments of the Holy Church

LOVE: We shall begin here, says Love, with the commandments of the holy Church, so that each may draw sustenance from this book with the help of God, Who commands us to love Him with all our heart, with all our soul, and with all our virtue; and ourselves as we ought; and our neighbors as ourselves.

Firstly, that we love Him with all our heart. That is to say that our thoughts are always truly in Him. And with all our soul. That is to say that upon pain of death we speak only the truth. And with all our virtue. That is that we do all our works purely for Him. And ourselves as we ought. That is, we do not consider our profit, in doing this, but rather the perfect will of God. And our neighbors as ourselves. This is that we neither do, nor think, nor say to our neighbors that which we would not have them do to us. These commandments are necessary for the salvation of all: from a lesser life can no one obtain grace.

Note here the example of the young man, who said to Jesus Christ that he had kept the commandments from childhood, and Jesus Christ said to him: you must do one thing more, if you want to be perfect. This: go and sell all that you have and give it to the poor and then follow Me thus, and you shall have the treasure of the heavens. This is the counsel of all perfection of the virtues, and whoever shall keep it shall dwell in perfect charity. . . .

5. Of the Life Called Peace of Charity in Annihilated Life

LOVE: Now there is another life, which we call peace of charity in annihilated life. Of it, says Love, we wish to speak, asking that one find:

(1) a soul
(2) who saves herself by faith without works,
(3) who is alone in love,
(4) who does nothing for God,
(5) who leaves God nothing to do,
(6) who can be taught nothing,
(7) from whom nothing can be taken,
(8) to whom nothing can be given,
(9) who has no will.

LOVE: Alas, says Love, and who will give this Soul what she needs, for it has never been given, nor shall it ever be?

LOVE: This Soul, says Love, has six wings like the seraphim. She no longer wants anything which comes by intermediary, this is the seraphim being: there is no intermediary between their love and the divine love. They have constant tidings without intermediary, and this Soul also, for she does not seek the divine science among the masters of this century, but by truly scorning the world and herself. O Gods, how great is the difference between the gift of a friend given by an intermediary and the gift of a friend to a friend without intermediary!

LOVE: This book spoke the truth about this Soul, when it said that she has wings like the seraphim. With two wings she covers the face of Jesus Christ, our Lord. That is to say that the more knowledge this Soul has of the divine goodness, the more perfectly she knows that she knows nothing in comparison to a single spark of His goodness, for He is not known except to Himself.

With two other wings she covers His feet. That is to say the greater her knowledge of what Jesus Christ suffered for us, the more perfectly she knows that she knows nothing in comparison to what He suffered for us, for He is not known except to Himself.

With two other wings the Soul flies, and dwells immobile and seated. That is to say that all she knows and loves and praises of the divine goodness are the wings with which she flies and dwells immobile—for she is always in the sight of God—and seated, for she dwells constantly in the divine will.

Oh, and of what would such a Soul be afraid? Certainly, she neither could nor should fear or doubt anything, although she is in the world, and it is possible for the world, the flesh, and the devil and the four elements and the birds of the air and the dumb beasts to torment her, tear her to pieces, or devour her, she can lose nothing if God remains with her. For He is everywhere, all-powerful, all-wise, and all-good. He is our father, our brother, and our loyal friend. He is without beginning. He is incomprehensible except to Himself. He is without end, three persons and one single God; and such is, says this Soul, the friend of our souls. . . .

11. How, at the Request of Reason, Love Gives Knowledge of This Soul to Contemplatives by Declaring Nine Points Which Have Been Mentioned Before

REASON: Now, Love, says Reason, I pray you, for the sake of the contemplatives who still desire to grow in divine knowledge and who are and remain in the desire of Love, to explain out of your courtliness the eleven points which this Soul who wants Tender Love has, in whom Charity dwells and establishes herself by annihilated life, by which the Soul is abandoned through pure Love.

LOVE: Reason, says Love, name them.

REASON: The first point, says Reason to Love, that you said is that one cannot find such a Soul.

LOVE: This is true, says Love. This means that this Soul knows only one thing: the root of all evil and the abundance of all sin, which is without number, without weight, and without measure. And sin is nothingness, and this Soul is completely stricken and frightened by her horrible faults, which are less than nothing, and through this understanding the Soul is less than nothing, as is what is hers; therefore one may conclude that this Soul cannot be found, for such a Soul is so annihilated by humility that according to her rightful judgment if God wanted to punish her for the thousandth of one of her faults, no creature who has ever sinned would merit so great a torment

163

or such unending confusion as she. Such humility, and no other, is true and perfect humility in the annihilated Soul.

LOVE: The second point is that this Soul saves herself by faith without works.

REASON: Oh, for God's sake! says Reason, what does this mean?

LOVE: This means, says Love, that this annihilated Soul has such a great inward knowledge by the virtue of faith that she is so occupied within herself sustaining what Faith has ministered to her of the power of the Father, and of the knowledge of the Son, and of the goodness of the Holy Spirit that no created thing, unless it passes quickly, can remain in her memory, because her other occupation has so invaded the understanding of this annihilated Soul. This Soul can work no more, and surely, she is also sufficiently pardoned and exonerated without working by believing that God is good and incomprehensible. This saves the Soul without works, for faith overcomes all work, according to Love's own witness.

LOVE: The third point is that she is alone in love.

REASON: Oh, for God's sake, Lady Love, says Reason, what does this mean?

LOVE: This means, says Love, that this Soul finds neither consolation, nor affection, nor hope in any creature created by God either in heaven or on earth, but only in the goodness of God. This creature neither begs nor asks anything of any creature. This is the phoenix, who is alone; for this Soul, who satisfies herself of herself, is alone in love.

LOVE: The fourth point is that this Soul does nothing for God.

REASON: Oh, for God's sake, says Reason, what does this mean?

LOVE: This means, says Love, that God can do nothing with her work, and this Soul does nothing but that with which God can do something. She does not care about herself; let God, Who loves her more than this Soul loves herself, care about her. This Soul has so great a faith in God that she has no fear of being poor, her friend is so rich. For Faith teaches her that she will find God such as she hopes Him to be, and she hopes through faith that He is wholly rich, thus she cannot be poor.

LOVE: The fifth point is that this Soul leaves God nothing to do that she can do.

REASON: Oh, for God's sake, Love, says Reason, what does this mean?

LOVE: This means, says Love, that she can do nothing but the will of God and also cannot will anything else, and thus she leaves God nothing to do. For she lets nothing enter her thoughts which is contrary to God, and thus she leaves God nothing to do.

LOVE: The sixth point is that she can be taught nothing.

REASON: Oh, for God's sake, says Reason, what does this mean?

LOVE: This means that this Soul has such great steadfastness that if she had all the knowledge of all the creatures that ever were and are and are to come, this would seem nothing to her in comparison with what she loves which has never been known, nor shall it ever be. This Soul loves better what is in God and what has never been given, nor shall ever be given, than she loves what she has and would have, were she to have all the knowledge that all the creatures that are, and are to come, will have.

THE SOUL: And still this is nothing, says the Soul, in comparison with what is really concerned, but nothing can be said about that.

LOVE: The seventh point is that nothing can be taken from her.

REASON: Oh, for God's sake, Love, says Reason, tell what this means.

LOVE: What does this mean? says Love. And what could be taken from her? Certainly nothing could be taken from her. For though honor, riches and friends, heart and body and life were taken from this Soul, still nothing would be taken from her if God dwells with her. Thus it is apparent that no one can take anything from her, whatever his strength.

LOVE: The eighth point is that she can be given nothing.

REASON: Love, for God's sake, says Reason, what does this mean?

LOVE: What does it mean? says Love. And what could she be given? If she were given all that ever has been given and shall be given, this would be nothing in comparison with what she loves and will love: only God Himself.

AND THE SOUL SPEAKS: Lady Love loves and will love in me.

LOVE: With all due respect, says Love, this I am not.

We shall say, says Love, for the sake of the auditors, that God better loves the more of this Soul in Himself than the less of her in Him.

BUT THE SOUL SPEAKS: There is no less, there is only all and this I may truly say.

LOVE: I say moreover, says Love, that if the soul had all the knowledge and the love and the praise of the divine Trinity which have ever been given or shall be given, this would be nothing in comparison with what she loves and will love; nor may this love ever be attained through knowledge.

THE SOUL SPEAKS TO LOVE: Oh, assuredly, sweet Love, says the Soul. Not even the smallest particle of it. For there is no other God than the one about Whom nothing can be perfectly known. For my God is this one alone about Whom a single word cannot be said and of Whom all those in paradise cannot understand a single point, whatever their knowledge of Him may be.

And in this is implied, says the Soul, the sovereign mortification of my spirit's love, and this is all the glory of my soul's love, and will be everlastingly, and that of all those who ever understood. This point sounds small, says the Soul, in comparison to the greater one about which no one speaks. But I want to speak about it and do not know what to say. In spite of this, Lady Love, she says, my love is such that I prefer to hear you spoken ill of than that nothing be said about you. And surely, this is what I am doing; I speak ill of you, for all that I say about you is but to speak ill of your goodness. But that I speak ill of you should be pardoned by you. For Lord, says the Soul, who speaks of you constantly surely speaks ill of you, and thus never says anything of your goodness; and I myself speak similarly. I cannot stop speaking of you, either by questions or by thoughts, or listening in order to hear if someone will tell me something of your goodness; but the more I hear you spoken of, the more I am bewildered. For it would be to me a great villainy, to let me believe that something of your goodness is told me, for they who believe this are deceived, for I know with certainty that nothing can be said about it, and God grant that I never be deceived, and never want to hear your divine goodness lied about, rather that I accomplish the undertaking of this book, whose mistress, Love, told me to finish in it all my undertakings. For inasmuch as I ask anything myself from Love for herself, I will be with myself in the life of the spirit, in the shadow of the sun, where the intentions of divine love and the divine generation are seen as subtle images.

But what am I saying? says the Soul. And surely, though I had all that has been told, it would still be nothing in comparison with what I love in Him, what He will give no one except Himself, what He must keep for His divine righteousness. And consequently I say, and it is true, that I can be given nothing, whatever it may be. And this complaint which you hear me voice, Lady Reason, says the Soul, is my all and my best, understand it well. Oh, what a sweet understanding! By God! Understand it wholly, for paradise is nothing other than this understanding.

LOVE: The ninth point, Lady Reason, says Love, is that this Soul has no will.

REASON: Oh, for the God of love, says Reason, what are you saying? You say that this Soul has no will?

LOVE: Oh, surely not, for all this Soul wills by consent is what God wills her to will, and this she wills in order to accomplish the will of God, not her own will; and she cannot will this by herself, rather it is the will of God which wills it in her; thus it is apparent that this Soul has no will, without the will of God, which causes her to will all that she should will. . . .

118. The Seven States of the Pious Soul Which Are Otherwise Called Beings

THE SOUL: I have promised, says the Soul, since Love took hold, to say something about the seven states that we call beings, for this they are. They are the degrees by which one climbs up from the valley to the summit of the mountain, which is so isolated that one sees only God there; and each degree is rounded by its being.

The first state, or degree, is that of the Soul touched by God through grace and stripped of her capacity to sin, who intends to keep upon her life, that is upon pain of death, the commandments God gives in the Law. And because of this this Soul beholds with great fear that God has commanded her to love Him with all her heart, and her neighbor as herself, as well. To this Soul this seems labor enough for her—all that she can do—and it seems that though she live a thousand years, it is enough for her strength to hold and keep the commandments.

THE FREE SOUL: I was once found at this point and in this state, says the Free Soul. No one is frightened to climb the heights, certainly not if he has a valiant heart full of noble courage. But the little heart from lack of love dares neither to undertake a great thing nor to climb high. Such people are cowards; this is not astonishing, for they remain in sloth which prevents them from seeking God, Whom they will never find if they do not seek Him diligently.

THE SECOND STATE: The second state or degree is that the Soul beholds what God advises to His special friends, beyond what He commands; he who can dispense with accomplishing all that he knows pleases his friend is no friend.

And then the creature abandons herself and attempts to go beyond the advice of men by the mortification of nature, by scorning riches, delights, and honors in order to accomplish the perfection of the Gospel's counsel, of which Jesus Christ is the example. Then she fears neither losing what she has, nor the words of men, nor the weakness of the body, for her friend did not fear these things nor can the Soul who has been taken by Him.

THE THIRD STATE: The third state is that the Soul beholds herself affected by the love of works of perfection, works which her spirit, out of love's burning desire, decides to multiply within herself. And this makes known the subtlety of the understanding of her love, which can give no gift to her friend to comfort him except what he loves. For no other gift has any value in love than to give a friend the most loved thing. Therefore the will of this creature loves nothing except works of goodness, steadfastly undertaking all great labors with which it can nourish its spirit. For it rightly seems to her that she loves nothing except works of goodness and thus does not know what to give Love, unless she makes this sacrifice for him. For no death would be martyrdom for her except abstaining from the work she loves, which is the delight of her pleasure and the life of her will, which feeds on it. Therefore she abandons these works which delight her so and puts the will which led such a life to death and forces herself, for the sake of martyrdom, to obey the will of others, to abstain from her work and her will, to fulfill the will of others in order to destroy her own will. And this is harder, very much harder than the two aforementioned states, for it is harder to overcome the works of the will of the spirit than it is either to overcome the will of the body or to do the will of the spirit. Thus one must, by breaking and crushing, reduce oneself to powder in order to enlarge the place where Love will want to be and must burden oneself with several beings in order to disburden oneself and attain one's being.

THE FOURTH STATE: The fourth state is that the Soul is drawn up by highness of love through meditation into delight of thought, and abandons all outward labors and obedience to others for highness of contemplation. Then the Soul is so difficult, noble, and delightful that she cannot suffer anything to touch her, except the touch of Love's pure delight which makes her singularly charming and gay, which makes her proud of an abundance of love. Then she is mistress of the radiance, that is to say the light of her soul, which causes her to be marvelously filled with love of great faith through the concord of union which put her in possession of her delights. . . .

THE FIFTH STATE: The fifth state is that the Soul beholds that God is what is, that of Whom all things are, and she is not, so she is not that of whom all things are. And these two considerations provoke in her a marvelous astonishment and she sees that He is all goodness who has put a free will in her who is not, but is all wickedness. . . .

THE SIXTH STATE: The sixth state is that the Soul neither sees herself, whatever the abyss of humility she may have within herself, nor God, whatever high goodness He may have. But God sees Himself in her through His divine majesty that illuminates this Soul of Himself, so that she sees that no one is but God Himself Who is that of Whom all things are; and what is is God Himself. And therefore she sees but herself; for who sees what is sees only God himself Who, through His divine majesty, sees Himself in the Soul herself. . . .

And the seventh state keeps Love within the Soul to give us everlasting glory, which we will not know until our soul has left our body.

CHAPTER EIGHTEEN

Birgitta of Sweden, *Revelations* (late 1300s)

Birgitta of Sweden (1303–73)

Also known as Bridget, Birgitta was born into one of the wealthiest families in Sweden. At thirteen she married, bore eight children, and led the life of a Swedish noblewoman, including a time as mistress in the royal household at Stockholm (c.1336). Her revelations began after her husband's death in 1344, and she founded the Brigittine order in 1346. Three years later, she journeyed to Rome, ostensibly to obtain approval from the pope for her new order, although that was not her sole reason for going. She also felt called to help purify the Church and return the papacy from Avignon to Rome. She remained in Rome to pursue this work until her death, gaining the ear of many powerful officials within the Church and secular government. Equally important was the affectionate regard with which she was held by the Roman people for working miracles and caring for the poor. She was widely recognized as having special intercessory powers with Christ and Mary, and she was considered by many to be an agent of God. After her death an elaborate tradition quickly established itself, rich with legends and miracles of Birgitta's early life.

Revelations

Birgitta's revelations were handed over to confessors who organized them into eight books. They cover a range of spiritual and ecclesial issues, some from her pilgrimage to the Holy Land, some on moral themes, and some on the Church in Italy and reform. Book V focuses specifically on theological questions with an incisive and insistent tone. Book VIII is almost entirely political in content, indicating that Birgitta did not see any sphere of life as being outside her realm. In the excerpt from Book V, Birgitta tells of a monk who, while standing on a high rung on a ladder to heaven, challenges God with interrogations on evil, suffering, and justice in creation and in the economy of salvation. Remember that Book V reflects the pervasive awareness of the Black Death then plaguing Europe.

In the excerpt from Book VII, Birgitta reports of a revelation from the Virgin Mary in response to the concerns of a devout Friar about his conscience. She affirms the power of the pope and the clergy regardless of their personal sinfulness.

THE FIFTH BOOK OF REVELATIONS OR BOOK OF QUESTIONS

THE NINTH INTERROGATION

First question. When these things had been said, the same religious appeared on his rung as before and said: "O Judge, I ask you: Why do you seem so unfair in your gifts and graces that you preferred your Mother Mary to every other creature and exalted her above the angels?"

2. *Second question.* "Item. Why did you give the angels a spirit without flesh and the gift of being in heavenly joy, whereas to man you gave an earthen vessel and a spirit—and birth with wailing, life with labor, and death with sorrow?"

3. *Third question.* "Item. Why did you give man a rational intellect and senses, whereas to animals you did not give reason?"

4. *Fourth question.* "Item. Why did you give life to animals, but not to the other created things that lack senses?"

5. *Fifth question.* "Item. Why is there not such light at night as there is in the day?"

6. *Response to the first question.* The Judge replied: "Friend, in my Godhead all that is going to exist or happen is foreseen and foreknown from the beginning as if it had already occurred. 7. The fall of man was foreknown, and out of God's justice it was permitted; but it was not caused by God and did not have to happen because of God's foreknowledge. Foreknown too from eternity was man's liberation, which was to happen out of God's mercy. 8. You now ask why I preferred my mother Mary to all others and loved her more than any other creature. It was because the

special mark of virtues was found in her. 9. When a fire is kindled and many logs surround it, the log most apt and efficient for combustion will be the quickest to catch the flame and burn. So it was with Mary. 10. For when the fire of divine love—which in itself is changeless and eternal—began to kindle and appear and when the Godhead willed to become incarnate, no creature was more apt and efficient for receiving this fire of love than the Virgin Mary; for no creature burned with such charity as she. 11. And although her charity was revealed and shown at the end of time, it was nevertheless foreseen before the beginning of the world. 12. And so, from eternity, it was predetermined in the Godhead that as no one was found comparable to her in charity, so too no one would be her equal in grace and blessing."

13. *Response to the second question.* "Item. As to why I gave the angel a spirit without flesh, I answer: In the beginning and before time and the ages, I created spirits in order that of their own free choice they might live according to my will and thus rejoice in my goodness and glory. 14. But some of them took pride in their goodness and did evil to themselves by using their free will in an inordinate way. And because there was nothing evil in nature and creation except the inordinancy of their individual wills, they therefore fell. 15. But other spirits chose to take their stand in humility under me, their God; and therefore they merited eternal stability. 16. For it is right and just that I, God, who am an uncreated spirit and the Creator and Lord of all, should also have in my service spirits more subtle and swift than other creatures. 17. And because it was not fitting for me to have any diminishment in my hosts, I therefore created, in place of those who fell, another creature—namely, man—who, through his free choice and his good will, might merit the same dignity that the angels deserted. 18. And so, if man had a soul and no flesh, he would not be able to merit so sublime a good nor even be able to labor. The body was joined to the soul for the attainment of eternal honor. 19. Therefore, man's tribulations increase in order that he may experience his free will and his infirmities, to the end that he may not be proud. 20. And so that he may desire the glory for which he was created and that he may undo the disobedience that he voluntarily committed, he has therefore been given, out of divine justice, a tearful entrance and a tearful exit and a life full of toils."

21. *Response to the third question.* "Item. As to why animals do not have a rational intellect as man does, I answer you: 22. Everything that has been created is for man's use or for his needs and sustenance or for his instruction and reproof or for his consolation and humiliation. 23. But if brutes had

intelligence as man does, they would certainly be a trouble to him, causing harm rather than profit. 24. Therefore, in order that all things may be subject to man—for whom all things were made—and that all things might fear him, while he himself is to fear no one but me, his God, animals have not been given a rational intellect."

25. *Response to the fourth question.* "Item. As to why insensate things have no life, I answer: Everything that lives is going to die, and every living thing moves unless it is impeded by some obstacle. 26. If, therefore, insensate things had life, they would move against man rather than for him. 27. And so, in order that everything might be for man's solace, higher beings—namely, the angels, with whom man shares reason and immortality of the soul—have been given to man for his protection; 28. and lower beings, whether they are sensate or not, have been given to him for his use and sustenance and instruction and training."

29. *Response to the fifth question.* "Item. As to why it is not always daylight, I will answer you by means of an example. Under every vehicle, i.e., a cart, there are wheels so that the burden placed upon it may be more easily moved; and the back wheels follow those in front. 30. A similarity exists in spiritual matters. For the world is a great burden, burdening man with worries and troubles. And no wonder; for when man disdained the place of rest, it was right that he experienced a place of work. 31. Therefore, in order that the burden of this world may be more easily borne by man, mercifully there comes a change and alternation of times—namely: day and night, summer and winter—for the sake of man's exercise and his rest. 32. When contrary things come together—namely, the strong and the weak—it is reasonable to condescend to the weak so that it can exist beside the strong; otherwise the weak would be annihilated. 33. So it also is with man. Even though, in the strength of his immortal soul, man could continue forever in contemplation and labor, nevertheless the strength of his weak body would fail. 34. For this reason, light has been made so that man, who has a common bond with higher and lower beings, may be able to subsist by laboring in the day and remembering the sweetness of the everlasting light that he lost. 35. Night has been made that he may rest his body with the will of coming to that place where there is neither night nor labor, but rather everlasting day and eternal glory." . . .

THIRTEENTH INTERROGATION

First question. Again the same religious appeared on his rung as before and said: "O Judge, I ask you: Why is your grace so quickly withdrawn from some while others are long tolerated in their wickedness?"

2. *Second question.* "Item. Why is grace granted to some in their youth while others, in old age, are deprived of it?"

3. *Third question.* "Item. Why are some troubled beyond measure while others are, as it were, secure from tribulation?"

4. *Fourth question.* "Item. Why are some given intelligence and an incomparable genius for learning while others are like asses without intellect?"

5. *Fifth question.* "Item. Why are some excessively hardened while others rejoice in wonderful consolation?"

6. *Sixth question.* "Item. Why is greater prosperity given in this world to the wicked rather than to the good?"

7. *Seventh question.* "Item. Why is one called in the beginning and another toward the end?"

8. *Response to the first question.* The Judge replied: "Friend, all my works are in my foreknowledge from the beginning; and all things that have been made were created for the solace of man. 9. But because man prefers his own will to my will, therefore, out of justice, the goods gratuitously given to him are taken from him in order that man may know that with God all things are rational and just. 10. And because many are ungrateful for my grace and become more undevout the more their gifts are multiplied, the gifts are therefore quickly taken from them in order that my divine plan may be more swiftly manifested and lest man abuse my grace to his own greater doom. 11. Item. As to why some are long tolerated in their wickedness, the reason is that amidst their evils, many have some tolerable trait. 12. For either they are of profit to some, or they are a caution to others. When Saul was denounced by Samuel, Saul's sin seemed slight in the sight of men while David's sin seemed greater. 13. However, under the pressure of testing, Saul disobediently abandoned me, his God, and consulted the pythoness. But David, in temptation, became more faithful, patiently enduring the things that bore down upon him and considering that they befell him for his sins. 14. The fact that I patiently endured Saul demonstrates Saul's ingratitude and my divine patience. The fact that David was chosen shows my foreknowledge and David's future humility and his contrition."

15. *Response to the second question.* "Item. As to why grace is taken away from some in their old age, I answer: All are given grace in order that the Giver of grace may be loved by all. 16. But because many, toward their end, are ungrateful for my divine grace—as Solomon was—it is therefore just that what was not carefully kept before the end should, in the end, be withdrawn. 17. For my gift and my divine grace are taken away sometimes

because of the recipient's negligence in attending to what he has received and to what he should give in return, sometimes as a caution for others so that everyone in the state of grace may always fear and feel dread at the fall of others. 18. For even the wise have fallen through negligence; and even some, who seemed to be my friends, have been supplanted because of their ingratitude."

19. *Response to the third question.* "Item. As to why some have greater tribulation, I answer: I am the Creator of all. Therefore no tribulation comes without my permission, as it is written: 20. I am God 'creating evil'—i.e., permitting tribulation—because no trouble befalls even the gentiles without me or without a rational cause. 21. For my prophets foretold many things concerning the adversities of the gentiles in order that they, being negligent and abusive of reason, might be taught by scourges and in order that I, God—permitting all—might be known and glorified by every nation. 22. If therefore I, God, do not spare the pagans from scourges, far less will I spare these who have more copiously tasted of the sweetness of my divine grace. 23. The fact that some have less tribulation, and others more, occurs so that mankind may turn away from sin and may, after troubles in the present, obtain consolation in the future. 24. For all who are judged and who judge themselves in this age will not come to future judgment. As it is written: They will pass 'from death into life.' 25. The fact that some are protected from the scourge occurs lest, having been scourged, they murmur and thus incur a heavier judgment, for there are many who do not deserve to be scourged in the present. 26. There are even some in this life who are not weighed down by any bodily or spiritual annoyance and who live as carelessly as if God did not exist or as if God spares them because of their works of justice. 27. But they should be greatly afraid and should grieve lest I, God, who spare them in the present, come unforeseen and damn them more harshly because they have no compunction. 28. There are some who have health in the flesh but are troubled in soul because of their contempt for God. Others enjoy neither bodily health nor inner consolation of soul, and yet they persevere in serving and honoring me according to their ability. Indeed, some—from their mother's womb and right up to the end—are afflicted by infirmities. 29. But I, their God, so moderate the tribulations of all these people that nothing happens without a cause and a recompense, for of those who slept before their temptations the eyes of many are opened in tribulation."

30. *Response to the fourth question.* "Item. As to why some have greater intelligence, I answer: The abundance of one's wisdom does not profit the

soul toward eternal salvation unless the soul also shines with a good life. On the contrary, it is more useful to have less knowledge and a better life. 31. Therefore, each person has been given a measure of rationality by means of which he can obtain heaven if he lives piously. However, rationality varies in many according to their natural and spiritual dispositions. 32. For just as, by means of divine fervor and the virtues, man makes progress toward perfection of the virtues, so too, through bad will and bad disposition of nature and wrong upbringing, man descends into vanities. 33. Many times nature suffers a defect when one strives against nature and one sins. Therefore, it is not without cause that in some, rationality is great but useless, as in those who have knowledge but not life. 34. In others, there is less knowledge but better practice. In some, of course, rationality and life are in agreement; but in others, on the contrary, there is neither rationality nor life. 35. This variety comes from my well-ordered and divine permission—sometimes, for the benefit of humans or for their humiliation and instruction; sometimes, because of ingratitude or temptation; sometimes, because of a defect of nature or latent sins; 36. sometimes, in order to avoid the occasion of a greater sin; and sometimes, because a nature is not suited to receive anything greater. Let everyone who has the grace of intelligence therefore fear that, because of it, he will be judged more heavily if he is negligent. 37. Let him who has no intelligence or talent rejoice and do as much as he can with the little that he has; for he has been freed from many occasions of sin. 38. In youth, Peter the apostle was forgetful and John was no trained expert; but they grasped true wisdom in their old age because they sought wisdom's beginning. 39. When young, Solomon was docile and Aristotle was subtle; but they did not grasp the beginning of wisdom because they neither glorified the Giver of knowledge as they ought, nor imitated the things that they knew and taught, nor learned for themselves, but for others. 40. Balaam, too, had knowledge but did not follow it; and therefore the she-ass rebuked his folly. Daniel when young, judged his elders. 41. Erudition, without a good life, does not please me; therefore, it is necessary that those who abuse rationality be corrected. For I, the God and Lord of all, give knowledge to mankind; and I correct both the wise and the foolish."

42. *Response to the fifth question.* "Item. As to why some are hardened, I answer: The fact that Pharaoh was hardened was his own fault, and not mine, because he would not conform himself to my divine will. 43. For obduracy is nothing other than the withdrawal of my divine grace; and grace is withdrawn because man has not given to me, God, that free thing

he has, namely, his own will, as you will be able to understand through an example. 44. There was a man who possessed two fields, of which the one remained uncultivated and the other, at certain times, bore fruit. 45. His friend said to him: 'Since you are wise and wealthy, I wonder why you do not cultivate your fields more diligently or hand them over to others for cultivation.' 46. He answered: 'One of these fields—no matter how much diligence I display—produces nothing but very bad herbs—which noxious beasts seize upon, and then the beasts befoul the place. 47. If I apply an enrichment, the field grows so insolent and wanton that even if it produces a modicum of grain, even more weeds spring up, which I disdain to gather because I desire no grain unless it is pure. 48. Therefore, the better plan is to leave such a field uncultivated; for then the beasts do not occupy the place and the beasts do not hide in the grass. And if some bitter herbs do sprout, they are useful for the sheep, for after tasting them, the sheep learn not to be fastidious about things that are sweet. 49. The other field is laid out according to the temperature of the seasons. A part of it is stony and needs enrichment; another part is moist and needs warmth; another part is dry and needs moisture. For that reason, I will to regulate my work according to the field's condition.' 50. I, God, am like that man. The first field is the free movement of the will given to man. He moves it more against me than for me. 51. And if man does some things that please me, in many more things he provokes me, for man's will and mine are not in agreement. 52. So too Pharaoh acted, for, although through sure signs he recognized my power, nonetheless he strengthened his resolution of standing fast in his wickedness against me. 53. Therefore, he experienced my justice, for it is just that he who does not make good use of trifles should not pride himself on things that are very great. 54. The second field is the obedience of a good mind and the rejection of one's own will. If such a mind is dry in devotion, it must wait for the rain of my divine grace. 55. If it is stony through impatience or obduracy, it must, with composure, endure purgation and rebuke. If it is moist through carnal wantonness let it embrace abstinence and be like an animal prepared for its owner's will; for in such a mind I, God, take much glory. 56. Therefore, the fact that some become hardened is caused by man's will being contrary to mine. For even though I will that all be saved, nevertheless this is not accomplished unless man has personally cooperated by making his entire will conform to my will. 57. The fact that not all are given equal grace and progress is an act of my hidden judgment, for I know and I regulate for each person what is expedient and necessary for him; and I restrain man's attempts lest he fall too deeply. 58. For many have the talent of grace and would be able to work; but they refuse. Others abstain from sin out of fear of punishment or because they do not have the means to sin or because sin does not amuse them. Therefore, to some, greater gifts are not given because I, who alone know the minds of human beings know how to distribute my gifts."

59. *Response to the sixth question.* "Item. As to why the wicked sometimes have greater prosperity in the world than the good, I answer: This is an indication of my great patience and charity and a testing for the just. 60. For if I gave temporal goods only to my friends, the wicked would despair and the good would grow proud. Therefore, temporal goods are given to all so that I, the Creator and giver of all, may be loved by all and so that, when the good grow proud, they may be instructed in justice by means of the wicked. 61. Indeed, let all understand that temporal things are not to be loved or preferred to me, God, but are to be had for sustenance alone; and let them be all the more fervent in my service, the less the stability that they find in temporal things."

62. *Response to the seventh question.* "Item. As to why one is called at the beginning and another at the end, I answer: I am like a mother who sees in her children the hope of life and gives stronger things to some and lighter things to others. With those for whom there is no hope she also sympathizes, and she does for them as much as she can. 63. But if the children become worse from the mother's remedy, what need is there then to labor? 64. This is the way I deal with man. One, whose will is foreseen as more fervent and whose humility and stability are foreseen as more constant, received grace in the beginning; and it will follow him to the end. 65. Another, who, amidst all his wickedness, still attempts and strives to become better, deserves to be called toward the end. But he who is ungrateful does not deserve admission to his mother's breasts." . . .

THE SEVENTH BOOK OF REVELATIONS

. . . Honor and thanks be given to almighty God and to the Blessed Virgin Mary, his most worthy Mother! It seemed to me, unworthy person that I am, that while I was absorbed in prayer, the Mother of God spoke to me, a sinner, these following words:

2. "Say to my friend the friar, who through you sent his supplication to me, that it is the true faith and the perfect truth that if a person, at the devil's instigation, had committed every sin against God and then, with true contrition and the purpose of amendment, truly repented these sins and

humbly, with burning love, asked God for mercy, 3. there is no doubt that the kind and merciful God himself would immediately be as ready to receive that person back into his grace with great joy and happiness as would be a loving father who saw returning to him his only, dearly beloved son, now freed from a great scandal and a most shameful death. 4. Yes, much more willingly than any fleshly father, the loving God himself forgives his servants all their sins if they assiduously repent and humbly ask him for mercy and they fear to go on committing sins, and, with all the longing of their hearts, desire God's friendship above all things.

5. "Therefore say to that same friar, on my behalf, that because of his good will and my prayer, God in his goodness has already forgiven him all the sins that he ever committed in all the days of his life. 6. Tell him also that because of my prayer the love that he has for God will always increase in him right up to his death and will in no way diminish. 7. Likewise, say to him that it pleases God my Son that he stay in Rome, preaching, giving good advice to those who ask, hearing confessions, and imposing salutary penances, unless his superior should send him sometimes out of the city for some lawful necessity. 8. For their transgressions, the same friar should charitably reprove his other brothers with good words, with salutary teachings, and, when he might be able to correct them, even with just rebukes, to the end that they may keep the rule and humbly amend their lives. 9. Furthermore, I now make known to him that his Masses and his reading and his prayers are acceptable and pleasing to God. 10. And therefore tell him that, just as he guards himself against any excess in food and drink and sleep, so he must diligently guard himself against too much abstinence, in order that he may not suffer any faintness in performing divine labors and services. 11. Also, he is not to have an overabundance of clothing but only necessary things, according to the Rule of Saint Francis, so that pride and cupidity may not ensue; for the less costly and valuable his clothes have been, the more lavish shall be his reward. 12. And let him humbly obey all of his superior's instructions that are not contrary to God and that the friar's own ability permits him to perform.

13. "Tell him also, on my behalf, what he will answer to those who say that the pope is not the true pope and that it is not the true Body of Jesus Christ my Son that the priests confect on the altar. He should answer those heretics in this way: 14. 'You have turned the backs of your heads to God, and thus you do not see him. Turn therefore to him your faces, and then you will be able to see him.' 15. For it is the true and Catholic faith that a pope who is without heresy is—no matter how stained he be with other sins—

never so wicked as a result of these sins and his other bad deeds that there would not always be in him full authority and complete power to bind and loose souls. 16. He possesses this authority through blessed Peter and has acquired it from God. For before Pope John, there were many supreme pontiffs who are now in hell. Nevertheless, the just and reasonable judgments that they made in the world are standing and approved in God's sight.

17. "For a similar reason, I also say that all those priests who are not heretical—although otherwise full of many other sins—are true priests and truly confect the Body of Christ my Son and that truly they touch God in their hands on the altar and administer the other sacraments even though, because of their sins and evil deeds, they are unworthy of heavenly glory in God's sight." . . .

Julian of Norwich, *Showings* (c.1373)

Julian of Norwich 1343–1413

Also known as Juliana, Julian was an Englishwoman who lived outside the walls of what is now known as St. Julian's Church in Norwich, a town thriving with both ecclesial and intellectual interests. She emerged as an outstanding theological writer who composed her work in vernacular English. She was most likely a member of some religious order, although no certain record of this exists. She shows a familiarity with the contemplative teaching of her day and a thorough knowledge of the Vulgate; her writings demonstrate greater exposure to the outside world than women living in strict enclosure would likely have had. Several sources confirm that Julian was appreciated for her spiritual counsel and advice as well as for her learning and erudition. She tells us that when she was thirty years old she had a grave illness, at the end of which she received fourteen "shewings," or revelations. Two other visions followed in subsequent days for a total of sixteen. She was eager to communicate the love and compassion of God to her contemporaries who were so burdened by the gulf of sin separating them from God.

Showings

It was twenty years after her revelations that Julian recorded them and reflected on their meaning. Throughout this text we see her own theological struggle with the nature of sin, its effect on human nature, and on a person's relationship with God. Given her own age's insistence on God's punishments for sin, she turns her attention to the Trinity and to Christ's role in mediating love and compassion for a fallen humanity. "Christ, our Mother," the second person of the Trinity, is, according to Julian, the creative force in the Trinity that allows for the reunification of human and divine love. Her writing combines the passion of visionary literature with theological carefulness. In these excerpts, Julian tells of the judgment of God and of the Church, and the persevering love that protects us.

SHOWINGS

The Forty-fifth Chapter

God judges us in our natural substance, which is always kept one in him, whole and safe, without end; and this judgment is out of his justice. And man judges us in our changeable sensuality, which now seems one thing and now another, as it derives from parts and presents an external appearance. And this judgment is mixed, for sometimes it is good and lenient, and sometimes it is hard and painful. And inasmuch as it is good and lenient it pertains to God's justice, and inasmuch as it is hard and painful, our good Lord Jesus reforms it by mercy and grace through the power of the blessed Passion, and so brings it into justice. And though these two are so reconciled and joined, still both will be known in heaven forever. The first judgment, which is from God's justice, is from his own great endless love, and that is that fair, sweet judgment which was shown in all the fair revelation in which I saw him assign to us no kind of blame. And though this was sweet and delectable, I could not be fully comforted only by contemplating it, and that was because of the judgment of Holy Church, which I had understood before, and which was continually in my sight. And therefore it seemed to me that by this judgment I must necessarily know myself a sinner. And by the same judgment I understood that sinners sometimes deserve blame and wrath, and I could not see these two in God, and therefore my desire was more than I can or may tell, because of the higher judgment which God himself revealed at the same time, and therefore I had of necessity to accept it. And the lower judgment had previously been taught me in Holy Church, and therefore I could not in any way ignore the lower judgment.

This then was my desire, that I might see in God in what way the judgment of Holy Church here on earth is true in his sight, and how it pertains to me to know it truly, whereby they might both be reconciled as might be glory to God and the right way for me. And to all this I never had any other answer than a wonderful example of a lord and a servant, as I shall tell later, and that was very mysteriously revealed. And still it was my desire and my will until the end of my life by grace to know these two judgments, as it pertains to me. For all heavenly things and all earthly things which belong to heaven are comprehended in these two judgments. And the more knowledge and understanding that we have by the gracious leading of the Holy Spirit of these two judgments, the more shall we see and know our feelings. And always, the more that we see them, the more, according to our nature by the working of grace, shall we long to be filled with endless joy and bliss, for we are made for this. And our natural substance is now full of blessedness in God, and has been since it was made, and will be without end.

The Fifty-Eighth Chapter

God the blessed Trinity, who is everlasting being, just he is eternal from without beginning, just so was it in his eternal purpose to create human nature, which fair nature first prepared for his own Son, the second person; and when he wished, by full agreement of the whole Trinity he created us all once. And in our creating he joined and united us to himself, and through this union we are kept as pure and as noble as we were created. By the power of that same precious union we love our Creator and delight in him, praise him and thank him and endlessly rejoice in him. And this is the work which is constantly performed in every soul which will be saved, and this is the godly will mentioned before.

And so in our making, God almighty is our loving Father, and God all wisdom is our loving Mother, with the love and the goodness of the Holy Spirit, which is all one God, one Lord. And in the joining and the union he is our very true spouse and we his beloved wife and his fair maiden, with which wife he was never displeased; for he says: I love you and you love me, and our love will never divide in two.

I contemplated the work of all the blessed Trinity, in which contemplation I saw and understood these three properties: the property of the fatherhood, and the property of the motherhood, and the property of the lordship in one God. In our almighty Father we have our protection and our bliss, as regards our natural substance, which is ours by our creation from without beginning; and in the second person, in knowledge and wisdom we have our perfection, as regards our sensuality, our restoration and our salvation, for he is our Mother, brother and saviour; and in our good Lord the Holy Spirit we have our reward and our gift for our living and our labour, endlessly surpassing all that we desire in marvellous courtesy, out of his great plentiful grace. For all our life consists of three: In the first we have our being, and in the second we have our increasing, and in the third we have our fulfillment. The first is nature, the second is mercy, the third is grace.

As to the first, I saw and understood that the high might of the Trinity is our Father, and the deep wisdom of the Trinity is our Mother, and the great love of the Trinity is our Lord; and all these we have in nature and in our substantial creation. And furthermore I saw that the second person, who is our Mother, substantially the same beloved person, has now become our mother sensually, because we are double by God's creating, that is to say substantial and sensual. Our substance is the higher part, which we have in our Father, God almighty; and the second person of the Trinity is our Mother in nature in our substantial creation, in whom we are grounded and rooted, and he is our Mother of mercy in taking our sensuality. And so our Mother is working on us in various ways, in whom our parts are kept undivided; for in our Mother Christ we profit and increase, and in mercy he reforms and restores us, and by the power of his Passion, his death and his Resurrection he unites us to our substance. So our Mother works in mercy on all his beloved children who are docile and obedient to him, and grace works with mercy, and especially in two properties, as it was shown, which working belongs to the third person, the Holy Spirit. He works, rewarding and giving. Rewarding is a gift for our confidence which the Lord makes to those who have laboured; and giving is a courteous act which he does freely, by grace, fulfilling and surpassing all that creatures deserve.

Thus in our Father, God almighty, we have our being, and in our Mother of mercy we have our reforming and our restoring, in whom our parts are united and all made perfect man, and through the rewards and the gifts of grace of the Holy Spirit we are fulfilled. And our substance is in our Father, God almighty, and our substance is in our Mother, God all wisdom, and our substance is in our Lord God, the Holy Spirit, all goodness, for our substance is whole in each person of the Trinity, who is one God. And our sensuality is only in the second person, Christ Jesus, in whom is the Father and the Holy Spirit; and in him and by him we are powerfully taken out of hell and out of the wretchedness on earth, and gloriously brought up into heaven, and blessedly united to our substance, increased in riches and nobility by all the power of Christ and by the grace and operation of the Holy Spirit.

The Eighty-Second Chapter

But here our courteous Lord revealed the moaning and the mourning of our soul, with this meaning: I know well that you wish to live for my love, joyfully and gladly suffering all the penance which may come to you; but since you do not live without sin, you are depressed and sorrowful, and if you could live without sin, you would suffer for my love all the woe which might come to you, and it is true. But do not be too much aggrieved by the sin which comes to you against your will.

And here I understood that the lord looked on the servant with pity and not with blame; for this passing life does not require us to live wholly without sin. He loves us endlessly, and we sin customarily, and he reveals it to us most gently. And then we sorrow and moan discreetly, turning to contemplate his mercy, cleaving to his love and to his goodness, seeing that his is our medicine, knowing that we only sin. And so by the meekness which we obtain in seeing our sin, faithfully recognizing his everlasting love, thanking him and praising him, we please him. I love you and you love me, and our love will never be divided in two; and it is for your profit that I suffer. And all this was revealed in spiritual understanding, he saying these blessed words: I protect you very safely.

And by the great desire which I saw in our blessed Lord that we shall live in this way, that is to say in longing and rejoicing, as all this lesson of love shows, I understood that all which is opposed to this is not from him, but it is from enmity. And he wants us to know it by the sweet light of grace of his substantial and natural love.

If there be any such lover on earth, who is continually protected from falling, I do not know, for it was not revealed to me. But this was revealed, that in falling and in rising we are always preciously protected in one love. For we do not fall in the sight of God, and we do not stand in our own sight; and both these are true, as I see it, but the contemplating of our Lord God is the higher truth. So we are much indebted to him, that he will in this way of life reveal to us this high truth, and I understood that while we are in this way, it is most profitable to us that we see these both together. For the higher contemplation keeps us in spiritual joy and true delight in God; the other, which is the lower contemplation, keeps us in fear, and makes us ashamed of ourselves.

But our good Lord always wants us to remain much more in the contemplation of the higher, and not to forsake the knowledge of the lower, until the time that we are brought up above, where we shall have our Lord Jesus for our reward, and be filled full of joy and bliss without end.

Catherine of Siena, *Dialogue* (1378)

Catherine of Siena (1347–80)

Born Catherine Benincasa, the twenty-fourth child of twenty-five in a Sienese dyer's family, Catherine received unusual spiritual gifts at an early age. She became a Dominican tertiary, remaining at home in a solitary life of prayer. Soon, however, she found her household growing with kindred spirits, interested in prayer and service to others. At the same time she became increasingly influential in the church, concerning herself with such issues as the Crusades, civil war, the Avignon papacy, and ecclesiastical reform. In 1370 she experienced a mystical death, strengthening her resolve that she was to be about the business of God. She urged the princes to quit their civil wars, and is credited with persuading Pope Gregory XI to return to Rome. Distressed about the divisions and corruptions within the Church, she worked for reform until the end of her life in 1380. She was declared Doctor of the Church in 1970.

Dialogue

In 1378 Catherine asked her secretaries to write down her religious experiences as she dictated them, often as she was in a state of ecstasy. Taken all together, these experiences tell of a dialogue between a soul who asks God four petitions, and God's replies. The writing gives evidence of not only ecstatic experience, but considerable reflection and commentary as well. God responds to her request that she suffer in the place of others

187

and explains to her the role of knowledge of self and of God in the soul's search for God. God also describes the bridge that joins heaven and earth, Jesus Christ. It is his teaching, Catherine informs us, that leads to a life of love, the path to the very height of heaven. Paragraph 47 sets out Catherine's views that it is the disposition of the will toward God, not status or religious office, that ensures holiness. She goes on in Section 113 with a stinging criticism of the clergy and corruption in the Church. Out of her profound sense of the great need both the Church and the world have for God's love and healing, the final excerpt expands her petition to God for mercy on the world and on the Church.

THE DIALOGUE

PROLOGUE
IN THE NAME OF CHRIST CRUCIFIED AND OF GENTLE MARY

A soul rises up, restless with tremendous desire for God's honor and the salvation of souls. She has for some time exercised herself in virtue and has become accustomed to dwelling in the cell of self-knowledge in order to know better God's goodness toward her, since upon knowledge follows love. And loving, she seeks to pursue truth and clothe herself in it.

But there is no way she can so savor and be enlightened by this truth as in continual humble prayer, grounded in the knowledge of herself and of God. For by such prayer the soul is united with God, following in the footsteps of Christ crucified, and through desire and affection and the union of love he makes of her another himself. So Christ seems to have meant when he said, "If you will love me and keep my word, I will show myself to you, and you will be one thing with me and I with you." And we find similar words in other places from which we can see it is the truth that by love's affection the soul becomes another himself.

To make this clearer still, I remember having heard from a certain servant of God that, when she was at prayer, lifted high in spirit, God would not hide from her mind's eye his love for his servants. No, he would reveal it, saying among other things, "Open your mind's eye and look within me, and you will see the dignity and beauty of my reasoning creature. But beyond the beauty I have given the soul by creating her in my image and likeness, look at those who are clothed in the wedding garment of charity, adorned with many true virtues: They are united with me through love. So I say, if you should ask me who they are, I would answer," said the gentle loving

188

Word, "that they are another me; for they have lost and drowned their own will and have clothed themselves and united themselves and conformed themselves with mine."

It is true, then, that the soul is united to God through love's affection.

Now this soul's will was to know and follow truth more courageously. So she addressed four petitions to the most high and eternal Father, holding up her desire for herself first of all—for she knew that she could be of no service to her neighbors in teaching or example or prayer without first doing herself the service of attaining and possessing virtue.

Her first petition, therefore, was for herself. The second was for the reform of holy Church. The third was for the whole world in general, and in particular for the peace of Christians who are rebelling against holy Church with great disrespect and persecution. In her fourth petition she asked divine providence to supply in general and in particular for a certain case which had arisen. . . .

4

I have shown you, dearest daughter, that in this life guilt is not atoned for by any suffering simply as suffering, but rather by suffering borne with desire, love, and contrition of heart. The value is not in the suffering but in the soul's desire. Likewise, neither desire nor any other virtue has value or life except through my only-begotten Son, Christ crucified, since the soul has drawn love from him and in virtue follows his footsteps. In this way and in no other is suffering of value. It satisfies for sin, then, with gentle unitive love born from the sweet knowledge of my goodness and from the bitterness and contrition the heart finds in the knowledge of itself and its own sins. Such knowledge gives birth to hatred and contempt for sin and for the soul's selfish sensuality, whence she considers herself worthy of punishment and unworthy of reward. So you see, *said gentle Truth,* those who have heartfelt contrition, love for true patience, and that true humility which considers oneself worthy of punishment and unworthy of reward suffer with patience and so make atonement.

You ask me for suffering to atone for the offenses my creatures commit against me. And you ask for the will to know and love me, supreme Truth. Here is the way, if you would come to perfect knowledge and enjoyment of me, eternal Life: Never leave the knowledge of yourself. Then, put down as you are in the valley of humility you will know me in yourself, and from this knowledge you will draw all that you need.

No virtue can have life in it except from charity, and charity is nursed and mothered by humility. You will find humility in the knowledge of yourself when you see that even your own existence comes not from yourself but from me, for I loved you before you came into being. And in my unspeakable love for you I willed to create you anew in grace. So I washed you and made you a new creation in the blood that my only-begotten Son poured out with such burning love. . . .

10

Do you know how these three virtues exist?

Imagine a circle traced on the ground, and in its center a tree sprouting with a shoot grafted into its side. The tree finds its nourishment in the soil within the expanse of the circle, but uprooted from the soil it would die fruitless. So think of the soul as a tree made for love and living only by love. Indeed, without this divine love, which is true and perfect charity, death would be her fruit instead of life. The circle in which this tree's root, the soul's love, must grow is true knowledge of herself, knowledge that is joined to me, who like the circle have neither beginning nor end. You can go round and round within this circle, finding neither end nor beginning, yet never leaving the circle. This knowledge of yourself, and of me within yourself, is grounded in the soil of true humility, which is as great as the expanse of the circle (which is the knowledge of yourself united with me, as I have said). But if your knowledge of yourself were isolated from me there would be no full circle at all. Instead, there would be a beginning in self-knowledge, but apart from me it would end in confusion.

So the tree of charity is nurtured in humility and branches out in true discernment. The marrow of the tree (that is, loving charity within the soul) is patience, a sure sign that I am in her and that she is united with me.

This tree, so delightfully planted, bears many-fragranced blossoms of virtue. Its fruit is grace for the soul herself and blessing for her neighbors in proportion to the conscientiousness of those who would share my servants' fruits. To me this tree yields the fragrance of glory and praise to my name, and so it does what I created it for and comes at last to its goal, to me, everlasting Life, life that cannot be taken from you against your will.

And every fruit produced by this tree is seasoned with discernment, and this unites them all, as I have told you.

11

Such are the fruits of action that I ask of the soul: that virtue should prove itself in response to need. This is what I told you long ago, if you remember, when you wanted to do great penance for me. You said, "What can I do to suffer for you?" And in your mind I answered, "I am one who is pleased by few words and many works." I wanted to show you that I am not much pleased with one who simply shouts, "Lord, Lord, I would like to do something for you!" nor with one who wishes to kill the body with great penances without slaying the selfish will. What I want is many works of patient and courageous endurance and of the other virtues I have described to you—interior virtues that are all active in bearing the fruit of grace.

Actions based on any other principle I would consider a mere "shouting of words." For these are finite works, and I who am infinite insist upon infinite works, that is, infinitely desirous love. I want works of penance and other bodily practices to be undertaken as means, not as your chief goal. By making them your chief goal you would be giving me a finite thing—like a word that comes out of the mouth and then ceases to exist—unless indeed that word comes out of the soul's love, which conceives virtue and brings it to birth in truth. I mean that finite works—which I have likened to words—must be joined with loving charity. Such works, undertaken not as your chief goal but as means, and not by themselves but in the company of true discernment, would please me.

It would not be right to make penance or other bodily works either your motivation or your goal, for, as I have already said, they are only finite. They are done in time that comes to an end, and sometimes one has to abandon them or have them taken away. In fact, it would not only not be meritorious but would offend me if you continued in these works when circumstances or obedience to authority made it impossible to do what you had undertaken. So you see how finite they are. Take them up, then, not as your goal but only as they are useful. For if you take them as a goal and then have to abandon them at some point, your soul will be left empty.

This is what the glorious Paul taught when he said in his letter that you should mortify your body and put to death your selfish will. In other words, learn to keep your body in check by disciplining your flesh when it would war against the spirit. Your selfish will must in everything be slain, drowned, subjected to my will. And the knife that kills and cuts off all selfish love to its foundation in self-will is the virtue of discernment, for when the soul comes to know herself she takes for herself what is her due, hatred and contempt for sin and for her selfish sensuality.

If you act so, you will be my delight, offering me not only words but many works; for, as I have told you, I want few words but many works. I say "many" rather than giving you any number, because when the soul is grounded in charity (which gives life to all the virtues) her desire must reach to the infinite. As for words, I said I want few not because I have no use for them, but to emphasize that any act in itself is finite and can please me only if it is taken as an instrument of virtue and not as virtuous in itself.

Let no one, therefore, make the judgment of considering those great penitents who put much effort into killing their bodies more perfect than those who do less. I have told you that penance is neither virtuous nor meritorious in itself. Were that the case, how unfortunate would be those who for legitimate reasons cannot perform actual works of penance! But the merit of penance rests completely in the power of charity enlightened by true discernment.

I am supreme eternal Truth. So discernment sets neither law nor limit nor condition to the love it gives me. But it rightly sets conditions and priorities of love where other people are concerned. The light of discernment, which is born of charity, gives order to your love for your neighbors. It would not permit you to bring the guilt of sin on yourself to benefit your neighbor. For that love would indeed be disordered and lacking in discernment which would commit even a single sin to redeem the whole world from hell or to achieve one great virtue. No, neither the greatest of virtues nor any service to your neighbor may be bought at the price of sin. The priorities set by holy discernment direct all the soul's powers to serving me courageously and conscientiously. Then she must love her neighbors with such affection that she would bear any pain or torment to win them the life of grace, ready to die a thousand deaths, if that were possible, for their salvation. And all her material possessions are at the service of her neighbors' physical needs. Such is the work of the light of discernment born of charity.

So you see, every soul desirous of grace loves me—as she ought—without limit or condition. And with my own infinite love she loves her neighbors with the measured and ordered charity I have described, never bringing on herself the evil of sin in doing good for others. Saint Paul taught you this when he said that charity cannot fully profit others unless it begins with oneself. For when perfection is not in the soul, whatever she does, whether for herself or for others, is imperfect.

It could never be right to offend me, infinite Good, under the pretext of saving my finite creation. The evil would far outweigh any fruit that might come of it, so never, for any reason, must you sin. True charity knows this, for it always carries the lamp of holy discernment.

Discernment is that light which dissolves all darkness, dissipates ignorance, and seasons every virtue and virtuous deed. It has a prudence that cannot be deceived, a strength that is invincible, a constancy right up to the end, reaching as it does from heaven to earth, that is, from the knowledge of me to the knowledge of oneself, from love of me to love of one's neighbors. Discernment's truly humble prudence evades every devilish and creaturely snare, and with unarmed hand—that is, through suffering—it overcomes the devil and the flesh. By this gentle glorious light the soul sees and rightly despises her own weakness; and by so making a fool of herself she gains mastery of the world, treading it underfoot with her love, scorning it as worthless.

When the soul has thus conceived virtue in the stirring of her love, and through her neighbors proved it and for their sakes brought it to birth, not all the world can rob her of that virtue. Indeed, persecution only serves to prove it and make it grow. But for that very reason, were the soul's virtue not evident and luminous to others in time of trial, it could not have been conceived in truth; for I have already told you clearly that virtue cannot be perfect or bear fruit except by means of your neighbors. If a woman has conceived a child but never brings it to birth for people to see, her husband will consider himself childless. Just so, I am the spouse of the soul, and unless she gives birth to the virtue she has conceived [by showing it] in her charity to her neighbors in their general and individual needs in the ways I have described, then I insist that she has never in truth even conceived virtue within her. And I say the same of vice: Every one of them is committed by means of your neighbors. . . .

THE BRIDGE

26

Then God eternal, to stir up even more that soul's love for the salvation of souls, responded to her:

Before I show you what I want to show you, and what you asked to see, I want to describe the bridge for you. I have told you that it stretches from heaven to earth by reason of my having joined myself with your humanity, which I formed from the earth's clay.

This bridge, my only-begotten Son, has three stairs. Two of them he built on the wood of the most holy cross, and the third even as he tasted the great bitterness of the gall and vinegar they gave him to drink. You will recognize in these three stairs three spiritual stages.

The first stair is the feet, which symbolize the affections. For just as the feet carry the body, the affections carry the soul. My Son's nailed feet are a stair by which you can climb to his side, where you will see revealed his inmost heart. For when the soul has climbed up on the feet of affection and looked with her mind's eye into my Son's opened heart, she begins to feel the love of her own heart in his consummate and unspeakable love. (I say consummate because it is not for his own good that he loves you; you cannot do him any good, since he is one with me.) Then the soul, seeing how tremendously she is loved, is herself filled to overflowing with love. So, having climbed the second stair, she reaches the third. This is his mouth, where she finds peace from the terrible war she has had to wage because of her sins.

At the first stair, lifting the feet of her affections from the earth, she stripped herself of sin. At the second she dressed herself in love for virtue. And at the third she tasted peace.

So the bridge has three stairs, and you can reach the last by climbing the first two. The last stair is so high that the flooding waters cannot strike it—for the venom of sin never touched my Son.

But though this bridge has been raised so high, it still is joined to the earth. Do you know when it was raised up? When my Son was lifted up on the wood of the most holy cross he did not cut off his divinity from the lowly earth of your humanity. So though he was raised so high he was not raised off the earth. In fact, his divinity is kneaded into the clay of your humanity like one bread. Nor could anyone walk on that bridge until my Son was raised up. This is why he said, "If I am lifted up high I will draw everything to myself."

When my goodness saw that you could be drawn in no other way, I sent him to be lifted onto the wood of the cross. I made of that cross an anvil where this child of humankind could be hammered into an instrument to release humankind from death and restore it to the life of grace. In this way he drew everything to himself: for he proved his unspeakable love, and the human heart is always drawn by love. He could not have shown you greater love than by giving his life for you. You can hardly resist being drawn by love, then, unless you foolishly refuse to be drawn.

I said that, having been raised up, he would draw everything to himself. This is true in two ways: First, the human heart is drawn by love, as I said, and with all its powers: memory, understanding, and will. If these three powers are harmoniously united in my name, everything else you do, in fact or in intention, will be drawn to union with me in peace through the movement of love, because all will be lifted up in the pursuit of crucified love. So my Truth indeed spoke truly when he said, "If I am lifted up high,

I will draw everything to myself." For everything you do will be drawn to him when he draws your heart and its powers.

What he said is true also in the sense that everything was created for your use, to serve your needs. But you who have the gift of reason were made not for yourselves but for me, to serve me with all your heart and all your love. So when you are drawn to me, everything is drawn with you, because everything was made for you.

It was necessary, then, that this bridge be raised high. And it had to have stairs so that you would be able to mount it more easily.

27

This bridge has walls of stone so that travelers will not be hindered when it rains. Do you know what stones these are? They are the stones of true solid virtue. These stones were not, however, built into walls before my Son's passion. So no one could get to the final destination, even though they walked along the pathway of virtue. For heaven had not yet been unlocked with the key of my Son's blood, and the rain of justice kept anyone from crossing over.

But after these stones were hewn on the body of the Word, my gentle Son (I have told you that he is the bridge), he built them into walls, tempering the mortar with his own blood. That is, his blood was mixed into the mortar of his divinity with the strong heat of burning love.

By my power the stones of virtue were built into walls on no less a foundation than himself, for all virtue draws life from him, nor is there any virtue that has not been tested in him. So no one can have any lifegiving virtue but from him, that is, by following his example and his teaching. He perfected the virtues and planted them as living stones built into walls with his blood. So now all the faithful can walk without hindrance and with no cringing fear of the rain of divine justice, because they are sheltered by the mercy that came down from heaven through the incarnation of this Son of mine.

And how was heaven opened? With the key of his blood. So, you see, the bridge has walls and a roof of mercy. And the hostelry of holy Church is there to serve the bread of life and the blood, lest the journeying pilgrims, my creatures, grow weary and faint on the way. So has my love ordained that the blood and body of my only-begotten Son, wholly God and wholly human, be administered.

At the end of the bridge is the gate (which is, in fact, one with the bridge), which is the only way you can enter. This is why he said, "I am the Way and

Truth and Life; whoever walks with me walks not in darkness but in light." And in another place my Truth said that no one could come to me except through him, and such is the truth.

I explained all this to you, you will recall, because I wanted to let you see the way. So when he says that he is the Way he is speaking the truth. And I have already shown you that he is the Way, in the image of a bridge. He says he is Truth, and so he is, and whoever follows him goes the way of truth. And he is Life. If you follow this truth you will have the life of grace and never die of hunger, for the Word has himself become your food. Nor will you ever fall into darkness, for he is the light undimmed by any falsehood. Indeed, with his truth he confounds and destroys the lie with which the devil deceived Eve. That lie broke up the road to heaven, but Truth repaired it and walled it up with his blood.

Those who follow this way are children of the truth because they follow the truth. They pass through the gate of truth and find themselves in me. And I am one with the gate and the way that is my Son, eternal Truth, a sea of peace.

But those who do not keep to this way travel below through the river—a way not of stones but of water. And since there is no restraining the water, no one can cross through it without drowning.

Such are the pleasures and conditions of the world. Those whose love and desire are not grounded on the rock but are set without order on created persons and things apart from me (and these, like water, are continually running on) run on just as they do. Though it seems to them that it is the created things they love that are running on by while they themselves remain firm, they are in fact continually running on to their end in death. They would like to preserve themselves (that is, their lives and the things they love) and not run away to nothingness. But they cannot. Either death makes them leave all behind, or by my decree these created things are taken away from them.

Such as these are following a lie by going the way of falsehood. They are children of the devil, who is the father of lies. And because they pass through the gate of falsehood they are eternally damned.

28

So you see, I have shown you truth and falsehood, that is, my way, which is truth, and the devil's way, which is falsehood. These are the two ways, and both are difficult.

How foolish and blind are those who choose to cross through the water when the road has been built for them! This road is such a joy for those who travel on it that it makes every bitterness sweet for them, and every burden light. Though they are in the darkness of the body they find light, and though they are mortal they find life without death. For through love and the light of faith they taste eternal Truth, with the promise of refreshment in return for the weariness they have borne for me. For I am grateful and sensitive. And I am just, giving each of you what you have earned: reward for good and punishment for sin.

Your tongue could never tell, nor your ears hear, nor your eyes see the joy they have who travel on this road, for even in this life they have some foretaste of the good prepared for them in everlasting life.

They are fools indeed who scorn such a good and choose instead to taste even in this life the guarantee of hell by keeping to the way beneath the bridge. For there the going is most wearisome and there is neither refreshment nor any benefit at all, because by their sinfulness they have lost me, the supreme and eternal Good. So there is good reason—and it is my will—that you and my other servants should feel continual distress that I am so offended, as well as compassion for the harm that comes to those who so foolishly offend me.

Now you have heard and seen what this bridge is like. I have told you all this to explain what I meant when I said that my only-begotten Son is a bridge, as you see he is, joining the most high with the most lowly.

29

When my only-begotten Son returned to me forty days after his resurrection, this bridge was raised high above the earth. For he left your company and ascended to heaven by the power of my divine nature to sit at his eternal Father's right hand. On the day of his ascension the disciples were as good as dead, because their hearts had been lifted up to heaven along with my Son, who is Wisdom. So the angel said to them: "Do not stay here, for he is seated at the Father's right hand."

When he had been raised on high and returned to me, his Father, I sent the Teacher, the Holy Spirit. He came with my power and my Son's wisdom and his own mercy. He is one thing with me, the Father, and with my Son. He came to make even more firm the road my Truth had left in the world through his teaching. So though my Son's presence was no longer with you, his teaching—the way of which he made for you this lovely and glorious bridge—remained, as did his virtues, the solid stones grounded in that teaching. First he acted, and from his actions he built the way. He taught you more by example than with words, always doing first what he talked about.

The Holy Spirit's mercy confirmed this teaching by strengthening the disciples' minds to testify to the truth and make known this way, the teaching of Christ crucified. Through them he reproved the world for its injustice and false judgments. But I will tell you more about this injustice and judgment later. . . .

So first I made a bridge of my Son as he lived in your company. And though that living bridge has been taken from your sight, there remains the bridgeway of his teaching, which, as I told you, is held together by my power and my Son's wisdom and the mercy of the Holy Spirit. My power gives the virtue of courage to those who follow this way. Wisdom gives them light to know the truth along the way. And the Holy Spirit gives them a love that uproots all sensual love from the soul and leaves only virtuous love. So now as much as before, through his teaching as much as when he was among you, he is the way and truth and life—the way that is the bridge leading to the very height of heaven. . . .

47

. . . But those who keep the commandments and counsels actually as well as in spirit go the way of perfect love. They follow in true simplicity the counsel my Truth, the incarnate Word, gave to that young man when he asked, "What can I do, Master, to win eternal life?" He said, "Keep the commandments of the Law." The other answered, "I do keep them." And he said, "Well, if you want to be perfect go and sell what you have and give it to the poor."

Then the young man was sad. He was still too much in love with what wealth he had, and that is why he was sad. But those who are perfect heed what he said. They let go of the world and all its pleasures. They discipline their bodies with penance and vigils, with constant humble prayer.

Those, however, who go the way of ordinary love without actually rising above material things (for they are not obliged to do so) do not thereby forfeit eternal life. But if they wish to have this world's goods they must possess them in the way I told you. To have these things is not sinful. After all, everything is good and perfect, created by me, Goodness itself. But I made these things to serve my rational creatures; I did not intend my creatures to make themselves servants and slaves to the world's pleasures. So if they would not go the way of great perfection, they may keep these things if they choose, but they will be servants, less than lords. They owe their first love to me. Everything else they should love and possess, as I told you, not as if they owned it but as something lent them.

I am not a respecter of persons or status but of holy desires. In whatever situation people may be, let their will be good and holy, and they will be pleasing to me.

Who are they who possess this world's goods in this way? Those who have cut the venomous sting off them by despising their selfish sensuality and loving virtue. Once they have cut off the venom of disorder from their will and set it in order with love and holy fear of me, they can choose and hold whatever situation they will and still be fit to have eternal life. It remains true that it is more perfect and more pleasing to me to rise above all this world's goods in fact as well as in spirit. But those who feel that their weakness will not let them reach such perfection can travel this ordinary way according to their own situation. My goodness has ordained it thus, so that no one in any situation whatever should have an excuse for sin.

Indeed they have no excuse. For I have made allowance for their passions and weaknesses in such a way that if they choose to remain in the world they can. They can possess wealth and hold positions of authority. They can be married and care for their children and toil for them. They can remain in any situation whatever, so long as they truly cut off the venomous sting of selfish sensuality that deals eternal death.

And it surely is venomous. For just as venom is painful to the body and ultimately causes death unless a person makes the effort to vomit it out and take some medicine, so it is with this scorpion of the world's pleasure. I am not speaking of material things in themselves. I have already told you that these are good and that they are made by me, the greatest Good, and so you can use them as you please with holy love and truthful fear. What I am speaking of is the venom of a perverted human will, which poisons souls and causes them death, unless they vomit it up through a holy confession, tearing their heart and affection free from it. Such confession is a medicine that heals the effects of this venom even while it tastes bitter to selfish sensuality. . . .

113

O dearest daughter, I have told you all this so that you may better know how I have dignified my ministers, and thus grieve the more over their wickedness. If they themselves had considered their dignity, they would not have fallen into the darkness of deadly sin nor muddied the face of their souls. Not only have they sinned against me and against their own dignity, but even had they given their bodies to be burned they would not have been able to repay me for the tremendous grace and blessing they have received, for it is impossible to have a greater dignity than theirs in this life.

They are my anointed ones and I call them my "christs," because I have appointed them to be my ministers to you and have sent them like fragrant flowers into the mystic body of holy Church. No angel has this dignity, but I have given it to those men whom I have chosen to be my ministers. I have sent them like angels, and they ought to be earthly angels in this life.

I demand purity and charity of every soul, a charity that loves me and others, and helps others in whatever way it can, serving them in prayer and loving them tenderly. But much more do I demand purity in my ministers, and that they love me and their neighbors, administering the body and blood of my only-begotten Son with burning love and hunger for the salvation of souls, for the glory and praise of my name.

Just as these ministers want the chalice in which they offer this sacrifice to be clean, so I demand that they themselves be clean in heart and soul and mind. And I want them to keep their bodies, as instruments of the soul, in perfect purity. I do not want them feeding and wallowing in the mire of impurity, nor bloated with pride in their hankering after high office, nor cruel to themselves and their neighbors—for they cannot abuse themselves without abusing their neighbors. If they abuse themselves by sinning, they are abusing the souls of their neighbors. For they are not giving them an example of good living, nor are they concerned about rescuing souls from the devil's hands, nor about administering to them the body and blood of my only-begotten Son, and myself the true Light in the other sacraments of holy Church. So, by abusing themselves they are abusing others. . . .

134

Then that soul was like one drunk with restlessness and on fire with love, her heart cut through with bitter sorrow. So she turned to the supreme eternal Goodness and said:

O eternal God, light surpassing all other light because all light comes forth from you! O fire surpassing every fire because you alone are the fire that burns without consuming! You consume whatever sin and selfishness you find in the soul. Yet your consuming does not distress the soul but fattens her with insatiable love, for though you satisfy her she is never sated but longs for you constantly. The more she possesses you the more she seeks you, and the more she seeks and desires you the more she finds and enjoys you, high eternal fire, abyss of charity!

O supreme eternal Good! What moved you, infinite God, to enlighten me, your finite creature, with the light of your truth? You yourself, the very fire of love, you yourself are the reason. For it always has been and always is love that constrains you to create us in your own image and likeness, and to show us mercy by giving your creatures infinite and immeasurable graces.

O Goodness surpassing all goodness! You alone are supremely good, yet you gave us the Word, your only-begotten Son, to keep company with us, though we are filth and darksomeness. What was the reason for this? Love. For you loved us before we existed. O good, O eternal greatness, you made yourself lowly and small to make us great! No matter where I turn, I find nothing but your deep burning charity.

Can I, wretch that I am, repay the graces and burning charity you have shown and continue to show, such blazing special love beyond the general love and charity you show to all your creatures? No, only you, most gentle loving Father, only you can be my acknowledgment and my thanks. The affection of your very own charity will offer you thanks, for I am she who is not. And if I should claim to be anything of myself, I should be lying through my teeth! I should be a liar and a daughter of the devil, who is the father of lies. For you alone are who you are, and whatever being I have and every other gift of mine I have from you, and you have given it all to me for love, not because it was my due.

O most gentle Father, when the human race lay sick with Adam's sin you sent as doctor the gentle loving Word, your Son. Now, when I lie sick in the weakness of my foolish indifference, you, God eternal, most mild and gentle doctor, have given me a medicine at once mildly sweet and bitter so that I may be healed and rise up from my weakness. It is mild to me because you have shown yourself to me with your mild charity. It is sweeter than sweet to me because you have enlightened my mind's eye with the light of most holy faith. In this light, as you have been pleased to reveal it, I have come to know what dignity and grace you have bestowed on the human race by administering [to us your Son], wholly God and wholly human, in the mystic body of holy Church, and I have come to know the dignity of the ministers you have appointed to administer you to us. . . .

Immeasurable Love! By revealing this you have given me a bittersweet medicine so that I might rise up once and for all from the sickness of foolish indifference and run to you with concern and eager longing. You would have me know myself and your goodness, and the sins committed against you by every class of people and especially by your ministers, so that I might draw tears from the knowledge of your infinite goodness and let them flow as a river over my wretched self and over these wretched living dead. Therefore it is my will, ineffable Fire, joyous Love, eternal Father, that my desire should never weary of longing for your honor and the salvation of souls. And I beg you, let my eyes never rest, but in your grace make of them two rivers for the water that flows from you, the sea of peace. Thank you, thank you, Father! In granting me both what I asked of you and what I did not ask because I did not know how, you have given me both the invitation and the reason to weep and to offer tender, loving, tormented longings in your presence with constant humble prayer.

Now, I beg you, be merciful to the world and to holy Church. I am asking you to grant what you are making me ask. Alas for my wretched sorrowful soul, the cause of all evil! Do not delay any longer in granting your mercy to the world; bow down and fulfill the longing of your servants. Alas! It is you who make them cry out: so listen to their voices. Your Truth said that we should call and we would be answered, that we should knock and the door would be opened for us, that we should ask and it would be given to us. O eternal Father, your servants are calling to you for mercy. Answer them then. I know well that mercy is proper to you, so you cannot resist giving it to whoever asks you for it. Your servants are knocking at the door of your Truth. They are knocking because in your Truth, your only-begotten Son, they have come to know your unspeakable love for humankind. Therefore your burning charity neither can nor should hold back from opening to those who knock with perseverance.

Open, then, unlock and shatter the hardened hearts of your creatures. If you will not do it for their failure to knock, do it because of your infinite goodness and for love of your servants who are knocking at your door for them. Grant it, eternal Father, because you see how they stand at the door of your Truth and ask. And for what are they asking? For the blood of this door, your Truth. In this blood you have washed away iniquity and drained the pus of Adam's sin. His blood is ours because you have made of it a bath for us, and you neither can nor will refuse it to those who ask it of you in truth. Give then the fruit of the blood to these creatures of yours. Put into the scales the price of your Son's blood so that the infernal demons may not carry off your little sheep. Oh, you are a good shepherd to have given us your only-begotten Son to be our true shepherd who in obedience to you laid down his life for your little sheep and made of his blood a bath for us. It is this blood that your servants, hungry as they are, are asking for at this door. They are asking you through this blood to be merciful to the world and make holy Church blossom again with the fragrant flowers of good holy shepherds whose perfume will dispel the stench of the putrid evil flowers.

You said, eternal Father, that because of your love for your creatures, and through the prayers and innocent sufferings of your servants, you would be merciful to the world and reform holy Church, and thus give us refreshment. Do not wait any longer, then, to turn the eye of your mercy. Because it is your will to answer us before we call, answer now with the voice of your mercy.

Open the door of your immeasurable charity, which you have given us in the door of the Word. Yes, I know that you open before we knock, because your servants knock and call out to you with the very love and affection you gave them, seeking your honor and the salvation of souls. Give them then the bread of life, the fruit of the blood of your only-begotten Son, which they are begging of you for the glory and praise of your name and for the salvation of souls. For it would seem you would receive more glory and praise by saving so many people than by letting them stubbornly persist in their hardness. To you, eternal Father, everything is possible. Though you created us without our help, it is not your will to save us without our help. So I beg you to force their wills and dispose them to want what they do not want. I ask this of your infinite mercy. You created us out of nothing. So, now that we exist, be merciful and remake the vessels you created and formed in your image and likeness; re-form them to grace in the mercy and blood of your Son.

CHAPTER TWENTY - ONE

Catherine of Genoa,
The Spiritual Dialogue
(late 1400s)

Catherine of Genoa (1447–1510)

Born Catherine Fieschi to a noble Italian family, Catherine showed a deep spirituality. At age thirteen, she had the "gift of prayer" and was deeply disappointed when she was denied entrance to an Augustinian convent on account of her age. At sixteen she entered a marriage advantageous to her family, a common practice, but one in which she found little joy. Catherine was not interested in pursuing the social life expected of a noblewoman, nor did she appreciate her husband's pleasure-seeking life. She had a life-changing experience ten years later when, during her Lenten confession, God revealed to her the greatness of divine love for her even in the light of her own sinfulness. As a result she turned her life toward contemplation and service of the poor and sick. She worked in a women's hospital, establishing an open-air infirmary during the plague of 1493, during which she was believed to have performed miracles of healing. Although she never joined a religious order, she had many followers during and after her lifetime.

The Spiritual Dialogue

Also called *Dialogues of the Soul and the Body,* this work contains Catherine's doctrine and spiritual insight, though there is no evidence that she composed the text. Still, there is no doubt the teaching is hers, as it was likely preserved by her spiritual director and her closest disciple. In the

Dialogues three characters, Body, Soul, and Self-Love, converse about the needs each has, and how they will survive together on the journey of life.

THE SPIRITUAL DIALOGUE

I saw the Body and Soul conversing and arguing with one another. And the Soul said: God made me to love and to be happy. I should like, then, to start out on a voyage to discover what I am drawn to. Come willingly with me, for you too will share my joy. We shall travel throughout the world together; if I find what pleases me I shall enjoy it. You will do the same; and he who finds more will be most happy.

BODY

Since I am subject to you, I will do as you wish;
remember, though, that without me you cannot do what
   you wish.
let us, therefore, understand each other at the outset;
in this way we shall have no arguments.
Once I have found what gives me joy, please keep your word.
I would not want to hear you grumble,
muttering that you want to go elsewhere
or insisting on looking for what interests you.
To do away with that possibility,
let us invite a third party to come along,
someone to resolve any differences we might have
—a just and unselfish person.

SOUL

Very well. Who will the third person be?

BODY

Self-Love.
He will give the body its due and share the body's joys.
He will do the same with you;
and so each of us will have what is meet and proper.

SOUL

And if we were to come across food we would both enjoy,
what then?

BODY

Then he who can eat more will do so,
    provided there is enough for two.
If that is not the case, Self-Love will give to each his due.
Considering our naturally different tastes, however,
it would be remarkable
if we came across food we both enjoyed.

SOUL

Very well.
I am not afraid of being won over to your preferences,
since by nature of the two I am the stronger.

BODY

True, you are the stronger of the two, but I am at home here.
There are many things here that I enjoy.
It will be easier for me to convert you to my preferences,
    I think,
than vice versa.
The things that give you joy
are not visible nor do they have any taste.

SOUL

Let us start out, then.
Each of us will have one week to do what he will—
as long as we do not offend our Creator,
something I will not do as long as I live.
Should I die—that is, if you have me offend God
—I will do all that you ask, be your servant, do your will,
take delight in what gives you delight.
Bound each to each,
we shall never again be separated in this world or the next,
but be together in good and evil.
Free Will will not loosen this bond.
Should I triumph over you, naturally you would act the same.

Agreed on this, the Body and the Soul set out in search of Self-Love. Having found him, they informed him of what they had concluded, and Self-Love commented:

SELF-LOVE

I am delighted to join you
and have no doubt that I will feel at home with you.
I will indeed give to each his due, and fairly.
Should one of you seek to win me over,
I in turn would favor the other.

The Body and the Soul answered that they would gladly travel all together and accept his judgment—with the proviso that no offense be given to God, and should any of them sin the other two would reprove him. The Soul then suggested that they start out and said:

Let me, since I am the more worthy, start with the first week.

BODY

I accept.
Act according to reason
and within those limits that Self-Love approves.

Now the Soul, still free from sin, began by taking thought on its creation, on all the benefits God had given it, on how it had been created for eternal bliss, and how, in worth, it was higher than the choirs of angels. It understood that it was almost divine by nature for, drawn to contemplation of things divine, it wanted to eat its bread with that of the angels. And so the Soul said to itself:

Just as I am not visible,
so I want my joy, my food, to be in things invisible.
That is what I was created for,
and in that I will find rest.
Spending the first week in contemplation
and looking down on things below,
I will make my way up to the heavens.
No other work interests me
—let him who finds joy in this do so,
and may others be patient.

And so for one week the Soul spent his time in contemplation, much to the discomfort of the Body and Self-Love. When the week was up, the Soul said:

I have done my part, now you do yours.
Tell me, how did you find the week?

They answered that it was not to their taste, that not only did they feel little

joy that week, but indeed thought they were going to die. (They hoped,
however, to avenge themselves.) And so the Body said to the Soul:

Come with me.

Now let me show you how many things God has done for me.

He showed the Soul the heavens with its ornaments, and the earth, the sea,
the air with its birds, all the kingdoms, dominions, cities, provinces, spiritual and temporal, great treasures and songs and music, as well as all sorts
of food for the nourishment of the Body; in a word, all the joys the Body
could experience. These goods would not be lacking as long as they were
in this world, and since they were created for the Body they could be
enjoyed without offending God. And the Body added:

Though you did not show me your beloved country,
I will show you mine.
For unless you share my joy,
I know that I cannot have what I wish.
I remember the agreement—let me remind you of it.
If you intended to go
and take residence in your beloved country
and leave me to starve in mine I would die.
The responsibility would be yours,
and so would the offense to God.
Self-Love and I would point that out
Now, and this is an advantage I have over you
I can enjoy all of these joys and pleasures
as long as I live.
When the end comes,
and should I be saved, as I earnestly wish to be,
I will then go on to enjoy your beloved country.
It is to my advantage, then, that you save yourself;
and please do not think
that I seek for anything contrary to God or reason.
Ask my friend, Self-Love, if that is not so.

And Self-Love answered:

In both instances, your motives and reasons appear quite sensible.
In charity, though,
each of you has gone outside the limits of the reasonable.
God asks that we love our neighbor as ourselves,
and you, Soul, were so little concerned
with the needs of the Body and of me

that we were in danger of death.
Learn to moderate yourself,
to take into account the needs
of your neighbor, the Body, and me as well—
for I, too, could not live in your beloved country.
Then, turning to the Body, Self-Love added:
As for you, you have shown the Soul many superfluous things.
Remember that all that which is superfluous
harms you as much as the Soul,
and that is true even if the Soul may not recognize it.
If we live according to our needs
we can live happily together.
If you heed my words I will continue to stay with you
and, with discretion, we will share common joys.
Otherwise, I will leave.
If you, the Soul, wish to be helped by the Body,
keep in mind that the Body has its needs;
if you ignore them it will protest.
Meet those needs
and it will be at peace with itself and with you.
The Soul answered:
To attend to the body's needs to such an extent gives me pause.
I am afraid that I, too, will begin to find delight in them
and, unaware of the danger, will settle for them.
Watching you and the Body
so hungry and so intent on what gives you joy,
I sense that I too will become earthbound.
The goods of the earth
do not lead to an increased taste for spiritual things.
(Help me, O God!)

BODY

As far as I am concerned, it seems to me
that Self-Love has spoken very well of our respective needs.
We should continue to stay together.
As far as your fears are concerned, remember
that if the things that God created could harm the Soul,
He would not have created them.
The will, moreover, is strong.

It has been created such
that it can only be impeded by itself.
God Himself does not coerce it.
This is why it is in your power
to grant or refuse what we ask of you,
and when and where it pleases you.
The reins are in your hands.
Give to each according to his needs
and pay no heed to the grumblers.

SOUL

Tell me, precisely
what are the needs that you claim you cannot do without?
I will then provide for them and in that way
no longer be fearful.

BODY

My needs are food, drink, sleep, dress.
That is, to be served in one way or another
so that, in turn, I can serve you.
In attending to your spiritual needs, however,
do not vex me.
When I am disgruntled, I cannot attend to those needs.
If God provided so many delightful things for me, the Body,
think of what he may have in store for you, the immortal Soul!
We can both do homage to God in this manner—
and when we have our differences
Self-Love will settle them.

SOUL

Very well.
Since I cannot do otherwise, I will provide for your needs.
I am afraid, though, that you are both plotting against me.
Your words are so utterly sensible on the surface
that they force me to be understanding;
yet, I wonder what you have in mind
when you insist that without me you can do nothing.
(Still, if this is a trap, please God, I shall escape.)
Let us, then, to the honor of God, go on with our voyage.
Now as they went about the world, each attending to his own

affairs, and seeking joy in what was most proper for him, the Soul took another week for itself. This time, however, it fared very differently from the first time. Its companions kept insisting on their needs, broke up the allotted time into little pieces, and in general brought the Soul down to their level.

To give up the contemplation of things divine in order to provide for animal needs greatly upset the Soul. The difference between its first week and this one, it felt, was the difference between black and white.

It was then the body's turn to take a week for itself. Because of the Soul's imposed fasts it was starving. Anticipating other such rigors in the future, the Body thought of fortifying itself. It acted resolutely and all the more so since the Soul, incapable of achieving the freedom of its first week, was adapting itself to the needs of the others. So whereas the Soul had had half a week for its needs, which had become weaker, the Body had a full week for itself.

The Soul then said to Self-Love:

In meeting your needs,
I notice that bit by bit my own convictions are weakening.
Are you not getting more than your due?
And in following you am I not going to be badly hurt?
Indeed not I alone, but all three of us?
You are the arbiter. What do you think?

Self-Love answered:

It is because you were aiming so unreasonably high
that you feel as if you are debasing yourself
to come down to our level.
With time, though, you will learn to moderate yourself,
to be more sensible.
Our company is not so bad as you seem to think at this point.
Fear not, God will provide.
You are to love God fully, not in this world but in the next.
Take what you can get, and on the best available terms.

SOUL

I see now that I have no defense against the two of you.
You are at home in the world.
Of what use is my week to me when you so insist on your needs
that there is no room for mine?
When it is your turn you want your week free and clear;

211

but when my turn comes up,
you find a thousand things to object to.
Since I can only get the worst of this arrangement,
I think it better to give up the idea of individual weeks.
Let each one of us find what is to his taste
and live there where he is happiest.
I will deal as courteously as I can with you, of course,
for I know how to do no other.

Content with the suggestion, the two accepted the proposal, saying to the Soul: Now each of us can live in peace, since you have recognized your errors.

And so once more they went about the world, one finding some things that gave him joy, the other doing the same. But the Body, moving around in his own country, found more and more things he considered necessary. Each day those appetites increased. The more the Body and Self-Love, especially the latter, insisted on them, the more the three became inseparable. All things seemed equally necessary and reasonable. If the Soul occasionally hesitated, the other two protested that they were being wronged; so that gradually the Soul found itself adrift on the limitless sea of earthly goods. Worldly pleasures and joys were all they would talk about. If the Soul happened to think of spiritual things and allude to them, it met with such criticism that it quickly ceased doing so and said to itself unhappily:

If I keep accompanying the Body and Self-Love,
how will I ever escape them?
In the name of their needs,
they will do whatever they wish with me. . . .

Having witnessed these many signs of the intensity and purity of God's love, the Soul paused and said to the Body and to Self-Love:

My brothers, God has manifested to me the truth of His love.
Now I am no longer principally concerned
with you or your needs, much less your words.
Had I listened to you I would be lost.
Had I not experienced it, I would never have believed
that under the guise of the good and the necessary
you led me to the brink of eternal death.
And so I will now do to you what you did to me.
I no longer have any human respect for you.
You are my mortal enemies,
and I will have no further dealings with you.

212

Like the damned, lose all hope.
I will make every effort to return to that life
from which I started out,
the one from which, through pretense, you had me turn away.
With God's help I will no longer be deceived by you.
Still, I hope to act in such a way
that each will have what is due him.
As you made me do what I should not have done,
so I will have you do what you would rather not do.
In this way, you may satisfy the spirit.
I hope to subject you completely to me—
that is, have you go against your natural bent.

On sensing that resolve in the Soul and realizing that the Soul had indeed been illumined, the Body and Self-Love, who could no longer deceive the Soul, were extremely distressed.

We are subject to you
They said—
Be just and do with us what you will.
If we cannot get by any other way, we will steal;
that is, you will do all you can against us
and we will repay you in kind.
In the end, each will get his due.

The Soul answered:

Let me offer you a consoling truth.
Now you are sore distressed,
but once you free yourself of superfluous things,
then you will rejoice in everything I have said and done.
You will share my good forever.
Be at peace, then, for in the end we shall enjoy the peace of God.
I will not fail to provide, moreover, for your just needs.
Keep in mind
that I wish to lead you to the greatest joy in life.
Nothing has quite satisfied you altogether up to now,
even after trying everything.
Now we may come together to a port of endless joy,
The peace within you will grow slowly.
It will, though, eventually overflow from the Soul into the Body;
and by itself, it would be enough to sweeten hell.
Before this fully comes about, however,

much will have to be done.
Let the help of God's light comfort you.
Now, no more words, but deeds.
The Body answered:
You seem so intense as you come toward me that you frighten me.
You might commit some excess, make us both suffer.
I will do what you wish,
but first let me remind you of one thing.
The precept following that of loving God, you remember,
is that of loving our neighbor.
This love, in the temporal order,
begins with the love of your own body,
which you are to maintain alive and healthy under pain of sin.
You should not, therefore, endanger life or health.
Both are needed in order to come to what you seek, your end.
Life, quite simply, is a necessity.
When I, the Body, die,
you will have no means of adding to your glory,
nor any time for cleansing yourself from your imperfections.
You will have to do that work in purgatory
—that is, suffer far more than you would in this world.
Nor can you do without your health.
When the body is healthy, the powers of the Soul are apt
to properly receive the light and inspiration of God;
and above all when joy overflows into the body.
When the body is sick, these powers are wanting.
You see, then, what is good for both of us.
In this way, each receives what is due him,
and both come to the port of salvation
without censure from heaven or earth.
The Soul replied:
Now I clearly see what I must do,
prompted by God's light and the voice of reason.
It is, however, a higher reason that I will listen to,
one that, hurting no one
and making it impossible for any to justly complain,
may grant to each his just needs.
No one, indeed,
who has submitted his appetites to higher reason

will find fault with what I will do.
Let me do as I will, then,
for you will lead a life far happier than you can possibly imagine.
In the beginning,
when I wanted to attend to the needs of the spirit,
I was in charge.
Through your deceit, you then bound yourself to me
and we agreed to do good together,
to have neither lord it over the other.
Gradually, however, you turned me into your slave.
Now I will once more be in charge.
If you wish to serve me, I will take care of all your needs;
if not, I will still be mistress and be served.
If needs be, I will compel you to be my servant—
and that will put an end to all arguments. . . .

Section III

1500 –1800 C.E.

CHAPTER TWENTY - TWO

Vittoria Colonna, *Poetry* (early 1500s)

Vittoria Colonna (1490–1547)

Vittoria Colonna was born into the wealthy house of Colonna, an Italian daughter of the Renaissance with appropriate education and status. She was married at seventeen, but her husband was gone to wars during much of their eighteen-year marriage. Her verse, both in Latin and Italian, was recognized as exhibiting fine style and insight. Colonna's pen was put to theological and political prose as well. Her family often had conflict of a political nature with the papacy, and she did not shy away from criticizing the corruption of the church, the worldliness of the clergy, and the taste for war present in her day. She took up the cause of the Capuchins, an order radically devoted to the ideal of poverty in the Franciscan tradition. In writing on their behalf to Cardinal Contarini, she said, "If those who trouble these friars had seen their humility, poverty, obedience, and charity, they would be ashamed."

Poetry

Using the sonnet form, Colonna addressed the most pressing issues of her day, secular and religious. The first sonnet below strikes at the military exploits of "the bride of Christ," the church that creates a "fetid stench." The second sonnet speaks to the doctrine of justification by faith, the Reformation battle cry, but Vittoria develops it, noting the role of faith, fear, and works in salvation. The next three sonnets reflect Colonna's devotional focus respectively on Mary, in whom, she has written, "creature and creator are united"; on the nativity; and on the cross as the center of Christian life. Finally, the last sonnet speaks to the experience of the woman who encountered Jesus at the well.

ON THE CHURCH

When the breath of God that moved above the tide
Fans the embers of my smouldering state,
And the winds of God begin to dissipate
The fetid stench of the church, his bride,
Then the swaggering knights prepare to ride.
The war begins. They gloat and cannot wait.
They think they are the masters of their fate
And would display their valor far and wide.
Then within they hear God's trumpet blow,
And they, whose gods were goblets and a crest,
Appalled by death, their headlong charge arrest.
They cannot lift the vizier to the rays
Which penetrate the heart beneath the vest.
Would they but discard their gear and ways!

ON JUSTIFICATION BY FAITH

One cannot have a lively faith I trow
Of God's eternal promises if fear
Has left the warm heart chilled and seer
And placed a veil between the I and Thou.
Nor faith, which light and joy endow
And works, which in the course of love appear,
If oft some vile, deep dolor drear
Injects itself into the here and now.
These human virtues, works and these desires
All operate the same, are but a shade,
Cast as a shadow, moving or at rest,
But when the light descends from heaven's fires
Kindling hope and faith within the breast
Then doubt and fear and dolor, these all fade.

220

THE ANNUNCIATION

Blessed angel with whom the Father swore
The ancient covenant now sealed anew.
Which gives us peace and shows the pathway true
To contemplate his gifts for evermore.
For this holy office held in store
With soul inclined and mind in constant view
By his high embassy he did imbue
The virgin's heart, which joyful I adore.
I beg you now behold the face and hands,
Humble response, tinged with chaste dread,
The ardent love and faith with pulsing beat
Of her, who come from out no earthly lands,
With humble heartfelt yearning, sweet desire replete,
Greets, adores, embraces all God said.

THE STAR

What joy, oh star and blessed sign
Twinkling on the cattle stall,
From the fabled east you call
Wise men to the birth divine!
Behold the King amid the kine
Swaddled in no lordly hall.
Above, what love surpassing all
Lifts our hearts and makes them thine!
The place, the beasts, the cold, the hay,
The lowly coverlet and bed
Of thy love what more could say?
Then, for the star which hither led
And gave such proof of thy design
To joyful praise our hearts incline.

THE CROSS

When writhe the Saviour's shoulders on the tree
And droops the holy body from the weight
Is there then no key to fit the gate
That heaven should not open for to see?

What grievous pangs he bore from sheer pity
Thus by his guiltless blood to recreate
Our spirits laved of all impurity!
Our surcease from war, within, wherever,
Comes from him, the author of our peace.
He is the sun whose brilliance blinds our eyes.
The Father's, secrets how he will release
To whom and where and when none can surmize.
Enough for us to know he cannot err.

THE WOMAN AT THE WELL

Oh blessed dame, to whom beside the fount
Where you had come to fill your jar he spake,
At whose word the sea and mountains quake,
No more of old nor on the sacred mount,
With hearty faith we now our wants recount,
With sweet tears or bitter supplicate
The Father, who will inward wishes take,
And silent prayers, as they were spoken, count.
But then was thy deep yearning met
When on thee fell that burning vibrant ray
Illumining Samaria and mankind.
In haste you ran thereat in each byway
That none this festive day should e'er forget
But honor him with heart and soul and mind.

Teresa of Avila,
The Interior Castle
(1577)

Teresa of Avila (1515–82)

Teresa was born into an aristocratic Spanish family. She left home at sixteen to be educated at an Augustinian convent and at twenty entered the Carmelite convent of the Incarnation at Avila. For nearly twenty years she led a fairly lax life there, as the originally austere Carmelite rule had been mitigated to allow for a comfortable apartment, entertaining friends and family, visiting wealthy women outside the cloister, and other personal pursuits. However, in 1555 she had a "second conversion," which meant a greater experience of God's presence, a deeper desire for prayer and serving others, and, eventually, the establishment of a small convent of her own, dedicated to a more primitive and demanding Carmelite rule. At the new St. Joseph's convent, the nuns were totally dependent upon alms and their own labor. This fueled a reform movement associated with the Catholic Reformation as she founded many communities for women and men intended to return to a more spiritual and rigorous rule. Her brand of Teresian spirituality left an enduring mark as seen in her mentorship of Saint John of the Cross. In 1970 she became, along with Catherine of Siena, one of two women declared "Doctor of the Church" by Pope Paul VI.

The Interior Castle

Written in 1577 and usually considered her most mature work, this text provides an exposition of the soul's progression toward God, through the many rooms of the castle until it reaches the very center, where union with God and full human being are found. According to Teresa, prayer and contemplation should lead to energy and action, not to passivity and lethargy. One's conversion is only the first step on a journey toward "spiritual marriage." She doesn't hesitate to use humor as the best defense against self-importance in her writing, and the insistent joy of her own life infuses her work.

THE INTERIOR CASTLE

. . . 1. Today while beseeching our Lord to speak for me because I wasn't able to think of anything to say nor did I know how to begin to carry out this obedience, there came to my mind what I shall now speak about, that which will provide us with a basis to begin with. It is that we consider our soul to be like a castle made entirely out of a diamond or of very clear crystal, in which there are many rooms, just as in heaven there are many dwelling places. For in reflecting upon it carefully, Sisters, we realize that the soul of the just person is nothing else but a paradise where the Lord says He finds His delight. So then, what do you think that abode will be like where a King so powerful, so wise, so pure, so full of all good things takes His delight? I don't find anything comparable to the magnificent beauty of a soul and its marvelous capacity. Indeed, our intellects, however keen, can hardly comprehend it, just as they cannot comprehend God; but He Himself says that He created us in His own image and likeness.

Well if this is true, as it is, there is no reason to tire ourselves in trying to comprehend the beauty of this castle. Since this castle is a creature and the difference, therefore, between it and God is the same as that between the Creator and His creature, His Majesty in saying that the soul is made in His own image makes it almost impossible for us to understand the sublime dignity and beauty of the soul.

2. It is a shame and unfortunate that through our own fault we don't understand ourselves or know who we are. Wouldn't it show great ignorance, my daughters, if someone when asked who he was didn't know, and didn't know his father or mother or from what country he came? Well now, if this would be so extremely stupid, we are incomparably more so when we do not strive to know who we are, but limit ourselves to considering only roughly these bodies. Because we have heard and because faith tells us so, we know we have souls. But we seldom consider the precious things that can be found in this soul, or who dwells within it, or its high value.

Consequently, little effort is made to preserve its beauty. All our attention is taken up with the plainness of the diamond's setting or the outer wall of the castle; that is, with these bodies of ours. . . .

5. Well, getting back to our beautiful and delightful castle we must see how we can enter it. It seems I'm saying something foolish. For if this castle is the soul, clearly one doesn't have to enter it since it is within oneself. How foolish it would seem were we to tell someone to enter a room he is already in. But you must understand that there is a great difference in the ways one may be inside the castle. For there are many souls who are in the outer courtyard—which is where the guards stay—and don't care at all about entering the castle, nor do they know what lies within that most precious place, nor who is within, nor even how many rooms it has. You have already heard in some books on prayer that the soul is advised to enter within itself; well that's the very thing I'm advising.

6. Not long ago a very learned man told me that souls who do not practice prayer are like people with paralyzed or crippled bodies; even though they have hands and feet they cannot give orders to these hands and feet. Thus there are souls so ill and so accustomed to being involved in external matters that there is no remedy, nor does it seem they can enter within themselves. They are now so used to dealing always with the insects and vermin that are in the wall surrounding the castle that they have become almost like them. And though they have so rich a nature and the power to converse with none other than God, there is no remedy. If these souls do not strive to understand and cure their great misery, they will be changed into statues of salt, unable to turn their heads to look at themselves, just as Lot's wife was changed for having turned her head.

7. Insofar as I can understand, the gate of entry to this castle is prayer and reflection. I don't mean to refer to mental more than vocal prayer, for since vocal prayer is prayer it must be accompanied by reflection. A prayer in which a person is not aware of whom he is speaking to, what he is asking, who it is who is asking and of whom, I do not call prayer however much the lips may move. Sometimes it will be so without this reflection, provided that the soul has these reflections at other times. Nonetheless, anyone who has the habit of speaking before God's majesty as though he were speaking to a slave, without being careful to see how he is speaking, but saying whatever comes to his head and whatever he has learned from saying at other times, in my opinion is not praying. Please God, may no Christian pray in this way. Among yourselves, Sisters, I hope in His Majesty that you will not do so, for the custom you have of being occupied with interior

things is quite a good safeguard against failing and carrying on in this way like brute beasts. . . .

8. Well now let's get back to our castle with its many dwelling places. You mustn't think of these dwelling places in such a way that each one would follow in file after the other; but turn your eyes toward the center, which is the room or royal chamber where the King stays, and think of how a palmetto has many leaves surrounding and covering the tasty part that can be eaten. So here, surrounding this center room are many other rooms; and the same holds true for those above. The things of the soul must always be considered as plentiful, spacious, and large; to do so is not an exaggeration. The soul is capable of much more than we can imagine, and the sun that is in this royal chamber shines in all parts. It is very important for any soul that practices prayer, whether little or much, not to hold itself back and stay in one corner. Let it walk through these dwelling places which are up above, down below, and to the sides, since God has given it such great dignity. Don't force it to stay a long time in one room alone. Oh, but if it is in the room of self-knowledge! How necessary this room is—see that you understand me—even for those whom the Lord has brought into the very dwelling place where He abides. For never, however exalted the soul may be, is anything else more fitting than self-knowledge; nor could it be even were the soul to so desire. For humility, like the bee making honey in the beehive, is always at work. Without it, everything goes wrong. But let's remember that the bee doesn't fail to leave the beehive and fly about gathering nectar from the flowers. So it is with the soul in the room of self-knowledge; let it believe me and fly sometimes to ponder the grandeur and majesty of its God. Here it will discover its lowliness better than by thinking of itself, and be freer from the vermin that enter the first rooms, those of self-knowledge. For even though, as I say, it is by the mercy of God that a person practices self-knowledge, that which applies to what is less applies so much more to what is greater, as they say. And believe me, we shall practice much better virtue through God's help than by being tied down to our own misery.

9. I don't know if this has been explained well. Knowing ourselves is something so important that I wouldn't want any relaxation ever in this regard, however high you may have climbed into the heavens. While we are on this earth nothing is more important to us than humility. So I repeat that it is good, indeed very good, to try to enter first into the room where self-knowledge is dealt with rather than fly off to other rooms. This is the right road, and if we can journey along a safe and level path, why should

we want wings to fly? Rather, let's strive to make more progress in self-knowledge, for in my opinion we shall never completely know ourselves if we don't strive to know God. By gazing at His grandeur, we get in touch with our own lowliness; by looking at His purity, we shall see our own filth; by pondering His humility, we shall see how far we are from being humble.

10. Two advantages come from such activity. First, it's clear that something white seems much whiter when next to something black, and vice versa with the black next to the white. The second is that our intellects and wills, dealing in turn now with self, now with God, become nobler and better prepared for every good. And it would be disadvantageous for us never to get out of the mire of our miseries. As we said of those who are in mortal sin, that their streams are black and foul smelling, so it is here; although not entirely—God deliver us—for we are just making a comparison. If we are always fixed on our earthly misery, the stream will never flow free from the mud of fears, faintheartedness, and cowardice. I would be looking to see if I'm being watched or not; if by taking this path things will turn out badly for me; whether it might be pride to dare begin a certain work; whether it would be good for a person so miserable to engage in something so lofty as prayer; whether I might be judged better than others if I don't follow the path they all do. I'd be thinking that extremes are not good, even in the practice of virtue; that, since I am such a sinner, I might have a greater fall; that perhaps I would not advance and would do harm to good people; that someone like myself has no need of special things.

11. Oh, God help me, daughters, how many souls must have been made to suffer great loss in this way by the devil! These souls think that all such fears stem from humility. And there are other things I could mention. The fears come from not understanding ourselves completely. They distort self-knowledge; and I'm not surprised if we never get free from ourselves, for this lack of freedom from ourselves, and even more, is what can be feared. So I say, daughters, that we should set our eyes on Christ, our Good, and on His saints. There we shall learn true humility, the intellect will be enhanced, as I have said, and self-knowledge will not make one base and cowardly. Even though this is the first dwelling place, it is very rich and so precious that if the soul slips away from the vermin within it, nothing will be left to do but advance. Terrible are the wiles and deceits used by the devil so that souls may not know themselves or understand their own paths.

12. I could give some very good proofs from experience of the wiles the devil uses in these first dwelling places. Thus I say that you should think

not in terms of just a few rooms but in terms of a million; for souls, all with good intentions, enter here in many ways. But since the devil always has such a bad intention, he must have in each room many legions of devils to fight souls off when they try to go from one room to the other. Since the poor soul doesn't know this, the devil plays tricks on it in a thousand ways. He's not so successful with those who have advanced closer to where the King dwells. But since in the first rooms souls are still absorbed in the world and engulfed in their pleasures and vanities, with their honors and pretenses, their vassals (which are these senses and faculties) don't have the strength God gave human nature in the beginning. And these souls are easily conquered, even though they may go about with desires not to offend God and though they do perform good works. Those who see themselves in this state must approach His Majesty as often as possible. They must take His Blessed Mother and His saints as intercessors so that these intercessors may fight for them, for the soul's vassals have little strength to defend themselves. Truly, in all states it's necessary that strength come to us from God. May His Majesty through His mercy give it to us, amen.

13. How miserable the life in which we live! Because elsewhere I have said a great deal about the harm done to us by our failure to understand well this humility and self-knowledge, I'll tell you no more about it here, even though this self-knowledge is the most important thing for us. Please God, I may have now said something beneficial for you.

14. You must note that hardly any of the light coming from the King's royal chamber reaches these first dwelling places. Even though they are not dark and black, as when the soul is in sin, they nevertheless are in some way darkened so that the soul cannot see the light. The darkness is not caused by a flaw in the room—for I don't know how to explain myself—but by so many bad things like snakes and vipers and poisonous creatures that enter with the soul and don't allow it to be aware of the light. It's as if a person were to enter a place where the sun is shining but be hardly able to open his eyes because of the mud in them. The room is bright but he doesn't enjoy it because of the impediment of things like these wild animals or beasts that make him close his eyes to everything but them. So, I think, must be the condition of the soul. Even though it may not be in a bad state, it is so involved in worldly things and so absorbed with its possessions, honor, or business affairs, as I have said, that even though as a matter of fact it would want to see and enjoy its beauty these things do not allow it to; nor does it seem that it can slip free from so many impediments. If a person is to enter the second dwelling places, it is important that he strive to give up unnec-

essary things and business affairs. Each one should do this in conformity with his state in life. It is something so appropriate in order for him to reach the main dwelling place that if he doesn't begin doing this I hold that it will be impossible for him to get there. And it will even be impossible for him to stay where he is without danger even though he has entered the castle, for in the midst of such poisonous creatures one cannot help but be bitten at one time or another.

15. Now then, what would happen, daughters, if we who are already free from these snares, as we are, and have entered much further into the castle to other secret dwelling places should turn back through our own fault and go out to this tumult? There are, because of our sins, many persons to whom God has granted favors who through their own fault have fallen back into this misery. In the monastery we are free with respect to exterior matters; in interior matters may it please the Lord that we also be free, and may He free us. Guard yourselves, my daughters, from extraneous cares. Remember that there are few dwelling places in this castle in which the devils do not wage battle. True, in some rooms the guards (which I believe I have said are the faculties) have the strength to fight; but it is very necessary that we don't grow careless in recognizing the wiles of the devil, and that we not be deceived by his changing himself into an angel of light. There's a host of things he can do to cause us harm; he enters little by little, and until he's done the harm we don't recognize him.

16. I've already told you elsewhere that he's like a noiseless file, that we need to recognize him at the outset. Let me say something that will explain this better for you.

He gives a Sister various impulses toward penance, for it seems to her she has no rest except when she is tormenting herself. This may be a good beginning; but if the prioress has ordered that no penance be done without permission, and the devil makes the Sister think that in a practice that's so good one can be rightly daring, and she secretly gives herself up to such a penitential life that she loses her health and doesn't even observe what the rule commands, you can see clearly where all this good will end up.

He imbues another with a very great zeal for perfection. Such zeal is in itself good. But it could follow that every little fault the Sisters commit will seem to her a serious breach; and she is careful to observe whether they commit them, and then informs the prioress. It could even happen at times that she doesn't see her own faults because of her intense zeal for the religious observance. Since the other Sisters don't understand what's going on within her and see all this concern, they might not accept her zeal so well.

17. What the devil is hereby aiming after is no small thing: the cooling of the charity and love the Sisters have for one another. This would cause serious harm. Let us understand, my daughters, that true perfection consists in love of God and neighbor; the more perfectly we keep these two commandments, the more perfect we will be. All that is in our rule and constitutions serves for nothing else than to be a means toward keeping these commandments with greater perfection. Let's forget about indiscreet zeal; it can do us a lot of harm. Let each one look to herself. Because I have said enough about this elsewhere, I'll not enlarge on the matter.

18. This mutual love is so important that I would never want it to be forgotten. The soul could lose its peace and even disturb the peace of others by going about looking at trifling things in people that at times are not even imperfections, but since we know little we see these things in the worst light; look how costly this kind of perfection would be. Likewise, the devil could tempt the prioress in this way; and such a thing would be more dangerous. As a result much discretion is necessary. If things are done against the rule and constitutions, the matter need not always be seen in a good light. The prioress should be cautioned, and if she doesn't amend, the superior informed. This is charity. And the same with the Sisters if there is something serious. And to fail to do these things for fear of a temptation would itself be a temptation. But it should be carefully noted—so that the devil doesn't deceive us—that we must not talk about these things to one another. The devil could thereby gain greatly and manage to get the custom of gossiping started. The matter should be discussed with the one who will benefit, as I have said. In this house, glory to God, there's not much occasion for gossip since such continual silence is kept; but it is good that we be on guard. . . .

CHAPTER TWENTY - FOUR

Jane de Chantal,
Letters of Spiritual Direction
(1625–39)

Jane de Chantal (1572–1641)

As a wealthy young Frenchwoman, de Chantal married an equally wealthy baron in 1592, becoming a wife and mother. She was certainly formed by and valued these roles, which she later brought to bear upon the women's religious community she would direct. When her husband died in 1601, she took a vow of celibacy. She came under the spiritual direction of Francis de Sales, and developed a friendship that would shape them both for the rest of their lives. In 1610, they collaborated to establish at Annecy the Visitation of Holy Mary, a community whose initial purpose was to visit the sick and poor, earning the name Visitandines. De Chantal spent the remainder of her life in this ministry, which counted eighty-six houses before her death, and was actively involved in spiritual direction of those devoted to conforming their lives to Christ's.

Letters

Jane de Chantal's letters of spiritual direction reveal the heart of her theology and devotion. Always at the center is Jesus, with the motto "Live, Jesus" opening her letters. To fully realize this phrase was to live with Jesus engraved upon the heart. This led to complete love for God and fulfillment of God's will. In these letters to her brother, André Fremyot, Archbishop of Bourges, she encourages him to sustain his new convictions of a deeper Christian life. In addition, de Chantal wrote letters of direction to a wide range of people, to lay and religious, to family members, to a military commander, and to Francis de Sales.

LETTERS

Live ˙ Jesus!

[Chambery, 1625]

My very dear Lord,

Since God, in His eternal goodness, has moved you to consecrate all your love, your actions, your works, and your whole self to Him utterly without any self-interest but only for His greater glory and His satisfaction, remain firm in this resolve. With the confidence of a son, rest in the care and love which divine Providence has for you in all your needs. Look upon Providence as a child does its mother who loves him tenderly. You can be sure that God loves you incomparably more. We can't imagine how great is the love which God, in His goodness, has for souls who thus abandon themselves to His mercy, and who have no other wish than to do what they think pleases Him, leaving everything that concerns them to His care in time and in eternity.

After this, every day in your morning exercise, or at the end of it, confirm your resolutions and unite your will with God's in all that you will do that day and in whatever He sends you. Use words like these: "O most holy Will of God, I give You infinite thanks for the mercy with which You have surrounded me; with all my strength and love, I adore You from the depths of my soul and unite my will to Yours now and forever, especially in all that I shall do and all that You will be pleased to send me this day, consecrating to Your glory my soul, my mind, my body, all my thoughts, words and actions, and my whole being. I beg You, with all the humility of my heart, accomplish in me Your eternal designs, and do not allow me to present any obstacle to this. Your eyes, which can see the most intimate recesses of my heart, know the intensity of my desire to live out Your holy will, but they can also see my weakness and limitations. That is why, prostrate before Your infinite mercy, I implore You, my Savior, through the gentleness and justice of this same will of Yours, to grant me the grace of accomplishing it perfectly, so that, consumed in the fire of Your love, I may be an acceptable holocaust which, with the glorious Virgin and all the saints, will praise and bless You forever. Amen."

During the activities of the day, spiritual as well as temporal, as often as you can, my dear Lord, unite your will to God's by confirming your morning resolution. Do this either by a simple, loving glance at God, or by a few words spoken quietly and cast into His heart, by assenting in words like: "Yes, Lord, I want to do this action because You want it," or simply, "Yes, Father," or, "O Holy Will, live and rule in me," or other words that the Holy Spirit will suggest to you. You may also make a simple sign of the cross over your heart, or kiss the cross you are wearing. All this will show that above everything, you want to do the holy will of God and seek nothing but His glory in all that you do.

As for the will of God's good pleasure, which we know only through events as they occur, if these events benefit us, we must bless God and unite ourselves to this divine will which sends them. If something occurs which is disagreeable, physically or mentally, let us lovingly unite our will in obedience to the divine good pleasure, despite our natural aversion. We must pay no attention to these feelings, so long as at the fine point of our will we acquiesce very simply to God's will, saying, "O my God, I want this because it is Your good pleasure." Chapter 6 of Book IX of the *Love of God* throws a clear light on this practice and invites us to be courageous and simple in performing it. Whatever good or evil befalls you, be confident that God will convert it all to your good.

As for prayer, don't burden yourself with making considerations; neither your mind nor mine is good at that. Follow your own way of speaking to our Lord sincerely, lovingly, confidently, and simply, as your heart dictates. Sometimes be content to stay ever so short a while in His divine presence, faithfully and humbly, like a child before his father, waiting to be told what to do, totally dependent on the paternal will in which he has placed all his love and trust. You may, if you wish, say a few words on this subject, but very quietly: "You are my Father and my God from whom I expect all my happiness." A few moments later (for you must always wait a little to hear what God will say to your heart): "I am Your child, all Yours; good children think only of pleasing their father; I don't want to have any worries and I leave in Your care everything that concerns me, for You love me, my God. Father, You are my good. My soul rests and trusts in Your love and eternal providence." Try to let yourself be penetrated by words like these.

When you have committed some fault, go to God humbly, saying to Him, "I have sinned, my God, and I am sorry." Then, with loving confidence, add: "Father, pour the oil of Your bountiful mercy on my wounds, for You are my only hope; heal me." A little later: "By the help of Your grace, I shall be more on my guard and will bless you eternally," and speak like this according to the different movements and feelings of your soul. Sometimes put yourself very simply before God, certain of His presence everywhere, and without any effort, whisper very softly to His sacred heart whatever your own heart prompts you to say.

When you are experiencing some physical pain or a sorrowful heart, try to endure it before God, recalling as much as you can that He is watching you at this time of affliction, especially in physical illness when very often the heart is weary and unable to pray. Don't force yourself to pray, for a simple adherence to God's will, expressed from time to time, is enough. Moreover, suffering borne in the will quietly and patiently is a continual, very powerful prayer before God, regardless of the complaints and anxieties that come from the inferior part of the soul.

Finally, my dear Lord, try to perform all your actions calmly and gently, and keep your mind ever joyful, peaceful and content. Do not worry about your perfection, or about your soul. God to whom it belongs, and to whom you have completely entrusted it, will take care of it and fill it with all the graces, consolations and blessings of His holy love in the measure that they will be useful in this life. In the next life He will grant you eternal bliss. Such is the wish of her to whom your soul is as precious as her own; pray for her, for she never prays without you, my Lord.

[Annecy, 8 May 1625]

My very honored and beloved Lord,

May the divine Savior, who ascends, glorious and triumphant, to sit at the right hand of His Father, draw to Himself our hearts and all our affections, in order to place them in the bosom of His love! How consoled I was when I read your letter and saw the graces and mercy that this good Savior has granted you! I have blessed Him and thanked Him for this; I do so again with all my heart, and I shall continue to thank Him unceasingly.

It is good when a soul loves solitude; it's a sign that it takes delight in God and enjoys speaking with Him. Don't you see, my dearest Lord, this is where the divine sweetness communicates its lights and more abundant graces. How great is the grace you have received in this self-examination and the renewal of your soul which you have made with such preparation! Now you experience the fruit of this: peace and contentment in your conscience which is so well prepared that God will be pleased to fill it with His most holy, precious favors. How strongly I feel about this and what great hope I have that it will lead you to utter integrity and perfection! You must respond faithfully to the lights that God will give you, no matter what it costs you, for really, the love which God, in His goodness, has for you, and which He manifests so openly by such excellent, solid graces, requires a reciprocal love, according to the measure of your weakness and poverty. This means that you must refuse nothing you recognize to be His will. This perfect abandonment of yourself in the arms of divine Providence, this loving acceptance of all that He wishes to do with you, and with everything, this peace of conscience, this holy desire to please Him by all kinds of virtuous acts, according to the opportunities He will give you, and especially acts of charity and humility—all this is the wood that will feed the fire of sacred love which you feel in your heart and continually desire. And in this holy exercise, do not forget me, my very dear Lord, so that some day—God knows when—we may see each other in that blessed eternity where we shall love Him and praise and bless Him with all our strength. . . .

Pont-à-Mousson, 1 June 1626

My very dear and very honored Lord,

I thank and praise our good God for the blessing He is pleased to have given us through the exchange made possible by our perfect friendship; for I assure you that if my letters enkindle in you the flame of love for the supreme Good, your very dear letters arouse the same feelings in me and make me wish more and more that our hearts be totally and constantly united to the good pleasure of God which we find so kind and favorable. Let us love this good pleasure, my dearest Lord, and let us see it alone in all that happens to us, embracing it lovingly. May this exercise be our daily bread. It can be practiced everywhere, and is particularly necessary for you because of the variety of obligations and contacts which you cannot avoid; for, in everything, by God's grace, you seek only Him and His most holy will.

Oh! how satisfying it is to read and reread what you tell me, my very dear Lord—of how you continue to practice your spiritual exercises with the same fervor and love you had when you began them, and how you keep your resolutions vigorous, despite the bustle of the court.

Confident of the Lord's goodness, I trust you will never retreat but will continually advance. Your assurance and testimony about this give my soul consolation and peace. That's why I beg you, my dearest Lord, always to mention something on this subject when you write to me. And don't think that this desire comes from mistrust, certainly not. I have no fear of that, now that your year of "novitiate" is over; and I have never doubted that God would grant you a holy perseverance, for the grace of your vocation in the service of His pure love is too extraordinary and abundant. Let us both appreciate and love this grace well, my very dear Lord, since it is the source of eternal life for us. It is so precious to me that I rank it second among all the God-given graces which impel me most strongly to do good and to long to see our life totally bound with Jesus Christ and hidden in God.

Do not think that by this I mean for us to retire into solitude, or to flee those occupations and legitimate contacts necessary to our vocations; oh, no, for I very much like each one to stay in his state of life and not throw himself into the excesses of a hermit's devotion, especially you, my dearest Lord, for whom this would be most inappropriate. But what I do mean is that we must want, above all, to adorn our souls with the virtues of our Savior, Jesus Christ, and also with that secret, intimate union of our hearts with God, which causes us to long for Him everywhere, as you are doing. As for that humility of heart which makes you think of yourself as a blade of hyssop in comparison to her whom you consider a cedar of Lebanon— though, in truth, she is but a shadow and lifeless image of virtue—my dear Lord, this is the humility which attracts God's Spirit to our souls and fills them with the treasure of all virtues. It is through humility that we live a hidden life, for she manages her good works in secret and holds in security, in the shelter of her protection, the little good that we do.

I didn't intend to write so much, dearest Lord, but that's how my heart always opens up to you. And certainly it is very softened by the holy and incomparable love God has given it for you. Always love this heart of mine well and continue to recommend it to the divine mercy. Be assured that I never cease desiring for you the fullness of His best graces in this life and a very high place before the throne of His glory and only desirable eternity. But all this, no doubt, I do with infinite love and affection.

[Annecy, 1633]

My very honored Lord,

Should we not adore God's will in profound submission, and lovingly kiss the rod with which He reproves His elect? Of course we should, and, despite nature's repugnance, we should praise and thank Him a thousand times because He is our good God who sends us both sorrows and joys with the same love, and ordinarily even has us draw more spiritual profit from affliction than from prosperity.

But how does it happen that, having this knowledge and experience, we still feel so keenly the death of those we love? I must admit, my dear Lord, that as I read the little note telling me of the death of our dearest darling daughter, I was so overcome that, had I been standing, I think I would have fallen. I can't remember that any grief ever gripped me this way. But when I read your letter, oh, Lord Jesus! My dear Lord, what a blow it was to my poor heart and how much your sorrow added to mine! It is understandable that you should feel this loss as you do, and at your age; what a sweet support you have lost in this daughter who so devotedly looked after your health and your every want. All this has touched me more than I can say, for whatever affects you affects me acutely. But when I consider that by means of these privations, lovingly accepted, God wishes to be Himself everything to us, that the least progress we make in His holy love is worth more than the whole world with all its consolations, and that in the most bitter trials which strip us of our greatest satisfactions, God treasures, above all, the union of our wills with His. When I consider all this, then, truly, my dear Lord, I find so many advantages to affliction, that I can't help admitting that the more we suffer, the more we are favored by God. I hope that by now you yourself will have perceived this and found comfort in this truth. Such is my wish for you, and I pray God with all my heart to grant you this grace.

My beloved and dearest Lord, our first reactions are inevitable, and our gentle Savior is not offended by them; but I hope that afterward He will fill you with a thousand delicate, holy consolations. This is what I continually beg of Him, just as I beg you, my dear Lord, to divert yourself as much as you can, and to find strength in the confident hope that we shall all be united in the joy of a blessed eternity. Surely, the virtuous life and saintly death of this very lovable daughter gives us hope that, by God's mercy, she has already attained this bliss. This should console us, for, in the end, dearest Lord, we are in this world only to attain such happiness, and the sooner we reach it, the better. I'm amazed that this truth still doesn't prevent our feeling so profoundly the death of our loved ones.

I am writing to M. and Mme. de Coulanges to whom this terrible loss must have been a great shock. I believe that the love they have always had for the poor little orphan will continue unchanged. When my thoughts turn to this child, I have to check myself. I trust that God, to whom I confide her, will be Father and Protector to her, and I give her over to the care of the Blessed Virgin with all my heart.

On this occasion, the sisters in both houses [Paris] have omitted nothing. Besides their own love for the dear deceased, they have felt keenly your sorrow and mine in this bereavement. I find some comfort in knowing that she will be buried in the very place where the heart of my poor son is kept. . . .

[Annecy, 1639]

My Lord,

I have learned, through our dear Sister Superior in Paris, how God has allowed you to share in the calamity with which, in His Providence, He has chastised His people, and how your gentle, loving acceptance of this affliction has touched everyone. No words can express the consolation this gives me; I see in it the special care that our Lord has for your progress in His holy love.

It is clear that through your temporal loss, you are richer in spiritual treasures, the least of which is worth more than the ownership of the entire world. I always remember what our blessed Father used to say: "An ounce of virtue practiced in time of tribulation is worth more than a hundred thousand pounds exercised in prosperity, because that is where real virtue is shown." Blessed be God forever, who has, in His mercy, visited you! How fortunate you are, my dearest Lord, to be able to say with so much courage and indifference: "The Lord gave me those abbeys, and the Lord has taken them away: blessed be the name of the Lord!" It is His grace that gives you this disposition. Once again, I bless and thank Him for it.

In your last letter, you were telling me how our Lord is asking you to move into the retirement you have felt drawn to for some time. Oh! how it comforts me to hear that! I hope you are taking care of your affairs so that you may do this in the manner you think will be most pleasing to God; but, I beg you, do not in any way alter your plan for a reasonable retirement, unless you come to see clearly that our Lord is asking something else of you.

I am forever in His love, yours, etc. . . .

CHAPTER TWENTY - FIVE

Juana Inés de la Cruz, *Respuesta a Sor Filotea de la Cruz* (1690)

Juana Inés de la Cruz (1651–95)

Inés Ramirez de Asbaje y Santillana was born on a small ranch southeast of Mexico City and was raised by her grandparents in the nearby town of Panoayan. As early as 1659 she desired greater opportunities to learn, so she was sent to relatives in Mexico City. Five years later she went to live at the residence of the viceroy, whose responsibility it was to educate and socialize chosen girls and boys. Her intellect was keen, and Sor Juana knew she wanted a life of scholarship, not matrimony. After a brief stint in a Carmelite convent, she was admitted to St. Paula's convent of the order of St. Jerome. She took the religious name of Juana Inés de la Cruz at her profession in 1669, and entered upon a comfortable life of study and friendship. The convent's rule was lax, allowing for well-appointed quarters, slaves and servants, private meals, and minimal labor. She pursued science, music, and literature, collecting her own library. She was soon in demand as a fine composer of poetry and was heralded as "the Tenth Muse" of New Spain. Her confessor, Antonio Núñez de Miranda, became concerned sometime around 1681/82 about the secular nature of much of Sor Juana's poetry. When he ordered her to stop writing, she dismissed him as her confessor, certain that the guidance of the Holy Spirit would suffice.

Nonetheless, opposition from high clerics did not go away. In 1690 a bishop published Sor Juana's theological critique of a Jesuit's sermon without her permission. In addition, he called upon her to devote herself to writing more appropriate for her sex and vocation. Her response, *Respuesta*

239

a Sor Filotea de la Cruz ("The Reply to Sor Philothea de la Cruz"), provides a wealth of autobiographical and theological commentary. However, in 1692 she put down her pen, returned to Nuñez de Miranda for spiritual direction, and never wrote again. She died April 17, 1695, from an illness contracted while nursing other sisters.

Respuesta a Sor Filotea de la Cruz

The bishop of Puebla, without Sor Juana's consent, had published her critical review of a sermon delivered forty years earlier by a well-known Portuguese Jesuit priest. Moreover, the bishop added a letter to her under the pseudonym Sor Filotea de la Cruz, which questioned the propriety of her writing. In response, Sor Juana wrote the *Respuesta,* a defense of her theological claims about human nature and purpose as well as a defense of her life of scholarly pursuit. While the bishop's challenge had suggested that a nun's life should be given to God and the church, Sor Juana construed that service broadly, collapsing the categories of sacred and secular. She argues that because God had made her a rational creature, it was her duty to become learned and use that gift for all humanity. In this excerpt Sor Juana addresses the character of human knowing and the persecution often attendant upon those seeking knowledge. She is a powerful writer, even in English translation, and speaks eloquently to the issues confronting her.

RESPUESTA A SOR FILOTEA DE LA CRUZ

. . . In this way I went on, continually directing the course of my study, as I have said, toward the eminence of sacred theology. To reach this goal, I considered it necessary to ascend the steps of human arts and sciences, for how can one who has not mastered the style of the ancillary branches of learning hope to understand that of the queen of them all? How, lacking logic, was I to understand the general and specific methodologies of which Holy Scripture is composed? How, without rhetoric, could I understand its figures, tropes, and locutions? How, without physics, all the natural questions concerning the nature of sacrificial animals, which symbolize so many things already explicated, and so many others? How, whether Saul's being cured by the sound of David's harp [1 Kings (1 Sam.) 16:23] came about by virtue of the natural power of music, or through supernatural powers which God was pleased to bestow on David? How, lacking arithmetic, could one understand such mysterious computations of years, days, months, hours, weeks, as those of Daniel and others, for the intelligence of which one needs to know the natures, concordances, and properties of numbers? How, without geometry, could one measure the sacred ark of the covenant and the holy city of Jerusalem, whose mysterious measurements form a cube in all its dimensions, and the marvelous proportional distribution of all its parts? How, without a knowledge of architecture, is one to understand Solomon's great temple of which God Himself was the artificer who provided the arrangement and layout, the wise king being only the overseer who carried it out? In it, no column's base was without its mystery, no column without its symbolic sense, no cornice without allusiveness, no architrave without meaning, and so on with all its parts, not even the most miniscule fillet serving solely as support or complement to the design of the whole, but rather itself symbolizing greater things. How will one understand the historical books without a full knowledge of the principles and divisions of which history consists? Those recapitulations in the narrative which postpone what actually occurred first? How will one understand the legal books without a complete acquaintance with both codes of law? How, without a great deal of erudition, all the matters of secular history mentioned in Holy Writ, all the customs of the Gentiles, the rites, the ways of speaking? How, without many rules and much reading of the Church Fathers, will one be able to understand the prophets' obscure forms of expression? And how, unless one is thoroughly versed in music, will one understand those musical proportions, with all their fine points, found in so many passages, especially in Abraham's petitions to God for the cities, asking whether He would forgive them, providing there were fifty righteous men, from which number he went down to forty-five, which is the sesquinone and is as from mi to re: thence to forty, which is the sesquioctave and as from re to mi; thence to thirty, which is the sesquitierce, or the proportion of the diatessaron; thence to twenty, which is the sesquialter, or that of the diapente; thence to ten, which is the duple, or diapason—and went no further, there being no other harmonic proportions. Now, how is this to be understood without music?

In the book of Job, God says to him: *Numquid coniungere valebis micantes stellas Pleiadas, aut gyrum Arcturi poteris dissipare? Numquid producis Luciferum in tempore suo, et Vesperum super filios terrae consurgere facis?* ["Shalt thou be able to join together the shining stars the Pleiades, or canst thou stop the turning about of Arcturus? Canst thou bring forth the day star in its time and make the evening star to rise upon the children of the earth?" (Job 38:31-32)]. Such terms will be incomprehensible without a knowledge of astrology. And it is not only these noble disciplines; no mechanical art goes unmentioned. In sum, how to understand the book which takes in all books, and the knowledge which embraces all types of knowledge, to the understanding of which they all contribute? After one has mastered them all (which is evidently not easy nor, in fact possible), a further circumstance going beyond all those mentioned is required: a continuing prayer and purity of life, so as to be visited by God with that cleansing of the spirit and illumination of the mind which the understanding of such lofty matters demands, in the absence of which none of the rest is any use.

. . . I should like to convince everyone by my own experience not only that different subjects do not interfere with one another, but that they actually support one another, since certain ones shed light on others, opening a way into them by means of variations and occult connections. It was to form this universal chain that the wisdom of their Author so put them in place that they appear correlated and bound together with marvelous concert and bonding. This is the chain that the ancients pretended emerged from Jupiter's mouth, on which all things were strung and linked together. So much is demonstrated by the Reverend Father Athanasius Kircher in his curious book *De Magnete* [On the Magnet]. All things proceed from God, who is at once the center and the circumference from which all existing lines proceed and at which all end up. . . .

. . . I must say, Madam, that sometimes I stop and reflect that anyone who stands out—or whom God singles out, for He alone can do so—is viewed as everyone's enemy, because it seems to some that he is usurping the applause due them or deflecting the admiration which they have coveted, for which reason they pursue him. . . .

What, if not this, was the cause of that furious hatred the Pharisees conceived for Christ, when they had so many reasons to feel just the opposite? . . .

When the soldiers made our Lord Jesus Christ their amusement, entertainment, and laughingstock, they brought a worn scarlet robe and a hollow reed and a crown of thorns to crown Him king in jest. Now then, the reed and the purple robe, though an affront, were not hurtful; why is the crown alone so? Is it not enough for it, like the other insignia, to be a sneering gibe, that being the object? No, because the sacred head of Christ and His divine brain were a storehouse of wisdom, and in the world it is not enough for a wise mind to be scorned: it must also be bruised and hurt. Let the head that is a treasure-house of wisdom expect no crowning other than the thorns!

What wreath can human intelligence expect when it sees what is bestowed on the divine? Roman arrogance crowned the various feats of arms of its captains with different crowns: the civic was for one who defended the citizenry; the military, for one who penetrated an opposing army; the mural, for one who scaled a city wall; the obsidional, for one who raised the siege of a city or an encircled army, encampment, or headquarters; the naval, the oval, the triumphal, for other feats, of which Pliny and Aulus Gellius tell. Seeing so many varieties of crown, I was uncertain what kind Christ's was. I think it must have been obsidional, which (as you, my Lady, know) was the most honored and was so called from *obsidio,* which means siege. This was not made of gold or silver but of the actual grass or plants of the field in which the operation was carried out. The feat of Christ was to make the Prince of Darkness lift his siege, which had the whole world encircled, as is said in the Book of Job: *Circuivi terram et ambulavi per eam* ["(And the Lord said to him, Whence comest thou? And he answered:) I have gone round about the earth, and walked through it" (Job 1:7)]; and told in Saint Peter: *Circuit, quaerens quem devoret* ["(The devil) . . . goeth about seeking whom he may devour" (1 Peter 5:8)]. Our Chieftain then came and made him lift the siege: *nunc princeps huius mundi eiecietur foras* ["Now shall the prince of this world be cast out" (John 12:31)]. Thus the soldiers crowned Him, not with gold or silver, but with the natural product of the world, which was the seat of the struggle, and which, after the curse—*spinas et tribulos germinabit tibi* ["Thorns and thistles shall it bring forth to thee" (Gen. 3:18)]—produced nothing but thorns. Thus the crown with which His mother, the Synagogue, crowned the valiant wise Conqueror was most fitting. The daughters of Zion came forth in tears to behold the sorrowful triumph, as they had come rejoicing to that of the other Solomon, for the triumph of the wise is obtained in sorrow and celebrated with weeping; that is how wisdom triumphs. It was Christ, as prince of the wise, who first tried out the crown, in order that, having been sanctified on His temples, it should lose its horror for other men of wisdom, and make them realize that they may aspire to no other honor.

The very Life was willing to go and give life to the deceased Lazarus. The disciples, not knowing His purpose, objected: *Rabbi, nunc quaerebant te Judaei lapidare, et iterum vadis illuc?* ["Rabbi, the Jews but now sought to stone Thee: and goest thou thither again?" (John 11:8)]. The Redeemer quieted their fears: *Nonne duodecim sunt horae diei?* ["Are there not twelve hours of the day?" (John 11:9)]. Up to this point they seem to have been afraid because they had in mind the precedent of the Jews' wanting to stone

Him for having reproved them by calling them thieves and not shepherds of their flocks. And thus, they feared that, if He went forth with the same end in view (reproofs, however well deserved, being usually taken ill), His life would be in danger. But once set right and made aware that His going is to restore life to Lazarus, what could have caused Thomas, showing as much bravery as Peter in the garden, to say: *Eamus et nos, ut moriamur cum eo* ["Let us also go, that we may die with Him" (John 11:16)]. Blessed apostle, what are you saying? The Lord is not going forth to die—why such misgivings? For Christ's aim is not to reprimand, but to perform an act of mercy, and they therefore can do Him no harm. The Jews themselves might have been your reassurance, for when He reproved them for wishing to stone Him, saying: *Multa bona opera ostendi vobis ex Patre meo, propter quod eorum opus me lapidatis?* ["Many good works I have shewed you from my Father; for which of those works do you stone me?" (John 10:32)], they answered Him: *De bono opere non lapidamus te, sed de blasphemia* ["For a good work we stone thee not, but for blasphemy" (John 10:33)]. So if they do not want to stone Him on account of His good works, and He is now going to do them such a good one in giving life to Lazarus, of what are they afraid and why? Would it not be better to say: Let us go and enjoy the fruit of gratitude for the good deed that our Master is about to perform? To see Him applauded and given thanks for the benefaction? To see their own astonishment at the miracle? And not to say to them something so evidently beside the point as: *Eamus et nos, ut moriamur cum eo.* But, alas, the Saint was well-advised to be afraid and spoke like an apostle. Is Christ not going to perform a miracle? What greater danger can there be? Pride finds it less intolerable to hear a reproof, than envy to see a miracle. In all I am saying, venerable Lady, I do not mean that I have been persecuted for being learned, only for my love of learning and letters, not because I have been successful in either. . . .

CHAPTER TWENTY - SIX

Madame Jeanne Guyon, *Spiritual Torrents* (late 1600s)

Madame Guyon (1648–1717)

Jeanne Marie Bouvier de la Motte was born in France and married at fifteen to Jacques Guyon de Chesney. Upon his death after twelve years of marriage, she more actively pursued her theological and religious interests. She embarked upon a life of spiritual quest that included certain challenges to conventional theological ideas. This began with the establishment of a community of Nouvelles Catholiques, or converted Huguenots, near Geneva in 1681. Guyon continued to travel throughout southern France and Italy, spreading her ideas about prayer and Christian life. She basically asserted that the soul's contemplation of God was the heart of Christian life, and that such contemplation should lead to a pure or disinterested love of God. She ran up against Church authorities who accused her of "quietism" and fanatical mysticism, and who kept her under close supervision. However, after her activity caused heated theological debate at the Conference of Issy (1694–95), she was imprisoned on Christmas Eve 1695. Released into the custody of her daughter in 1703, she died in 1717. Guyon was a powerful laywoman whose spiritual experiences and theological writings concerning the working of God in the soul spoke to many of her day, and offered a model of Christian life and thought.

Spiritual Torrents

In this treatise, Madame Guyon set forth her basic notions about the nature of the human soul and the avenues, differentiated in detail, through which God leads it. The Paris Edition of 1790 includes thirteen chapters divided into two parts. In this excerpt, Guyon expounds upon the transition from the human state to the divine, which is life in God. To illustrate, she describes the torrent, which, taken up by the sea, loses itself yet gains the treasures of the sea. Indifference is then proper for the soul, for no longer are such distinctions as devotion and action, or virtue and meanness, significant. The soul is one with God and cannot act as a separate self. This resurrection of the soul in God leads to profound liberty of life, perhaps the most controversial consequence of her claims.

SPIRITUAL TORRENTS

PART I

. . .

CHAPTER IX. FOURTH DEGREE OF THE PASSIVE WAY OF FAITH, WHICH IS THE COMMENCEMENT OF THE DIVINE LIFE . . .

When the torrent begins to lose itself in the sea, it can easily be distinguished. Its movement is perceptible, until at length it gradually loses all form of its own, to take that of the sea. So the soul, leaving this degree, and beginning to lose itself, yet retains something of its own; but in a short time it loses all that it had peculiar to itself. The corpse which has been reduced to ashes is still dust and ashes; but if another person were to swallow those ashes, they would no longer have an identity, but would form part of the person who had taken them. The soul hitherto, though dead and buried, has retained its own being; it is only in this degree that it is really taken out of itself.

All that has taken place up to this point has been in the individual capacity of the creature; but here the creature is taken out of his own capacity to receive an infinite capacity in God Himself. And as the torrent, when it enters the sea, loses its own being in such a way that it retains nothing of it, and takes that of the sea, or rather is taken out of itself to be lost in the sea; so this soul loses the human in order that it may lose itself in the divine, which becomes its being and its subsistence, not essentially, but mystically. Then this torrent possesses all the treasures of the sea, and is as glorious as it was formerly poor and miserable.

It is in the tomb that the soul begins to resume life, and the light enters insensibly. Then it can be truly said that "The people which sat in darkness saw great light; and to them which sat in the region and shadow of death light is sprung up" (Matt. iv. 16). There is a beautiful figure of this resurrection in Ezekiel (chap. xxxvii.), where the dry bones gradually assume life: and then there is that other passage, "The hour is coming, and now is, when the dead shall hear the voice of the Son of God; and they that hear shall live" (John v. 25). O you who are coming out of the sepulchre! you feel within yourselves a germ of life springing up little by little: you are quite astonished to find a secret strength taking possession of you: your ashes are reanimated: you feel yourselves to be in a new country. The poor soul, which only expected to remain at rest in its grave, receives an agreeable surprise. It does not know what to think: it supposes that the sun must have shed upon it a few scattered rays through some opening or chink, whose brightness will only last for a moment. It is still more astonished when it feels this secret vigour permeating its entire being, and finds that it gradually receives a new life, to lose it no more for ever, unless it be by the most flagrant unfaithfulness.

But this new life is not like the former one: it is a *life in God*. It is a perfect life. The soul *lives no longer* and works no longer of itself, but *God* lives, acts, and operates in it (Gal. ii. 20); and this goes on increasing, so that it becomes perfect with God's perfection, rich with God's riches, and loving with God's love.

The soul sees now that whatever it owned formerly had been in its own possession: now it no longer possesses, but is possessed: it only takes a new life in order to lose it in God; or rather it only lives with the life of God; and as He is the principle of life, the soul can want nothing. What a gain it has made by all its losses! It has lost the created for the Creator, the nothing for the All in all. All things are given to it, not in itself, but in God; not to be possessed by itself, but to be possessed by God. Its riches are immense, for they are God Himself. It feels its capacity increasing day by day to immensity: every virtue is restored to it, but in God.

It must be remarked, that as it was only spoiled by degrees, so it is only enriched and vivified by degrees. The more it loses itself in God, the greater its capacity becomes; just as the more the torrent loses itself in the sea, the more it is enlarged, having no other limits than those of the sea: it participates in all its properties. The soul becomes strong and firm: it has lost all means, but it has found the end. This divine life becomes quite natural to it. As it no longer feels itself, sees itself, or knows itself, so it no longer sees or understands or distinguishes anything of God as distinct or outside of itself. It is no longer conscious of love, or light, or knowledge; it only knows that God is, and that it no longer lives except in God. All devotion is action, and all action is devotion: all is the same; the soul is indifferent to all, for all is equally God. Formerly it was necessary to exercise virtue in order to perform virtuous works; here all distinction of action is taken away, the actions having no virtue in themselves, but all being God, the meanest action equally with the greatest, provided it is in the order of God and at His time: for all that might be of the natural choice, and not in this order, would have another effect, leading the soul out of God by unfaithfulness. Not that it would be brought out of its degree or its loss, but out of the divine plan, which makes all things one and all things God. So the soul is *indifferent* as to whether it be in one state or another, in one place or another: all is the same to it, and it lets itself be carried along naturally. It ceases to think, to wish, or to choose for itself; but remains content, without care or anxiety, no longer distinguishing its inner life to speak of it. Indeed it may be said not to possess one: it is no longer in itself; it is all in God. It is not necessary for it to shut itself up within itself; it does not hope to find anything there, and does not seek for it. If a person were altogether penetrated with the sea, having sea within and without, above and below on every side, he would not prefer one place to another, all being the same to him. So the soul does not trouble itself to seek anything or to do anything; that is, of itself, by itself, or for itself. It remains as it is. But what does it do? Nothing—always nothing. It does what it is made to do, it suffers what it is made to suffer. Its peace is unchangeable, but always natural. It has, as it were, passed into a state of nature; and yet how different from those altogether without God!

The difference is, that it is compelled to action by God without being conscious of it, whereas formerly it was nature that acted. It seems to itself to do neither right nor wrong, but it lives satisfied, peaceful, doing what it is made to do in a steady and resolute manner.

God alone is its guide; for at the time of its loss, it lost its own will. And if you were to ask what are its desires, it could not tell. It can choose for itself no longer: all desire is taken away, because, having found its centre, the heart loses all natural inclination, tendency, and activity, in the same way as it loses all repugnance and contrariety. The torrent has no longer either a declivity or a movement: it is in repose, and at its end. . . .

PART II

CHAPTER I . . .

I omitted to say that this is where true liberty begins; not, as some imagine, a liberty which necessitates idleness; that would be imprisonment rather than liberty, fancying ourselves free because, having an aversion to our own works, we no longer practise them. The liberty of which I speak is of a different nature; it does all things easily which God would have done, and the more easily in proportion to the duration and the painfulness of the incapacity to do them which we have previously experienced. . . .

It is the same with spiritual resurrection; everything is restored, with a wonderful power to use it without being defiled by it, clinging to it without appropriating it as before. All is done in God, and things are used as though they were not used. It is here that true liberty and true life are found. "If we have been planted in the likeness of Christ's death, we shall be also in the likeness of His resurrection" (Rom. vi. 5). Can there be freedom where there are powerlessness and restrictions? No; "If the Son shall make you free, ye shall be free indeed," but with His liberty. . . .

CHAPTER TWENTY - SEVEN

Susanna Wesley,
Letters and *Writings*
(1709–25)

Susanna Wesley (1669–1742)

Born Susanna Annesley in London, she was brought up in a Puritan
(Nonconformist) household as the daughter of learned and pious parents.
Her father trained her in biblical and classical languages as well as other
arts and sciences, thus providing an education far beyond that of most girls
of her day. It is no surprise, given her learning and strong-mindedness, that
she informed her father when she was twelve that she had concluded that
the Established Church of England was the true church of God and that she
would convert from her Nonconformist upbringing. She remained a faithful
member of the Church of England the rest of her life. She married Samuel
Wesley, a minister in the Church of England, and moved to his rural parish
at Epworth, leaving behind a gentle and cultured urban life for one that
would be fraught with poverty and violence. She bore nineteen children,
only nine of whom lived to adulthood, and ran this large household on
extremely limited means. She took personal responsibility for educating her
children, daughters as well as sons, establishing a sort of "home school" and
a daily regimen of learning, chores, and devotions. Her influence on all of
her children continued well into their adulthood as she corresponded with
them on personal, social, moral, and theological matters. She continued to
read, reflect, and write throughout her adult life as well. She commented in
her private journal that, could she ask one thing of God, it would be to not
have "so much hurry and distraction; and that I might have more leisure to

retire from the world, without injuring my husband or children," not for private pleasure, but for contemplation and devotion.

Letters and Writings

Her hand upon the ministry of her sons John and Charles Wesley showed not only in their methodical (thus the name Methodist) ways, but also in the emphasis they placed on the serious responsibility each person must take for her or his own spiritual life. The many letters between Wesley and her sons reflect a close and affectionate relationship that allowed for disagreement and challenge. The following excerpts from her letters demonstrate Wesley's own theological insights on the nature of human being, predestination, the nature of God, and salvation, which were written by way of correction and instruction to John. In addition, Wesley composed a commentary on the Apostles' Creed that "comprehends the main of what a Christian ought to believe" and "may inform you what you should intend when you make the solemn confession of our most holy faith." Portions of this commentary are included here.

LETTERS AND WRITINGS

Wroote, Jan. 8, 1725.

"Dear Son,—I cannot recollect the passages you mention: but believing you do the author, I positively aver that he is extremely in the wrong in that impious, not to say blasphemous, assertion, That God by an irresistible decree hath determined any man to be miserable, even in this life. His intentions, as himself, are holy, and just, and good; and all the miseries incident to men here or hereafter spring from themselves. The case stands thus:—This life is a state of probation, wherein eternal happiness or misery is proposed to our choice; the one as the reward of a virtuous, the other as a consequence of a vicious, life. Man is a compound being, a strange mixture of spirit and matter; or rather a creature, wherein those opposite principles are *united without mixture,* yet each principle, after an incomprehensible manner, subject to the influence of the other.—The true happiness of man, under this consideration, consists in a due subordination of the *inferior* to the *superior* powers; of the *animal* to the *rational* nature; and of *both* to GOD.

"This was his original righteousness and happiness that was lost in Adam: and to restore man to this happiness, by the recovery of his original

251

righteousness, was certainly God's design in admitting him to the state of trial on the world, and of our redemption by Jesus Christ. And surely this was a design truly worthy of God! and the greatest instance of mercy that even Omnipotent goodness could exhibit to us.

"As the happiness of man consists in a due subordination of the *inferior* to the *superior* powers, &c, so the inversion of this order is the true source of human misery. There is in us all a natural propension toward the *body* and the world. The beauty, pleasures, and ease, of the *body* strangely charm us; the wealth and honours of the world allure us: and all, under the manage of a subtle malicious adversary, give a prodigious force to present things; and if the animal life once get the ascendant of our reason, it utterly deprives us of our moral liberty, and by consequence makes us wretched. Therefore for any man to endeavour after happiness, in gratifying all his bodily appetites in opposition to his reason, is the greatest folly imaginable: because he seeks it where God has not designed he shall ever find it. But this is the case of the generality of men: they live as mere animals, wholly given up to the interests and pleasures of the body; and all the use of their understanding is, to make provision for the *flesh* to fulfil the lusts thereof, without the least regard to future happiness or misery.

"It is true, our eternal state lies under a vast disadvantage to us in this life, in that, that it is *future* and *invisible*: and it requires great attention and application of mind, frequent retirement, and intense thinking, to excite our affections, and beget such an habitual sense of it as is requisite to enable us to walk steadily in the paths of virtue, in opposition to our corrupt nature, and all the vicious customs and maxims of the world. Our blessed Lord who came from heaven *to save us from our sins,* as well as the *punishment* of them, as knowing that it was impossible for us to be *happy* in either world, unless we were *holy,* did not intend by commanding us to take up the cross, that we should bid adieu to all joy and satisfaction indefinitely: but he opens and extends our views beyond time to eternity. He directs us where to place our joys; how to seek satisfaction durable as our being; which is not to be found in gratifying, but in retrenching our sensual appetites; not in obeying the dictates of our irregular passions, but in correcting their exorbitancy, bringing every appetite of the body and power of the soul under subjection to his laws, if we would follow him to heaven. And because he knew we could not do this without great contradiction to our corrupt animality, therefore he enjoins us to take up this cross, and to fight under his banner against the flesh, the world, and the devil. And when, by the grace of God's Holy Spirit, we are so far conquerors, as that we never willingly offend, but still press after greater degrees of Christian perfection, sincerely endeavouring to plant each virtue in our minds, that may through Christ render us pleasing to God; we shall then experience the truth of Solomon's assertion, 'The ways of virtue are ways of pleasantness, and all her paths are peace.'

"I take Kempis to have been an honest weak man, who had more zeal than knowledge, by his condemning all mirth or pleasure as sinful or useless, in opposition to so many direct and plain texts of Scripture. Would you judge of the lawfulness or unlawfulness of pleasure; of the innocence or malignity of actions; take this rule,—Whatever weakens your reason, impairs the tenderness of your conscience, obscures your sense of God, or takes off the relish of spiritual things: in short, whatever increases the strength and authority of your *body* over your *mind* that thing is sin to *you,* however innocent it may be in itself. And so on the contrary.

"'Tis stupid to say nothing is an affliction to a good man. That is an affliction that makes an affliction either to good or bad. Nor do I understand how any man can thank God for present misery; yet do I very well know what it is to rejoice in the midst of deep afflictions; not in the affliction itself, for then it would necessarily cease to be one: but in this we may rejoice, that we are in the hand of a God who never did, and never can, exert his power in any act of injustice, oppression, or cruelty; in the power of that superior wisdom which disposes all events, and has promised that all things shall work together for good (for the spiritual and eternal good) of those that love him. We may rejoice in hope that Almighty goodness will not suffer us to be tempted above that we are able; but will with the temptation make a way to escape, that we may be able to bear it. In a word, we may and ought to rejoice that God has assured us he will never leave or forsake us, but if we continue faithful to him, he will take care to conduct us safely, through all the changes and chances of this mortal life, to those blessed regions of joy and immortality, where sin and sorrow can never enter."

Wroote, July 18, 1725

"———I have often wondered that men should be so vain to amuse themselves by searching into the decrees of God, which no human wit can fathom; and do not rather employ their time and powers in working out their salvation, and making their own calling and election sure. Such studies tend more to confound than inform the understanding; and young people had best let them alone. But since I find you have some scruples concerning our article of predestination, I will tell you my thoughts of the matter; and if they satisfy not, you may desire your father's direction, who is surely better qualified for a casuist than me.

"The doctrine of *predestination*, as maintained by rigid Calvinists is very shocking; and ought utterly to be abhorred, because it charges the most holy God with being the author of sin. And I think you reason very well and justly against it; for it is certainly inconsistent with the justice and goodness of God to lay any man under either a physical or moral necessity of committing sin, and then punish him for doing it.—Far be this from the Lord!—Shall not the Judge of all the earth do right?

"I do firmly believe that God from all eternity hath elected some to everlasting life: but then I humbly conceive, that this election is founded in his foreknowledge, according to that in the eighth of Romans, ver. 29, 30, *Whom he did foreknow, he also did predestinate to be conformed to the image of his Son:—Moreover whom he did predestinate, them he also called; and whom he called, them he also justified; and whom he justified, them he also glorified.*

"*Whom,* in his eternal prescience, God saw would make a right use of their powers and accept of offered mercy, *he did predestinate,*—adopt for his children, his peculiar treasure. And that they might be *conformed to the image of his only Son,* he *called them* to himself by his eternal word, through the preaching of the Gospel; and internally by his Holy Spirit: which *call* they obeying, repenting of their sins, and believing in the Lord Jesus, he *justifies* them,—absolves them from the guilt of all their sins, and acknowledges them as just and righteous persons, through the merits and mediation of Jesus Christ. And *having* thus *justified,* he receives them to *glory,* to heaven.

"This is the sum of what I believe concerning predestination, which I think is agreeable to the analogy of faith; since it does in no wise derogate from the glory of God's free grace, nor impair the liberty of man. Nor can it with more reason be supposed that the prescience of God is the cause that so many finally perish, than that our knowing the sun will rise to-morrow is the cause of its rising." . . .

"Gainsborough, Nov. 27, 1735.

"——— God is Being itself! the I Am! and therefore must necessarily be the Supreme Good! He is so infinitely blessed, that every perception of his blissful presence imparts a vital gladness to the heart. Every degree of approach toward him is, in the same proportion, a degree of happiness. And I often think that were he always present to our mind, as we are present to him, there would be no pain, nor sense of misery. I have long since chose him for my only good! my all! my pleasure, my happiness in this world, as well as in the world to come! And although I have not been so faithful to his grace as I ought to have been; yet I feel my spirit adheres to its choice, and aims daily at cleaving steadfast unto God. . . .

Commentary on the Apostles' Creed

Epworth, Jan. 13, 1709-10.

. . . "Or how should we have had any certainty of our salvation unless God had revealed these things unto us? The *soul* is *immortal,* and must survive all time, even to eternity; and consequently it must have been miserable to the utmost extent of its duration, had we not had that sacred treasure of knowledge which is contained in the books of the Old and New Testament; a treasure infinitely more valuable than the whole world, because therein we find all things necessary for our salvation. There also we find many truths, which though we cannot say it is absolutely necessary that we should know them, (since it is possible to be saved without that knowledge,) yet it is highly convenient that we should; because they give us great light into those things which are necessary to be known, and solve many doubts which could not otherwise be cleared.

"Thus we collect from many passages of Scripture, that before God created the *visible world,* or ever he made man, he created a higher, rank of *intellectual beings,* which we call *angels* or *spirits*; and these were those *bright morning* stars mentioned in *Job,* which sang together; those *sons of God which shouted for joy when the foundations of the earth were laid.* To these he gave a law or rule of action, as he did afterward to the rest of his creation; and they being *free agents,* having a principle of liberty, of choosing or refusing, and of acting accordingly, as they must have, or they could not properly be called either good or evil; for upon this principle of freedom or liberty the principle of election or choice is founded; and upon the *choosing* good or evil depends the being virtuous or vicious, since liberty is the formal essence of moral virtue, that is, it is the *free choice* of a rational being that makes them either good or bad: nor could any one that acts by necessity be even capable of rewards or punishments. . . .

"But the infinite goodness of God, who delighteth that his mercy should triumph over his justice, though he provided no remedy for the fallen angels; yet man being a more simple kind of creature, who perhaps did not sin so maliciously against so much knowledge as those apostate spirits did;

he would not suffer the whole race of mankind to be ruined and destroyed by the fraud and subtilty of Satan: but he laid help upon one that is mighty, that is able and willing to save to the uttermost all such as shall come unto God through him. And this Saviour was that seed of the woman, that was promised should bruise the head of the serpent, break the power of the devil, and bring mankind again into a salvable condition. And upon a view of that satisfaction which Christ would make for the sins of the whole world was the penalty of Adam's disobedience suspended, and he admitted to a second trial; and God renewed his covenant with man, not on the former condition of perfect obedience, but on condition of faith in Christ Jesus, and a sincere though imperfect obedience of the laws of God. I will speak something of these two branches of our duty distinctly.

"By faith in Christ is to be understood an assent to whatever is recorded of him in Holy Scripture; or is said to be delivered by him, either immediately by himself, or mediately by his prophets and apostles; or whatever may by just inferences, or natural consequences, be collected from their writings. But because the greater part of mankind either want leisure or capacity to collect the several articles of faith, which lie scattered up and down throughout the Sacred Writ, the wisdom of the CHURCH hath thought fit to sum them up in a short form of words, commonly called THE APOSTLES' CREED, which, because it comprehends the main of what a Christian ought to believe, I shall briefly explain unto you: and though I have not time at present to bring all the arguments I could to prove the being of God, his divine attributes, and the truth of revealed religion; yet this short paraphrase may inform you what you should intend when you make the solemn confession of our most holy faith; and may withal teach you that it is not to be said after a formal customary manner, but seriously, as in the presence of the almighty God, who observes whether the *heart* join with the *tongue*, and whether your mind do truly assent to what you profess when you say,

I BELIEVE IN GOD.

I do truly and heartily assent to the being of a God, one supreme independent power, who is a Spirit infinitely wise, holy, good, just, true, unchangeable.

"I do believe that this God is a necessary self-existent being; necessary, in that he could not but be, because he derives his existence from no other than himself, but he always is

THE FATHER.

And having all life, all being in himself, all creatures must derive their existence from him; whence he is properly styled the Father of all things, more especially of all spiritual natures, angels and souls of men; and since he is the great *parent* of the universe, it naturally follows that he is

ALMIGHTY.

And this glorious attribute of his omnipotence is conspicuous in that he hath a right of making any thing which he willeth, after that manner which best pleaseth him, according to the absolute freedom of his own will; and a right of possessing all things so made by him as he pleaseth: nor can his almighty infinite power admit of any *weakness, dependence,* or *limitation*; but it extendeth to all things; is boundless, incomprehensible, and eternal. And though we cannot comprehend, or have any adequate conceptions of what so far surpasseth the reach of human understanding, yet it is plainly demonstrable that he is *omnipotent* from his being the

MAKER OF HEAVEN AND EARTH,

Of all things visible: nor could any thing less than almighty power produce the smallest, most inconsiderable thing out of nothing. Not the least spire of grass, or most despicable insect, but bears the divine signature, and carries in its existence a clear demonstration of the Deity. For could we admit of such a wild supposition as that anything could *make* itself, it must necessarily follow that a thing had being before it had a being, that it could *act* before it was, which is a palpable contradiction: from whence among other reasons we conclude, that this beautiful world, that celestial arch over our heads, and all those glorious heavenly bodies, sun, moon, and stars, &c, in fine, the whole system of the universe, were in the beginning made, or created out of nothing, by the eternal power, wisdom, and goodness of the ever blessed God, according to the counsel of his own will; or, as St. Paul better expresses it, Colos. i, 16: 'By him were all things created that are in heaven, and that are in earth, visible and invisible, whether they be thrones, or dominions, or principalities, or powers: all things were created by him.'

AND IN JESUS.

Jesus signifies a *Saviour* ; and by that *name* he was called by the angel Gabriel before his birth, for to show us that he came into the world to save us from our sins, and the punishment they justly deserve; and to repair the damage human nature had sustained by the fall of Adam; that as in Adam all died, so in Christ all should be made alive; and so he became the second general head of all mankind. And as he was promised to our parents in paradise; so was his coming signified by the various types and sacrifices under the law, and foretold by the prophets long before he appeared in the world.

"And this *Saviour,* this Jesus, was the promised Messiah, who was long the hope and expectation of the Jews, the

CHRIST,

which in the original signifies *anointed.* Now among the Jews it was a custom to *anoint* three sorts of persons, prophets, priests, and kings; which anointing did not only show their designation to those offices, but was also usually attended with a special influence, or inspiration of the Holy Spirit, to prepare and qualify them for such offices. Our blessed Lord, who was by his almighty Father sanctified, and sent into the world, was also *anointed,* not with *material* oil, but by the descent of the Holy Ghost upon him, to signify to us that he was our *prophet, priest,* and *king*; and that he should first, as our PROPHET, fully, clearly, reveal the will of God for our salvation, which accordingly he did. And though the Jews had long before received the law by Moses; yet a great part of that law was purely *typical* and *ceremonial*; and all of it that was so was necessarily vacated by the coming of our Saviour: and that part which was *moral,* and consequently of perpetual obligation, they had so corrupted by their misrepresentations and various traditions, that it was not pure and undefiled, as God delivered it on Mount Sinai, which occasioned the words of our Lord, 'Think not that I am come to destroy the law and the prophets; I am not come to destroy, but to fulfil:' to accomplish the predictions of the prophets concerning himself; and to rescue the moral law from those false glosses they had put on it. Though the rest of the world were not altogether without some precepts of morality; yet they lay scattered up and down, in the writings of a few wiser and better than the rest: but morality was never collected into a complete system, till the coming of our Saviour; nor was life and immortality brought fully to light till the preaching of the Gospel.

"He was also our PRIEST, in that he offered up himself a sacrifice to Divine justice in our stead; and by the perfect satisfaction he made, he did *atone* the displeasure of God, and purchase eternal life for us, which was forfeited by the first man's disobedience.

"And as he is our *prophet* and *priest,* so likewise he is our KING, and hath an undoubted right to govern those he hath redeemed by his blood; and as such he will conquer for us all our spiritual enemies, sin and death, and all the powers of the kingdom of darkness; and when he hath perfectly subdued them, he will actually confer upon us, eternal happiness. This satisfaction and purchase that Christ hath made for us is a clear proof of his *divinity,* since no mere man is capable of meriting any thing good from God; and therefore we are obliged to consider him in a state of equality with the Father, being

HIS ONLY SON.

"Though we are all children of the almighty Father, yet hath he one only Son, by an eternal and incomprehensible generation, which *only Son* is Jesus the Saviour; being equal to the Father, as touching his Godhead; but inferior to the Father as touching his manhood. God of God, Light of Light, Very God of Very God; begotten, not made. And this only Son of God we acknowledge to be

OUR LORD;

In that he is co-equal and co-essential with the Father, and by him were all things made. Therefore since we are his *creatures,* we must, with the Apostle St. Thomas, confess him to be *our Lord* and *our God.* But beside this right to our allegiance, which he hath by creation, he hath redeemed us from death and hell, and he hath purchased us with his own blood: so that upon a *double account,* we justly call him Lord, namely, that of *creation* and *purchase.* And as the infinite condescension of the eternal Son of God in assuming our nature was mysterious, and incomprehensible, surpassing the wisest of men or angels to conceive how such a thing might be; so it was requisite and agreeable to the majesty of God, that the conception of his sacred person should be after a manner altogether differing from ordinary generations; accordingly it was he

WHICH WAS CONCEIVED BY THE HOLY GHOST;

Whose miraculous conception was foretold by the angel, when his blessed mother questioned how she who was a *virgin* could conceive. *The Holy Ghost shall come upon thee, and the power of the highest shall overshadow thee; therefore also that holy thing which shall be born of thee shall be called the Son of God.* And as all the sacrifices which represented our Saviour under the law, were to be without spot or blemish; so likewise Christ, the great Christian sacrifice, was not only infinitely pure and holy, not only in his Divine, but also in his human nature, he was perfectly immaculate, having none but God for his Father being

BORN OF THE VIRGIN MARY,

Whose spotless purity no age of the catholic Church hath presumed to question. That the promised Messiah should be born of a virgin is plain from Jer. xxxi, 22, 'The Lord hath created a new thing upon the earth; a woman shall compass a man.' And from Isaiah vii. 14. 'Behold a virgin shall conceive and bear a son, and shall call his name Immanuel.' And this *seed of the woman* must necessarily have assumed our nature, or he could never have been our Jesus, the Savior of the world; for the Divine nature of the *Son* of God is infinitely happy, utterly incapable of any grief, pain, or sense of misery. Nor could its union with humanity any way defile or pollute it or derogate the least from its infinite perfection; so it was only as *man* that he

SUFFERED

those infirmities and calamities incident to human nature.

"What transactions passed between the almighty Father and his eternal Son concerning the redemption of the world we know not: but we are sure that by an express agreement between them, he was from eternity decreed to *suffer* for mankind. And in several places of the Old Testament it was written of the Son of man, that he must *suffer* many things. And the Spirit of Christ that was in the prophets testified before hand the *sufferings* of Christ; particularly in Isaiah liii, we have a sad, but clear, description of the *sufferings* of the Messiah. Indeed, his whole life was one continual scene of misery. No sooner was he born, than he was persecuted by Herod, and forced to flee into Egypt, in the arms of a weak virgin, under the protection of a foster-father. And when he returned into his own country he for thirty years lived in a low condition, probably employed in the mean trade of a carpenter, which made him in the eyes of the world despicable, of no reputation. And when after so long an obscurity he appeared unto men, he entered upon his ministry with the severity of forty days' abstinence.

"Behold the eternal Lord of nature transported into a wild and desolate wilderness, exposed to the inclemency of the air, and tempted by the *apostate spirits!*

"The almighty Being, who justly claims a right to the whole creation, was himself hungry, and athirst; often wearied with painful travelling from place to place. And though he went about doing good; and never sent any one away from him, who wanted relief, without healing their diseases, and casting out those evil spirits which afflicted them; yet was he despised, and rejected of men! The possessor of heaven and earth, the sovereign disposer of all things, from whose bounty all creatures receive what they enjoy of the necessary accommodations of life, was reduced to such a mean estate, that the foxes had holes, and the birds of the air had nests, yet the Son of man had not where to lay his head! All his life he was a man of sorrow, and acquainted with grief. . . .

I BELIEVE IN THE HOLY GHOST;

That he is a person of a real and true subsistence, neither created nor begotten, but proceeding from the Father and the Son:—true and eternal God, who is essentially holy himself, and the author of all holiness in us, by sanctifying our natures, illuminating our minds, rectifying our wills and affections: who co-operateth with the word and sacraments, and whatever else is a mean of conveying grace into the soul. He it was that spoke by the prophets and apostles, and it is he who leadeth us into all truth. He helpeth our infirmities, assures us of our adoption, and will be with

THE HOLY CATHOLIC CHURCH

to the end of the world. The catholic Church is composed of all congregations of men whatever, who hold the faith of Jesus Christ and are obedient to his laws, wherein the pure word of God is preached, and the sacraments duly delivered by such ministers as are regularly consecrated and set apart for such ordinances, according to Christ's institution. And as this Church is called *holy* in respect of its *author,* Jesus,————*end,* glory of God, and salvation of souls, institution of the ministry, administration of the sacraments, preaching of the pure word of God; and of the members of this Church, who are renewed and sanctified by the Holy Spirit, and united to Christ, the supreme head and governor of the Church.

"It is styled catholic, because it is not, like that of the Jews, confined to one place and people; but is disseminated through all nations, extendeth throughout all ages, even to the end of the world. And as there is but one head; so the members, though many, are one body, united together by the same spirit, principally by the three great Christian virtues, faith, hope, and charity. For as we hold the same principles of faith, do all assent to the same truths once delivered to the saints; so have we the same hopes and expectations of eternal life which are promised to all. And as our Lord gave the same mark of distinction to all his disciples,—'By this shall all men know that ye are my disciples if ye love one another;' so this universal love which is diffused throughout the whole body of Christ is the union of charity; and the same ministry and the same orders in the Church make the unity of discipline. But since Christ hath appointed only one way to heaven; so we are not to expect salvation out of the Church which is called catholic, in opposition to heretics and schismatics. And if an angel from heaven should preach any other doctrine than Christ and his apostles have taught, or appoint any other sacraments than Christ hath already instituted, let him be accursed.

"And as the mystical union between Christ and the Church, and the spiritual conjunction of the members with the head, is the fount of that union and communion which the saints have with each other, as being all under the influence of the same head; so death, which only separates bodies for a time, cannot dissolve the union of minds; and therefore it is not only in relation to the saints on earth, but including also those in heaven, we profess to hold

THE COMMUNION OF SAINTS.

Accordingly we believe that all saints, as well those on earth as those in heaven, have communion with God, the Father, Son, and Holy Ghost; with the blessed angels, who not only join in devotion with the *Church triumphant* above, but are likewise sent forth to minister to those who are the heirs of salvation while they remain in this world. And perhaps we do not consider as we ought to do, how much good we receive by the ministration of the holy angels; nor are we sufficiently grateful to those guardian spirits that so often put by ill accidents, watch over us when we sleep, defending us from the assaults of evil men and evil angels. And if they are so mindful of our preservation in this world, we may suppose them much more concerned for our eternal happiness: 'There is joy among the angels in heaven over one sinner that repenteth:'—they are present in our public assemblies, where we in a more especial manner hold communion with them; and it is there we join with all the company of the heavenly host in praising and admiring the supreme Being whom we jointly adore. What knowledge the saints in heaven have of things or persons in this world we cannot determine, nor after what manner we hold communion with them it is not at present easy to conceive.

"That we are all members of the same mystical body of Christ we are very sure; and do all partake of the same vital influence from the same head, and so we are united together; and though we are not actually possessed of the same happiness which they enjoy, yet we have the same Holy Spirit given unto us as an earnest of our eternal felicity with them hereafter. And though their faith is consummated by vision, and their hope by present possession, yet the bond of Christian charity still remains; and as we have great joy and complacency in their felicity, so no doubt they desire and pray for us.

"With the saints on earth we hold communion by the word and sacraments, by praying with and for each other; and in all acts of public or private worship we act upon the same principles and the same motives, having the same promises and hopes of

THE FORGIVENESS OF SINS,

Through Jesus Christ, the Mediator of the new covenant, who gave his life a sacrifice by way of compensation and satisfaction to Divine justice, by which God became reconciled to man, and cancelled the obligation which every sinner lay under to suffer eternal punishment; and he hath appointed in his Church *baptism* for the first remission, and *repentance* for the constant forgiveness of all following trespasses. And now have we confidence toward God, that not only our souls shall be freed from the guilt and punishment of sin by faith in Jesus: but also our bodies may rest in hopes of

THE RESURRECTION OF THE BODY,

That the same almighty power which raised again our blessed Lord, after he had lien three days in the grave, shall again quicken our mortal bodies; shall reproduce the same individual body that slept in the dust, and vitally unite it to the same soul which informed it while on earth. . . .

THE LIFE EVERLASTING.

By everlasting life is not only meant that we shall die no more; for in this sense the damned shall have everlasting life as well as the saints: they shall always have a being, though in intolerable torments; which is infinitely worse than none at all.

"But we are to understand by the life everlasting a full and perfect enjoyment of solid inexpressible joy and felicity,—*Eye hath not seen, nor ear heard, neither hath it entered into the heart of man to conceive, what God hath prepared for those that love him.*

"The soul shall be perfectly sanctified, nor shall it be possible to sin any more. All its faculties shall be purified and exalted: the understanding shall be filled with the beatific vision of the adorable Trinity; shall be illuminated, enlarged, and eternally employed and satisfied in the contemplation of the sublimest truths. *Here* we see as in a glass,—have dark and imperfect perceptions of God: but *there* we shall behold him as he is, shall know as we are known. Not that we shall fully comprehend the Divine nature, as he doth ours; that is impossible; for he is infinite and incomprehensible, and we though in heaven shall be finite still; but our apprehension of his being and perfections shall be clear, just, and true. *We shall see him as he is*: shall never be troubled with misapprehensions or false conceptions of him more: those dark and mysterious methods of Providence which *here* puzzle and confound the wisest heads to reconcile them with his justice and goodness shall be *there* unriddled in a moment; and we shall clearly perceive that all the evils which befall good men in this life were the corrections of a merciful Father; that the furnace of affliction, which now seems so hot and terrible to nature, had nothing more than a lambent flame, which was not designed to consume us; but only to purge away our dross, to purify and prepare the mind for its abode among those blessed ones that passed through the same trials before us into the celestial paradise. And we shall for ever adore and praise that infinite power and goodness which safely conducted the soul through the rough waves of this tempestuous ocean to the calm haven of peace and everlasting tranquillity. Nor shall we have the same *sentiments there* which we had *here*: but shall clearly discern that our afflictions *here* were our choicest mercies. Our *wills* shall no longer be averse from God's, but shall be for ever lost in that of our blessed Creator's. No conflicts with unruly passions; no pain or misery shall ever find admittance into that heavenly kingdom. . . .

"I have purposely omitted many arguments for the *being of God,* the *Divine authority of Scripture,* the *truth of revealed religion,* or *future judgment.* The last article I have left very imperfect, because I intend to write *on all these subjects* for the use of my children when I have more leisure. I shall only add a few words to prepare your mind for the *second part* of my discourse, *Obedience to the Laws of God,* which I shall quickly send you.

"As the defilement of our natures is the source and original of all our actual iniquities and transgressions of the laws of God; so the first regular step we can take toward amendment is to be deeply sensible of, grieved and humbled for, our original sin. And though (I believe) the *damning guilt* of that sin is washed away by baptism, by those who die before they are capable of known and actual transgressions; yet experience shows us that the *power* of it does still survive in such as attain to riper years; and this is what the apostle complains of in Romans vii.

"This is the *carnal nature*; that law in our members, which wars against the law of the mind, and brings into captivity to the law of sin.

"And when the work of conversion or regeneration is begun by the Holy Spirit, yet still corrupt nature maintains a conflict with Divine grace: nor shall this enemy be entirely conquered, till death shall be swallowed up of victory; till this mortal shall have put on immortality. . . . "

Section IV

1800–1947 C.E.

Ann Lee,
Testimonies
(1826)

Ann Lee (1736–84)

Ann Lee (or Lees) was born in Manchester, England, in 1736, but nothing about her was written until at least thirty years after her death. We know that she received no formal education and that she worked at a variety of manual jobs. She was attracted by Quakerism and converted in 1756. After her marriage to A. Standerin in 1762, she bore four children in four years' time, all of whom died in infancy. Lee came increasingly to see concupiscence as the root of all forms of evil—war, disease, poverty, oppression. She began to promote celibacy so actively that she was imprisoned, during which time she had a vision of Christ commissioning her to continue his earthly work, and to preach freedom from sexual cohabitation. Upon her release she became leader of a small band of "Shaking Quakers" (later to be known as Shakers) who called her "Mother Ann" and found embodied in her the Second Coming of Jesus Christ. Anyone could experience this inner resurrection through confession and celibacy, thereby becoming free of carnal lust. Continued persecution and imprisonment convinced the group to leave England for America in 1774, where they established an egalitarian community committed to celibacy, common resources, and strict patterns of religious life. Through the next century, the Shakers attracted many converts and founded eighteen societies before the Civil War.

A Testimony

These testimonies, though not written by Ann Lee, represent the content and implications of her teachings as lived out in the lives of her followers. The text was compiled by her followers in 1826 as *Testimonies Concerning the Character and Ministry of Mother Ann Lee*. As with the earlier Testimonies, published in 1816, the purpose of this material was not so much to provide historical data concerning Ann Lee as it was to provide a theological and ecclesial confession of sorts—a confession of what Shakerism was, of how lives had been touched, and of how Mother Ann had shaped the community and continued to shape it after her death.

TESTIMONIES CONCERNING THE CHARACTER AND MINISTRY OF MOTHER ANN LEE

TESTIMONY OF HANNAH COGSWELL.

I received faith in the present testimony of the gospel in the fore part of January, 1781. I was then in my eighteenth year. I went to Watervliet to visit Mother and the Elders, and was received into their family. . . .

I can say, for one, that I have not been led blindfold by a vain imagination these forty-five years past. I know by the revelation of God in my own soul, that Mother was the Lord's anointed, and that Christ really began his second appearance in her, and dwelt in her, and that her body was a temple for the Holy Spirit. (See I Cor. vi. 19.) However incredible this may appear to an unbelieving world, we know that we are not left in darkness and doubt concerning these things; they are as clear and certain to us as the light of the sun in a clear day. Here we find the promise of Christ verified: "He that followeth me shall not walk in darkness." (John viii. 12.)

I know of a certainty, that Mother Ann had the gift of prophecy and the revelation of God, by which she was able to search the hearts of those who came to see her; for I have myself been an eye and ear witness of it. I have known some to come to her under a cloak of deception, thinking to conceal their sins in her presence; and I have seen her expose them by the searching power of truth, and set their sins before them; so that they have been constrained to confess, with guilt and shame, that she had told them the truth, and to acknowledge that the light and revelation of God was in her. I am not insensible of the spirit of unbelief which prevails in the world against the spirit of truth, and especially against testimonies of this kind;

but I can say with the apostle Paul, "I speak forth the words of truth and soberness;" my eyes have seen and my ears have heard what I have stated; it is no vain imagination. . . .

TESTIMONY OF ANNE MATHEWSON.

My father's name was Philip Mathewson; I was born at Providence, in Rhode-Island, June 24th, 1763. In my childhood and youth I was instructed by my parents in the principles of morality and religion. In my youthful days I had a feeling sense of my lost state, and became greatly awakened and exercised in my mind about religion. My earnest desire was to find some way of deliverance from sin—some religion which I could depend on for salvation. . . .

When I heard of Mother Ann and the Elders, from the very nature of the report, I fully believed them to be the true followers of Christ, and from the operation of the Divine Spirit in my soul I was fully confirmed in it, and felt a great desire to go and see them. In February, 1782, I visited them for the first time, at Harvard, being then in my 19th year. The first night after my arrival, I lodged in the same room with Mother. She received me with kindness, and taught me the way of God. I felt full confidence in her testimony, and had a privilege to confess my sins. This I did in the sincerity of my soul, as doing it to God, in the presence of his witnesses, and found great releasement of mind by it. I then felt a full assurance of salvation, provided I kept my faith and obedience, which, through the mercy of God, I have never lost to this day. . . .

Their conduct and conversation was at all times according to the gospel. I have enjoyed many precious privileges with them, and have received much heavenly instruction and much good and wholesome counsel from them, both in public and private. They were always faithful in their duty, at all times, "both in season and out of season." In teaching, admonishing, reproving, encouraging and comforting, they spared no pains. Mother Ann, especially, was always alive in the work of God. Her spirit seemed wholly devoted to God. In reproving sin and all manner of evil, she was like a flaming sword; yet she knew well how to separate between the precious and the vile. She would not indulge any evil propensity in herself nor in others; yet her charity to souls disposed to repent and turn to God, would often seem to melt her soul in tears. I cannot feel the least doubt or scruple of her being a chosen woman anointed of the Lord, any more than I can doubt her existence. . . .

The present generation of people boast much of living in an enlightened age, and of being blessed with the bright effusions of the gospel of light; and yet how few there are who appear to understand even the plain and simple comparisons which Jesus Christ made of the natural things of time and sense! There are many who do not seem to understand that *a tree is known by its fruit;* that a thorn-bush cannot bring forth grapes, nor figs grow on thistles; "O faithless and perverse generation!—How is it that ye do not understand?" Many Bible Societies have been formed, and missionaries have been sent abroad with the professed object of spreading the sacred truths of the gospel of Christ, as recorded in the scriptures; yet blindness and ignorance are so prevalent at home, that the people "are like the heath in the desert;" they know not whence good cometh. It is indeed lamentable that darkness, depravity and loss, have so covered the earth—that such a vast portion of the human race are so involved in blindness that they do not know the day of their visitation. How evident it is that the Jews did not know, tho they were called God's chosen people: for if they had known that Christ was the Lord from Heaven, they would not have crucified him. (I Cor. ii. 8.) And did the Gentiles of that day know any better? Or do those of the present day know any better?

There are but few, in this day, who will pretend to deny the agency of the first woman in leading mankind into sin. Why then should it be thought incredible, that the agency of a woman should necessarily be first in leading the human race out of sin? Mother Ann's testimony and example, and all her fruits, evidently show that she was led by a spirit totally opposite to that which led and influenced the first woman. To the truth of this, all who have heard her testimony and seen her example, and faithfully followed it, can bear witness; because they have in reality, been led out of sin thereby; and they are able to testify that, "she taught as never *woman* taught before." . . .

TESTIMONY OF AMOS STOWER.

. . . In obedience to their doctrine, I confessed my sins to God in the presence of the Elders; and by them I was taught obedience to my parents, and faithfulness in all things; and their instructions felt like the word of God to me. By continuing in obedience to that word, I have proved it to be the word of God in very deed: for by it I obtained the power of salvation from sin. Hence I know of a certainty that the testimony which I received from these parents in the gospel, is the power of God unto salvation, and must of necessity come from God through their ministration.

Their doctrine is indeed crossing to the elements of an evil nature in every soul that receives it; which is a further proof that it proceeds not from an evil source, but from the source of all goodness. And the effect it produces in every faithful soul, is a full confirmation that it is indeed the true doctrine of Christ; because it makes such souls the real heirs and possessors of those blessings which he promised to his faithful followers. It makes them poor in spirit; it makes them hunger and thirst after righteousness; it makes them peace-makers, and the like. It also saves them from the corruptions of the flesh through lust; from evil surmising and jealousy; from envying and strife; from hatred and malice; from evil speaking and all intemperate language; from intemperance in eating and drinking; and from every thing which is contrary to the law of Christ.

The gospel of Christ which we have received from Mother Ann Lee and those with her, as well as from their successors in the ministry, is in truth and reality, our only hope of eternal life. And this gospel is a durable and abiding treasure in every faithful Believer. It is "a well of water springing up to everlasting life," which continually nourishes and supports the Soul in those scenes of trial and tribulation which it must pass through in the work of regeneration.

We were instructed in the beginning of our faith, to prove the way of God for ourselves; that we might have rejoicing in ourselves, and not in another. This I have done, and have found the benefit of it. We were told that when we came to see the branches flourish, we might then know that the root is holy. And truly, when we see the branches grow and flourish in righteousness, from such a small and humble beginning, we must know, for ourselves, that the foundation was righteous, and in righteousness hath the hand of God planted it. We were also told that, if we would hearken to the voice of the Lord our God, and do whatsoever we were taught, we should be protected.

These promises have been amply fulfilled in every faithful soul who has travelled in reconciliation to the cross of Christ, revealed through Mother Ann and her successors in the gospel. And their preaching and labors in the vineyard of Christ have not been in vain: for we have thereby "tasted the good word of God and the powers of the world to come." And this has been an abiding substance with every true and faithful Believer, by day and by night, from the first of our faith. . . .

TESTIMONY OF THANKFUL BARCE.

. . . Mother and the Elders always maintained a strong testimony against all sin. They taught us to abstain from "the lust of the flesh, the lust of the eye and the pride of life;"—to take up our crosses against deceit and lies—against all fraud, theft and intemperance—against wars and fightings, and every kind of evil. They taught us to confess and forsake our sins; and if we had wronged or injured any of our fellow creatures, to go and make restitution to the full satisfaction of the injured party, and thus fulfil the strict demands of the moral law; and follow Christ in the regeneration, by a daily cross against the nature of evil.

By becoming personally and intimately acquainted with them, I found their lives and conversation to correspond with their testimony. According to their teaching, I confessed my sins to God, and told these his faithful witnesses what I had done: for I fully believed that in the *communion of saints,* there was *forgiveness of sins.* By faithful obedience to what I was taught, I received the gifts of God, and found that power over my own sinful passions that I was never able to find before, and which gave me peace and justification. I visited Mother Ann at different times, and in different places; and I never saw any thing in her or the Elders, as far as respected their christian precepts and examples, but displayed a spirit of love and peace, gentleness and meekness, forbearance and long suffering. And tho their testimony was sharp and powerful against the fallen nature of man; yet they were kind and merciful to the humble and penitent soul that was convicted of sin, and sought the mercy of God. If I ever saw the image of Christ displayed in human clay, I saw it in Mother Ann. I considered her a perfect pattern of piety to all who saw her.

When the wicked came to take Mother and the Elders to prison, I was present, and was an eye witness to the scene; and to us it was truly a mournful scene. She prayed earnestly that they might be able to endure with patience all that should come upon them. She often prayed for her persecutors, when they came to abuse her, in these words: "Father, forgive them; for they know not what they do." I feel under no necessity of asking those who seldom or never saw Mother Ann, what kind of person she was; because I know for myself. I was with Mother and the Elders several weeks at Hancock and Richmond; and was knowing to their being accused of swearing and blasphemy, drunkenness and fighting; but I saw none of these things among them. I there saw several mobs who came to take Mother; and I knew they were under the influence of *something* which made them act very inhumanly. Had she been lewd woman, as they said, they never would have persecuted her as they did. It was the purity and innocence of her life, and the pointed plainness of her testimony against the sins and abominations in which they lived, that excited their enmity against her, and caused them to revile and persecute her.

I was with her, day and night, for weeks together; and I knew her purity and innocence too well to give credit to the false accusations of the wicked against her. I was with her at Ashfield, and saw the mighty power of God among the people, through her ministration. I have known her to search out sin, and expose the secret thoughts of the heart, by the discerning power of God, and have seen sinners tremble before her heart searching testimony. When she was at Nathan Goodrich's, in Hancock, I was there, and prepared victuals for her and the Elders, and took care of her room, and saw and knew every thing she had in the room, and had a fair opportunity to know that she had nothing to support drunkenness or any kind of intemperance. I know of a certainty that Christ did commence his second appearance in Mother Ann, "without sin unto salvation." And I am thankful to God that I have seen her and believed her testimony: for it has saved me from sin, and still affords me daily peace and consolation. . . .

TESTIMONY OF COMSTOCK BETTS.

When I first heard of the testimony maintained by Mother Ann Lee and the Elders with her, and understood the nature of it, my mind was forcibly struck with doctrines which, tho new and strange, appeared so consistent with truth and reason, and so much in harmony with the testimony of Jesus Christ and his apostles. Their testimony was, that Christ had come "the second time, without sin unto salvation;" that they had come as God's witnesses to the people and were sent to teach the way of salvation; that all sin and every kind of iniquity was condemned; that they had obtained power over sin; that the call of God to the people was, to confess all their sins to God, in the presence of his witnesses, and to forsake them forever. They also taught the necessity of confessing sin, and of hating and crucify-ing the carnal nature of the flesh, as the only means by which souls could enter in at the strait gate, and walk in the narrow way that leads to eternal life.

All this appeared reasonable and right to me: for I did not believe that any one could follow Christ in the regeneration, while living in any known sin. But my natural feelings, at that time, were very far from yielding obedience to this work. And I presume I never should have been one of this despised and persecuted people called Shakers, if I could have found any other way, short of this humiliating way of the cross, in which I could have felt any real hope of acceptance with God. But I confess I could see no way of salvation, only in obedience to this testimony. Many of the people who lived near me had embraced this testimony, and set out in this way, more than three years, before I confessed my sins. I frequently attended their meetings, and their worship appeared very solemn and heavenly to me. I felt more and more affected with my case: for I knew that I was a sinner, and expected, if I should continue in my sins, that I must go to hell. . . .

Accordingly, in August, 1783, I went to Daniel Goodrich, sen. who was a leader among the people, and confessed my sins to him. Soon after this, I went to see Mother and the Elders, at Watervliet, and was received with great kindness and charity. After tarrying several days, being greatly satisfied with what I had heard and seen, and feeling an increase of the work of God in my own soul, I returned home in peace. I soon went a second time, and had much opportunity with Mother and the Elders, which I esteemed as a great privilege. In both of these visits, I was greatly satisfied with the godly example which was manifested in all their words and works. Their feelings seemed wholly devoted to do the will of God. I felt so well satisfied with what I had heard and seen, that I went to Mother and begged the privilege of living there, which she granted. . . .

TESTIMONY OF JOHN WARNER.

. . . As their testimony was plain, powerful and explicit, and pointedly declared that every one would receive a reward according to his works; that, "he that covereth his sins should not prosper; but whoso confesseth and forsaketh them should have mercy;" I was at length induced to yield to the power of conviction. I therefore determined, as in the presence of him who searcheth the secrets of all hearts to make a sacrifice, once for all, and bring my deeds to light, by coming to an open confession every secret sin that I had ever committed. This I did, in truth and honesty, according to the best of my understanding and memory. In so doing, I felt immediately released from the guilt and condemnation under which I had long labored, and found a sensible and undoubted forgiveness of my past life. I then resolved, from my heart, to break off from the friendship of the world, with all its vain allurements, and to follow Christ in the regeneration. And I have found an increasing victory over the propensities of a carnal nature, from that day to this.

This experience, (if I had no other evidence,) I find fully sufficient to confirm my faith and confidence in the present work of God, beyond the shadow of a doubt. Those truths which have been confirmed by a long experience of actual obedience and the constant testimony of a living witness within, can never be doubted. This testimony assures me that Jesus Christ, that despised Nazarene, who was accused by the rebellious Jews, and haughty scribes and Pharisees, as a wine-bibber, and a friend of publicans and sinners, was the first pillar in the regeneration, to call souls from darkness to light, and from the power of Satan unto God. And this same testimony equally assures me that Ann Lee, that despised female, who is equally accused by rebellious sinners, and modern scribes and Pharisees, of intoxication and lewdness, was anointed of God as the second heir in the all important work of redemption, as all can bear witness who, from the heart, have obeyed her heavenly precepts, and followed her Christ-like example. . . .

CHAPTER TWENTY - NINE

Jarena Lee, *Autobiography* (early 1800s)

Jarena Lee (b. 1783)

Born February 11, 1783, at Cape May, New Jersey, Lee left home at age seven to become a maid in a household some sixty miles from her home. Though Lee is recognized as the first female preacher in the African Methodist Episcopal Church, she was never actually ordained. Her call to preach came when she was twenty-four. At that time she approached Richard Allen, then leader of what would become African Methodism, who denied her a preaching license. There were no formal precedents for female preachers, according to Allen, but Lee was encouraged to hold prayer meetings and to exhort. This she did ably, traveling extensively to "exhort" and teach. Lee and many other women within the A.M.E. tradition had successful preaching ministries, though none were ever licensed or ordained. In 1836 she published a detailed record of her call and her ministry.

An Account of Her Call to Preach the Gospel

The full title of this work, *The Life and Religious Experience of Jarena Lee, a Coloured Lady, Giving an Account of Her Call to Preach the Gospel. Revised and Corrected from the Original Manuscript, Written by Herself,* gives the reader some expectation about the breadth of the material covered as well as the central importance of call to Jarena Lee. She takes her opening text for this autobiographical work from a passage from Joel: "And it shall come to pass, that I will pour out my Spirit upon all flesh; and your sons, and your *daughters* shall prophesy" (Joel 2:28). Certainly her lengthy career as a preacher and evangelist bore the fruit of this conviction that she was a daughter called. This account, published in 1836, details some of her early religious experiences in the African Methodist Episcopal Church and the struggle of her soul with God's acceptance of her. In this excerpt she also expounds briefly upon the role of sanctification in the Christian life, her call to preach and, finally, the "operation of the Spirit," even in one with no schooling.

THE LIFE AND EXPERIENCES OF JARENA LEE . . .

. . . I inquired of the head cook of the house respecting the rules of the Methodists, as I knew she belonged to that society, who told me what they were; on which account I replied, that I should not be able to abide by such strict rules not even one year;—however, I told her that I would go with her and hear what they had to say.

The man who was to speak in the afternoon of that day, was the Rev. Richard Allen, since bishop of the African Episcopal Methodists in America. During the labors of this man that afternoon, I had come to the conclusion, that this is the people to which my heart unites, and it so happened, that as soon as the service closed he invited such as felt a desire to flee the wrath to come, to unite on trial with them—I embraced the opportunity. Three weeks from that day, my soul was gloriously converted to God, under preaching, at the very outset of the sermon. The text was barely pronounced, which was: "I perceive thy heart is not right in the sight of God" [Acts 8:21], when there appeared to *my* view, in the centre of the heart *one* sin; and this was *malice,* against one particular individual, who had strove deeply to injure me, which I resented. At this discovery I said, *Lord* I forgive *every* creature. That instant, it appeared to me, as if a garment, which had entirely enveloped my whole person, even to my fingers ends, split at the crown of my head, and was stripped away from me, passing like a shadow, from my sight—when the glory of God seemed to cover me in its stead.

That moment, though hundreds were present, I did leap to my feet, and declare that God, for Christ's sake, had pardoned the sins of my soul. Great was the ecstasy of my mind, for I felt that not only the sin of *malice* was pardoned, but all other sins were swept away together. That day was the first when my heart had believed, and my tongue had made confession unto salvation—the first words uttered, a part of that song, which shall fill eternity with its sound, was *glory to God*. For a few moments I had power to exhort sinners, and to tell of the wonders and of the goodness of him who had clothed me with *his* salvation. During this, the minister was silent, until my soul felt its duty had been performed, when he declared another witness of the power of Christ to forgive sins on earth, was manifest in my conversion. . . .

Although at this time, when my conviction was so great, yet I knew not that Jesus Christ was the Son of God, the second person in the adorable trinity. I knew him not in the pardon of my sins, yet I felt a consciousness that if I died without pardon, that my lot must inevitably be damnation. If I would pray—I knew not how. I could form no connexion of ideas into words; but I knew the Lord's prayer; this I uttered with a loud voice, and with all my might and strength. I was the most ignorant creature in the world; I did not even know that Christ had died for the sins of the world, and to save sinners. Every circumstance, however, was so directed as still to continue and increase the sorrows of my heart, which I now know to have been a godly sorrow which wrought repentance, which is not to be repented of. Even the falling of the dead leaves from the forests, and the dried spires of the mown grass, showed me that I too must die, in like manner. But my case was awfully different from that of the grass of the field, or the wide spread decay of a thousand forests, as I felt within me a living principle, an immortal spirit, which cannot die, and must forever either enjoy the smiles of its Creator, or feel the pangs of ceaseless damnation. . . .

I continued in this happy state of mind for almost three months, when a certain coloured man, by name William Scott, came to pay me a religious visit. He had been for many years a faithful follower of the Lamb; and he had also taken much time in visiting the sick and distressed of our colour, and understood well the great things belonging to a man of full stature in Christ Jesus.

In the course of our conversation, he inquired if the Lord had justified my soul. I answered, yes. He then asked me if he had sanctified me. I answered, no; and that I did not know what that was. He then undertook to instruct me further in the knowledge of the Lord respecting this blessing.

He told me the progress of the soul from a state of darkness, or of nature, was threefold; or consisted in three degrees, as follows:—First, conviction for sin. Second, justification from sin. Third, the entire sanctification of the soul to God. I thought this description was beautiful, and immediately believed in it. He then inquired if I would promise to pray for this in my secret devotions. I told him, yes. Very soon I began to call upon the Lord to show me all that was in my heart, which was not according to his will. Now there appeared to be a new struggle commencing in my soul, not accompanied with fear, guilt, and bitter distress, as while under my first conviction for sin; but a labouring of the mind to know more of the right way of the Lord. I began now to feel that my heart was not clean in his sight; that there yet remained the roots of bitterness, which if not destroyed, would ere long sprout up from these roots, and overwhelm me in a new growth of the brambles and brushwood of sin.

By the increasing light of the Spirit, I had found there yet remained the root of pride, anger, self-will, with many evils, the result of fallen nature. I now became alarmed at this discovery, and began to fear that I had been deceived in my experience. I was now greatly alarmed, lest I should fall away from what I knew I had enjoyed; and to guard against this I prayed almost incessantly, without acting faith on the power and promises of God to keep me from falling. I had not yet learned how to war against temptation of this kind. Satan well knew that if he could succeed in making me disbelieve my conversion, that he would catch me either on the ground of complete despair, or on the ground of infidelity. For if all I had passed through was to go for nothing, and was but a fiction, the mere ravings of a disordered mind, then I would naturally be led to believe that there is nothing in religion at all.

From this snare I was mercifully preserved, and led to believe that there was yet a greater work than that of pardon to be wrought in me. I retired to a secret place (after having sought this blessing, as well as I could, for nearly three months, from the time brother Scott had instructed me respecting it) for prayer, about four o'clock in the afternoon. I had struggled long and hard, but found not the desire of my heart. When I rose from my knees, there seemed a voice speaking to me, as I yet stood in a leaning posture—"Ask for sanctification." When to my surprise, I recollected that I had not even thought of it in my whole prayer. It would seem Satan had hidden the very object from my mind, for which I had purposely kneeled to pray. But when this voice whispered in my heart, saying, "Pray for sanctification," I again bowed in the same place, at the same time, and said, "Lord *sanctify* my soul for Christ's sake?" That very instant, as if lightning had darted through me, I sprang to my feet, and cried, "The Lord has sanctified my soul!" There was none to hear this but the angels who stood around to witness my joy—and Satan, whose malice raged the more. That Satan was there, I knew; for no sooner had I cried out, "The Lord has sanctified my soul," than there seemed another voice behind me, saying, "No, it is too great a work to be done." But another spirit said, "Bow down for the witness—I received it—*thou art sanctified!*" The first I knew of myself after that, I was standing in the yard with my hands spread out, and looking with my face toward heaven.

I now ran into the house and told them what had happened to me, when, as it were, a new rush of the same ecstasy came upon me, and caused me to feel as if I were in an ocean of light and bliss.

During this, I stood perfectly still, the tears rolling in a flood from my eyes. So great was the joy, that it is past description. There is no language that can describe it, except that which was heard by St. Paul, when he was caught up to the third heaven, and heard words which it was not lawful to utter.

MY CALL TO PREACH THE GOSPEL.

Between four and five years after my sanctification, on a certain time, an impressive silence fell upon me, and I stood as if some one was about to speak to me, yet I had no such thought in my heart. But to my utter surprise there seemed to sound a voice which I thought I distinctly heard, and most certainly understood, which said to me, "Go preach the Gospel!" I immediately replied aloud, "No one will believe me." Again I listened, and again the same voice seemed to say, "Preach the Gospel; I will put words in your mouth, and will turn your enemies to become your friends."

. . . Two days after, I went to see the preacher in charge of the African Society, who was the Rev. Richard Allen. . . .

I now told him, that the Lord had revealed it to me, that I must preach the gospel. He replied by asking, in what sphere I wished to move in? I said, among the Methodists. He then replied, that a Mrs. Cook, a Methodist lady, had also some time before requested the same privilege; who it was believed, had done much good in the way of exhortation, and holding prayer meetings; and who had been permitted to do so by the verbal license of the preacher in charge at the time. But as to women preaching, he said that our Discipline knew nothing at all about it—that it did not call for women preachers. This I was glad to hear, because it removed the fear of the cross—but no sooner did this feeling cross my mind, than I found that a love of souls had in a measure departed from me; that holy energy which burned within me, as a fire, began to be smothered. This I soon perceived.

O how careful ought we to be, lest through our by-laws of church government and discipline, we bring into disrepute even the word of life.

For as unseemly as it may appear now-a-days for a woman to preach, it should be remembered that nothing is impossible with God. And why should it be thought impossible, heterodox, or improper, for a woman to preach? seeing the Saviour died for the woman as well as the man.

If a man may preach, because the Saviour died for him, why not the woman? seeing he died for her also. Is he not a whole Saviour, instead of a half one? as those who hold it wrong for a woman to preach, would seem to make it appear. . . .

THE SUBJECT OF MY CALL TO PREACH RENEWED.

. . . But here I feel myself constrained to give over, as from the smallness of this pamphlet I cannot go through with the whole of my journal, as it would probably make a volume of two hundred pages; which, if the Lord be willing, may at some future day be published. But for the satisfaction of such as may follow after me, when I am no more, I have recorded how the Lord called me to his work, and how he has kept me from falling from grace, as I feared I should. In all things he has proved himself a God of truth to me; and in his service I am now as much determined to spend and be spent, as at the very first. My ardour for the progress of his cause abates not a whit, so far as I am able to judge, though I am now something more than fifty years of age.

As to the nature of uncommon impressions, which the reader cannot but have noticed, and possibly sneered at in the course of these pages, they may be accounted for in this way: It is known that the blind have the sense of hearing in a manner much more acute than those who can see: also their sense of feeling is exceedingly fine, and is found to detect any roughness on the smoothest surface, where those who can see can find none. So it may be with such as I am, who has never had more than three months schooling; and wishing to know much of the way and law of God, have therefore watched the more closely the operations of the Spirit, and have in consequence been led thereby. But let it be remarked that I have never found that Spirit to lead me contrary to the Scriptures of truth, as I understand them. "For as many as are led by the Spirit of God are the sons of God."—Rom. viii. 14.

I have now only to say, May the blessing of the Father, and of the Son, and of the Holy Ghost, accompany the reading of this poor effort to speak well of his name, wherever it may be read. AMEN.

CHAPTER THIRTY

Phoebe Palmer,
Entire Devotion to God
(1845)

Phoebe Palmer (1807–74)

Born in New York City as Phoebe Worrall, Palmer grew up in a cultured and educated environment. In 1827 she married a doctor, Walter Clark Palmer, and found in this happy marriage a kindred spirit who shared her participation in Methodist gatherings and study. Soon she provided leadership, teaching and speaking to groups about salvation and the doctrine of "entire sanctification." After a time of deep despair following the death of her child, she experienced a "second blessing." Palmer held that the first blessing of grace was bestowed in conversion, and that complete consecration to Christ—that is, giving one's all as an altar to God—brought the second blessing of entire sanctification. Such sanctification assured one that love was the pure motive of the consecrated self. This conviction was not so much based on personal mystical experience as it was on Palmer's confidence in God's promises in Scripture concerning being made holy. She was active in social reform, initiating several social ministries to New York's slums, and founding the Five Points Mission in 1850, which included a chapel, a school, and free housing. She sought equal rights for women, though she never took an actively public stand on slavery. Her leadership in prayer meetings, Bible study, and testimony makes her a significant founder of the holiness movement of the nineteenth century.

Entire Devotion to God

This text was first published in 1845 under the title *Present to My Christian Friend on Entire Devotion to God,* and it quickly became a classic. The reader hears the warmth and affection of Palmer's voice, and has the sense that the author is, indeed, speaking directly to him or her, a fact that accounts in part for the popularity of the book. As important, however, is the insistent call that her friend decide to seek holiness and come to "entire devotion to God." For Palmer such a decision includes the subsequent fulfillment of the claims of the holy life attendant upon entire devotion. She argues carefully and thoroughly, grounding her claims in Scripture, but not tediously so. Her tone is sometimes beseeching, sometimes enthusiastic, as she lays out her central theological claims concerning Christian faith and life.

ENTIRE DEVOTION TO GOD

INTRODUCTION

MY BELOVED CHRISTIAN FRIEND—

Will you accept of this little token of regard from one deeply interested in your welfare? I have received your friendship as a precious gift from God. Yes, "Jesus gives me my friends," and I have resolved on valuing and also cherishing your friendship as a precious gift from Him. You will feel with me that friendships thus bestowed are Divine responsibilities. Then, beloved one, let us be faithful to each other; and may our communings during our short sojourn here be so directed as shall in the highest possible degree tell towards our mutual well-being in eternity.

I would not needlessly sadden your heart, but my thoughts are now dwelling on the certainty of that period when our friendship on earth will close. Perhaps before the expiration of the present year you or I may be called suddenly, "in such an hour as we think not," to meet the Son of Man. My intense solicitude for you moves me to faithfulness beyond what cold formality might warrant.

Permit me, then, beloved one, to ask, Are you ready? Have you on the white robe? No longer think of holiness as a doctrine peculiar to a *sect*, but rather as a doctrine peculiar to the *Bible,* as the only fitness for admission to the society of the bloodwashed in Heaven.

If you are not a *holy* Christian, you are not a *Bible* Christian. I have been much concerned that till this period you should have remained indefinite in your experience on this point. In endeavouring to show the Standard of Bible fitness for Heaven, and the manner of attaining it, I have taken it in my way to answer three questions, which I am sure you will regard as infinitely important. . . .

I.

HOLINESS

Dost thou turn away with half-hearted eye, yielding to an impression indefinitely formed, that this, for the present, is a subject that does not demand special attention? Let us for a few moments examine the foundation on which this impression rests, and know whether it is warranted. We will take the word of God for our text-book, and not, "What does my neighbour, or what does my Christian friend, think of the *doctrine* of holiness?" No; for thereby we should be in danger of being influenced by the traditions of men. To the law and to the testimony, and not to the experience or practice of this or that professor, however high in experience or station. What does God say to *me* on this subject? What does He NOW require of me in relation to it? And how should these requirements affect my *present* conduct? And then let us firmly purpose, in the strength of the Lord Jehovah, that every future effort shall be correspondingly directed.

Let us take a declaration from the word of God—a declaration which, at a glance, covers the ground we would occupy, involving requirements weighty and far-reaching as eternity—"Follow peace with all men, and *holiness,* without which no man shall see the Lord." Had attention been called to this article by the words, "To one who intends to seek God, or to make sure work for Heaven," your heart would probably at once, as your eye met the article, have said, "Why, that is something for *me.*" Then you need not be assured that the attainment of the end is utterly impossible without the use of the means. Thus you at once come in possession of the knowledge that it is absolutely necessary that *you* should be *holy,* if you would God.

But perhaps you may say, "I am convinced that holiness is necessary, and I intend to have it before I am called into the presence of God." Ah! hear His voice saying unto thee, "Watch: for ye know not what hour your Lord doth come." Think of the many, both of the prepared and the unprepared, who have been called without a moment's warning to meet God.

Scores will be in the eternal world before the return of this day next week, who expect it as little as yourself; and the voice still continues to say, "What I say unto you I say unto *all,* 'Watch.' "

Perhaps you are saying, "I would be holy; I would not leave the attainment of it for any future period, not one day; no, not one hour would I delay;

284

but I cannot get my eye distinctly fixed on the object. At times I get a glimpse, but mainly it seems to stand as an attainment quite beyond my reach; and too often do I find myself giving way to the persuasion that it cannot be well apprehended, except by those more deeply experienced in the things of God." Let me assure you, dear friend, that as surely as you heed holiness *now,* so surely it is for you *now.* The provisions of the Gospel are all suited to the exigencies of the present time. Are you commanded to be ready for the coming of your Lord *now?* Then holiness is a blessing which it is now your privilege and also your duty to enjoy.

We will now endeavour, as promised, to answer three important questions. First, What is implied in Gospel holiness or sanctification? Second, How may we enter upon the enjoyment of a state of holiness? Third, What will be the advantages to ourselves and others of living in possession of it?

II.

WHAT IS GOSPEL HOLINESS, OR SANCTIFICATION?

GOSPEL holiness is that *state* which is attained by the believer when, through *faith* in the infinite merit of the Saviour, body and soul, with every ransomed faculty, are ceaselessly presented, a living sacrifice, to God; the purpose of the soul being steadily bent to know nothing among men, save Christ and Him crucified, and the eye of faith fixed on "the Lamb of God which taketh away the sin of the world. In obedience to the requirement of God, the sacrifice is presented *through* Christ, and the soul at once proves that "He is able to save them to the *uttermost* that come unto God by Him."

Holiness implies salvation from sin, a redemption from *all* iniquity. The soul, through faith, being laid upon the *altar* that *sanctifieth* the gift, experiences, *constantly* the all-cleansing efficacy of the blood of Jesus. And through this it knows the blessedness of being presented faultless before the throne, and mingles its triumphant ecstasies with the bloodwashed company: "Unto Him that loved us, and washed us from our sins in His own blood, and hath made us kings and priests unto God and His Father, to Him be glory and dominion for ever and ever. Amen."

Though saved from all sin at present, yet the soul that has been brought into the *experience* of this state well knows that it is not saved to the uttermost. It finds that, in the entire surrender of the world, it has but "laid aside every weight." And now, with undeviating purpose and unshackled feet, it runs with increasing rapidity and delight in the way of His commandments, gaining new accessions of wisdom, power, and love, with every other grace, daily.

"Holiness," "sanctification," and "perfect love" are terms intimately related in meaning. The terms *holiness* and *sanctification,* being frequently used by Divine inspiration, we may presume to be most significantly expressive of the state to which it is the duty of every believer to attain.

"Sanctification" being a word of much the same prominence as "holiness" in the blessed Word, it may be well to devote a few moments to its investigation, as it will doubtless throw an increase of light on the endeavour to ascertain the *nature* of the blessing.

As we have frequent occasion to observe in Scripture, the term "sanctify," in its most simple definition, means setting apart for any specified purpose. Thus it was that Moses was commanded to sanctify the children of Israel. "And the Lord said unto Moses, Go unto this people, and sanctify them today and tomorrow, and let them wash their clothes, and be ready against the third day: for the third day the Lord will come down in the sight of all the people upon Mount Sinai" (Exod. xix. 10, 11).

The Israelites also were required to sanctify themselves: "Sanctify yourselves therefore and be ye holy: for I am the Lord your God" (Lev. xx. 7). The Saviour sanctified Himself for the redemption of the world: "And for their sakes I sanctify Myself, that they also might be sanctified through the truth" (John xvii. 19). God also is represented as sanctifying His people: "I am the Lord that doth sanctify you" (Exod. xxxi. 13). "And the very God of peace sanctify you wholly" (I Thess. v. 23). "Even as Christ also loved the Church and gave Himself for it, that He might sanctify and cleanse it" (Eph. v. 25, 26). The Saviour prays that His disciples may be sanctified through the truth: "Sanctify them through Thy truth: Thy word is truth" (John xvii. 17). Peter also speaks of the sanctification of the elect, according to the foreknowledge of God, unto obedience and sprinkling of the blood of Jesus (1 Peter i. 2). Paul as above speaks of the sanctification of the Church, cleansed with the washing of water by the Word (Eph. v. 26, 27). The Corinthian brethren are also exhorted to cleanse themselves from all filthiness of the flesh and spirit, by taking hold on the promises (2 Cor. vii. 1). The vessels in the Temple were all, by the special appointment of God, set apart for holy purposes; and though a variety of uses was designated, yet they were sanctified exclusively for the holy service of the sanctuary.

Thus it is that the Christian, redeemed from all iniquity, not with corruptible things, such as silver and gold, but by the precious blood of Jesus, is, by the most explicit *declarations* and *obligations,* required to come out and be separate. "And what agreement hath the temple of God with idols? for ye are the temple of the living God: as God hath said, I will dwell in them, and walk in them; and I will be their God, and they shall be My people. Wherefore come out from among them and be ye separate, saith the Lord, and touch not the unclean thing, and I will receive you" (2 Cor. vi. 16, 17). "Go ye out of the midst of her; be ye clean, that bear the vessels of the Lord" (Isaiah lii. 11). "Know ye not that your body is the temple of the Holy Ghost which is in you, which ye have of God, and ye are not your own? For ye are bought with a price: therefore glorify God in your body, and in your spirit, which are God's" (1 Cor. v. 19, 20). "For this is the will of God, even your sanctification" (1 Thess. iv. 3, 4). "If ye were of the world, the world would love his own; but because ye are not of the world, but I have chosen you out of the world, therefore the world hateth you" (John xv. 19). Yet "sanctification," as applied to believers, comprehends inconceivably greater blessedness than a mere nominal setting apart of body and soul, with every power, to God. The sacrifice, or service, however well intended, could not for a moment be acceptable without the washing of regeneration, and the renewing of the Holy Ghost.

And then, in order to be continually washed, cleansed, and renewed after the image of God, the sacrifice must be *ceaselessly* presented. This is implied in the expression, "a *living* sacrifice;" it is thus we are made priests unto God. Through Jesus Christ, the Lamb of God, that taketh away the sins of the world; the Way, the Truth, and the Life, the Door by which we enter in; the Lamb slain from the foundation of the world; the sacrifice ascends unto God a sweet savour of Christ. It is thus that the triumphant believer momentarily realizes the blessed fulfillment of the prayer: "And the very God of peace sanctify you wholly; and I pray God your whole spirit, and soul, and body, be preserved *blameless* unto the coming of our Lord Jesus Christ. Faithful is He that calleth you, who also will do it." Amen. Even so, Lord Jesus.

III.

HOW MAY WE ENTER INTO THE ENJOYMENT OF HOLINESS?

Having become convinced that holiness is a state of soul which the Scriptures clearly set forth as an attainment which it is your duty and privilege to be living in the enjoyment of, it is necessary that the *intention* be fully fixed to *live* a holy life.

This will require deep searchings of heart, and will not admit of a secret reserve of this or the other thing, when there is a doubt that the object may be prejudicial to the soul's best interests. The matter must be brought to bear the scrutinizing eye of God; and *must* be decided upon faithfully, though the decision involve a surrender literally painful as that of parting with a right hand or right eye.

Some may be inclined to think this is narrowing the way too much, and with shrinking of heart may solicitously inquire, "Lord, are there few that be saved?" while the Saviour, beholding the many hindrances, replies, "Strive to enter in at the strait gate: for *many,* I say unto you, shall *seek* to enter in, and shall not be able." And why not able? Has the command gone forth, "Be ye holy in all manner of conversation?" (1 Peter i. 15). And has a command with such an infinite weight of consequences (Heb. xii. 14) pending on its non-fulfilment, been issued from the throne where eternal love, power, and wisdom preside, and yet the *ability* for its performance not been given? No! it is the Almighty God, boundless in love, goodness, and power, that says, "Walk before Me, and be thou perfect."

But the words of our Saviour will bring us yet more directly to the point, and will stamp the assertion with the signet of truth, that the *intention* to be holy, resolutely fixed in the mind, is a very *necessary* step toward insuring the object. "If any man will do his will he shall know of the doctrine" (John vii. 17). This, taken in connection with "For the word of the Lord is quick and powerful, and sharper than any two-edged sword, piercing even to the dividing asunder of the thoughts and intents of the heart" (Heb. iv. 12), will yet more fully assure us of the necessity of subjecting ourselves to the deep searchings of the Spirit with the intention decidedly fixed to know nothing among men "save Christ and Him crucified."

We have frequent occasion to observe with the sinner that the last point of extremity, previous to obtaining comfort, is the resolve that though he seek till the hour of his death, and never obtain forgiveness, he will not go back to the world and seek his pleasures there, but will endeavour to serve the Lord, and seek, in the use of all the appointed means, the knowledge of pardon. So with the believer; he must have all his energies concentrated in the one endeavour and *intention* of living a life of entire devotion to God. . . .

Make no provision for future emergencies; give up *all,* whether known or unknown. Resolve that, as duty shall be made plain, you will follow on, in obedience to the command, though death may await you.

If you are thus resolved to "count all things but loss for the excellency of the knowledge of Christ Jesus" your Lord, there is no reason why you may not enter into the enjoyment of this state *this* hour. Jesus, your intercessor, stands at the right hand of the Majesty on high, pleading your cause. He—

"Points to His side, and lifts His hands,

And shows that you are graven there."

Do you feel a fearful shrinking, which you would fain overcome? Look away *from earth,* from *self,* and fix your eye upon your compassionate JESUS. Obey constantly the admonition, "Looking unto Jesus." "And we have *known* and *believed* the love that God hath to us. . . . Herein is our love made perfect." Observe it is not enough to *know,* but we must also *believe* this love. Satan will with all his forces oppose you. Make up your mind to expect this. A door, great and effectual, is opened before you; but there are many adversaries. "The kingdom of Heaven suffereth violence, and the violent take it by *force."* Think of the many evidences your Saviour has given of His infinite willingness and ability to impart this Full Salvation to your soul. When He bowed His head upon the cross, and said, "It is finished," then a full and complete Salvation, a *redemption from all iniquity,* was made possible for every soul of man. And what shall hinder your now receiving it, if by faith you now lay hold on the *terms* of the covenant, as, in the hallowed presence, and through the Almighty strength, and in the name of the Father, Son, and Holy Spirit, you let *this* be the solemn hour *when you enter into the bonds of an everlasting covenant to be wholly the Lord's for time and for eternity?*

Perhaps you never felt a more piercing sense of your helplessness; but you are now to lay hold on almighty strength. "He giveth power to the faint, and to them that have no might He increaseth strength."

Some desponding, longing one, who may read this communication, may, up to this time have been an unfaithful, cold-hearted professor, so that coming out to profess this state of grace may cause many, whose companionship has before been courted, to say, "Is Saul also among the prophets?" But you are now giving yourself wholly away to Christ, and in His great love He is now saying unto you, "Ye are not of the world, but I have chosen you out of the world," "and ordained you, that ye should go and bring forth *fruit*; and that your fruit should remain; that whatsoever ye shall ask of the Father in My name, He may give it you." Oh, is not this enough? Mr. Wesley says, "By this *token* you may know whether you seek the blessing by faith or by works. If by works, you want something to be done first before you are made holy. You think, 'I must first be, or do, thus or thus, before I am sanctified.' If you seek it by faith, seek it as *you are*; and if as you *are,* then expect it *now!*

It is of great importance that you look at this great Salvation as a *present* Salvation, received momentarily from above. The blood of Jesus *cleanseth*; not that it can or will cleanse at some *future* period, but it *cleanseth now,* while you lay your all upon that "altar that sanctifieth the gift." You keep your offering there, even all your redeemed powers—body, soul, and spirit—mind, memory, and will—time, talents, and influence. And as in devotion all these redeemed powers return ceaselessly to God, *through* Christ, it is your *duty to believe.* Do not imagine that you have something indefinite, you know not what, to believe. No; it is the truth just stated you are called implicitly to believe; and if you do not believe, you dishonour God, and grieve the Spirit of love. The inconsistency of your unbelief is here: in obedience to the requirement of God, you, through the assistance of His grace, have been enabled to come out and be separate, resolved to touch not, taste not, handle not the unclean thing. If you had enabled *yourself* to do this, then there might be a shadow of consistency in your unbelief; but now that you have done it through the *power of God,* assured that, apart from his grace, there dwelleth no good thing in you, how unreasonable the thought that He will not fulfil His part of the engagement! *"I will receive you,"* is His own declaration. "I will sprinkle clean water upon you, and ye shall be clean; from all your filthiness and from all your idols will I cleanse you." "Now is the accepted time, and now is the day of Salvation." Then venture upon the truth of His word; you cannot believe God in vain. "The *faith SHALL* bring the *power;"* but do not expect to *feel* the power *before* you have exercised the faith. This would be expecting the fruit before the tree is planted; the power to *live* and *dwell* in God comes *through believing.*

Holiness is a state of soul in which all the powers of the body and mind are consciously given up to God; and the witness of holiness is that testimony which the Holy Spirit bears with our spirit that the offering is accepted through Christ. The work is accomplished the moment we lay our all upon the altar. Under the old covenant dispensation it was ordained by God that whatsoever touched the altar should be holy: "Seven days thou shalt make an atonement for the altar, and sanctify it; and it shall be an altar most holy: whatsoever toucheth the altar shall be holy" (Exod. xxix. 37). And in allusion to this our Saviour says, "The altar that sanctifieth the gift" (Matt. xxiii. 19). As explanatory of this subject, Dr. Clarke says, "This may be understood as implying that *whatsoever was laid on the altar became the Lord's property, and must be wholly devoted to sacred purposes."* Under the new covenant dispensation, the Apostle to the Hebrews says, *"We have an altar whereof they have no right to eat which serve the tabernacle"* (Heb. xiii. 10). Dr. Clarke again says, "The *Christian altar is the Christian sacrifice, which is CHRIST JESUS,* with all the benefits of His passion and death." "Hallelujah! Glory be to God in the highest!"

Will you come, dear disciple of Jesus, and venture even *now* to lay your all upon this blessed altar? He will not spurn you away. No; "His side an open fountain is;" "His nature and His name is love." Surely you will now begin to say—

> "O Love, thou bottomless abyss!
> My sins are swallowed up in Thee;
> Cover'd is my unrighteousness,
> Nor spot of guilt remains on me:
> While Jesus' blood through earth and skies,
> 'Mercy, free, boundless mercy,' cries."

Lucretia Mott,
Likeness to Christ
(1849)

Lucretia Mott (1793–1880)

Born Lucretia Coffin in Nantucket, Massachusetts, she married James Mott, who shared her commitment to several important social issues of the day. Throughout her adult life she was a champion of freedom, both theological and social. She became a Quaker preacher, a ministry not closed to women, and focused her preaching and writing on the practical implications of Jesus' teachings, which, as she saw it, gave mandates for a social agenda. She worked actively for the abolition of slavery and for equal rights for women, serving as president of the American Equal Rights Association from 1866 to 1868. Her home was a frequent way station for runaway slaves, and she helped to establish the Anti-Slavery Convention of American Women, although she watched its meeting hall burned down by a mob in 1838. For Mott, doctrinal orthodoxy would always take a back seat to social justice. Her insistence on freedom from human bondage in all forms made her a controversial figure in her own day. Still, her Quaker tradition, with its history of women's ministry and commitment to justice, gave her considerable strength. Her life certainly gave strength to the Quaker tradition as well.

Likeness to Christ

Mott's speeches and sermons, a wealth of material, have been published in their entirety (see bibliography, p. 347). This sermon, "Likeness to

Christ," contains many of the themes present throughout her entire sermon corpus. The opening sentence sets forth the thesis: "It is time that Christians were judged more by their likeness to Christ than their notions of Christ." Mott had little patience with sermonizing that bespoke empty piety, theological nit-picking, or sectarian wrangling. Her call was always to action, with an urgency not unlike the preachers of the first Christian centuries. At the heart of her theology was the notion that one is not to know about Christ, but rather, one is to know Christ, such that one conforms the faithful life to Christ's life. By this test, most Christian "professors" fail miserably, according to Mott. Make no mistake—for Mott this failure is not simply one of Christian practice, but it is failure of belief and theological truth. Likeness to Christ is faith that works by love.

LIKENESS TO CHRIST

SERMON, DELIVERED AT CHERRY STREET MEETING,

PHILADELPHIA, SEPTEMBER 30, 1849

It is time that Christians were judged more by their likeness to Christ than their notions of Christ. Were this sentiment generally admitted we should not see such tenacious adherence to what men deem the opinions and doctrines of Christ while at the same time in every day practise is exhibited anything but a likeness to Christ. My reflections in this meeting have been upon the origin, parentage, and character of Jesus. I have thought we might profitably dwell upon the facts connected with his life, his precepts, and his practice in his walks among men. Humble as was his birth, obscure as was his parentage, little known as he seemed to be in his neighborhood and country, he has astonished the world and brought a response from all mankind by the purity of his precepts, the excellence of his example. Wherever that inimitable sermon on the mount is read, let it be translated into any language and spread before the people, there as an acknowledgement of its truth. When we come to judge the sectarian professors of his name by the true test, how widely do their lives differ from his?

Instead of going about doing good as was his wont, instead of being constantly in the exercise of benevolence and love as was his practice, we find the disposition too generally to measure the Christian by his assent to a creed which had not its sign with him nor indeed in his day. Instead of engaging in the exercise of peace, justice and mercy, how many of the professors are arrayed against him in opposition to those great principles

even as were his opposers in his day. Instead of being the bold nonconformist (if I may so speak) that he was, they are adhering to old church
usages, and worn-out forms and exhibiting little of a Christ like disposition
and character. Instead of uttering the earnest protests against wickedness in
high places, against the spirit of proselytism and sectarianism as did the
blessed Jesus—the divine, the holy, the born of God, there is the servile
accommodation to this sectarian spirit and an observance of those forms
even long after there is any claim of virtue in them; a disposition to use
language which shall convey belief that in the inmost heart of many they
reject.

Is this honest, is this Christ like? Should Jesus again appear and preach
as he did round about Judea and Jerusalem and Galilee, these high professors would be among the first to set him at naught, if not to resort to the
extremes which were resorted to in his day. There is no danger of this now,
however, because the customs of the age will not bear the bigot out in it, but
the spirit is manifest, which led martyrs to the stake, Jesus to the cross,
Mary Dyer to the gallows. This spirit is now showing itself in casting out
the name one of another, as evil, in brother delivering up brother unto
sectarian death. We say if Jesus should again appear—He *is* here; he *has*
appeared, from generation to generation and his spirit is now as manifest,
in the humble, the meek, the bold reformers, even among some of obscure
parentage.

His spirit is now going up and down among men seeking their good, and
endeavoring to promote the benign and holy principles of peace, justice,
and love. And blessing to the merciful, to the peace maker, to the pure in
heart, and the poor in spirit, to the just, the upright, to those who desire
righteousness is earnestly proclaimed, by these messengers of the Highest
who are now in our midst. These the preachers of righteousness are no more
acknowledged by the same class of people than was the messiah to the
Jews. They are the anointed of God, the inspired preachers and writers and
believers of the present time. In the pure example which they exhibit to the
nations, they are emphatically the beloved sons of God. It is, my friends,
my mission to declare these things among you at the hazard of shocking
many prejudices. The testimony of the chosen servants of the Highest in our
day is equally divine inspiration with the inspired teaching of those in
former times. It is evidence of the superstition of our age, that we can
adhere to, Yea that, we can bow with profound veneration to the records of
an Abraham, the sensualist Solomon, and the war-like David, inspired
though they may have been, and I am not disposed to doubt it, more than to

the equal inspiration of the writers of the present age. Why not acknowledge the inspiration of many of the poets of succeeding ages, as well as of Deborah and Miriam in their songs of victory of Job and David in their beautiful poetry and psalms, or of Isaiah and Jeremiah in their scorching rebukes and mournful lamentations? These are beautifully instructive but ought they to command our veneration more than the divine poetic language of many, very many, since their day, who have uttered truth equally precious? Truth speaks the same language in every age of the world and is equally valuable to us. Are we so blindly superstitious as to reject the one and adhere to the other? How much does this society lose by this undue veneration to ancient authorities, a want of equal respect to the living inspired testimonies of latter time? Christianity requires that we bring into view the apostles of succeeding generations, that we acknowledge their apostleship and give the right hand of fellowship to those who have been and who are sent forth of God with great truths to declare before the people; and also to practise lives of righteousness, exceeding the righteousness of the scribes and pharisees, and even of many of the chosen ones of former times. The people in their childish and dark state, just emerging out of barbarism, were not prepared to exhibit all those great principles in the near approach to fulness, to the perfection that is called for at our hands. There is this continued advance toward perfection from age to age. The records of our predecessors give evidence of such progress. When I quote the language of William Penn, "it is time for Christians to be judged more by their likeness to Christ than their notions of Christ," I offer the sentiment of one who is justly held in great regard if not veneration by this people, and whose writings may be referred to with as much profit as those of the servants of God in former ages; and we may well respect the memory of him and his contemporaries as well as of many not limited to our religious society, who have borne testimony to the truth.

It is of importance to us also, to speak of those whom we know, those whose characters we have [fuller] acquaintance with, than we can have with such as lived in ages past, that we should bring into view the lives of the faithful in our generation.

Jesus bore his testimony—doing always the things which pleased his Father. He lived his meek, his humble and useful life—drawing his disciples around him, and declaring great truths to the people who gathered to hear him.

His apostles and their successors were faithful in their day—going out into the world, and shaking the nations around them. Reformers since their time have done their work in exposing error and wrong, and calling for priests of righteousness in place of vain forms. The bold utterance of Elias Hicks and his contemporaries aroused the sectarian and theological world in our day. Their demand for a higher righteousness was not in vain. Their examples of self-denials and faithfulness to duty should be held up for imitation. We overestimate those who have lived and labored in days long past, while we value not sufficiently the labors of those around us, who may have as high a commission as had their predecessors.

Let us not hesitate to regard the utterance of truth in our age, as of equal value with that which is recorded in the scriptures. None can revere more than I do, the truths of the Bible. I have read it perhaps as much as any one present, and, I trust, with profit. It has at times been more to me than my daily food. When an attempt was made some twenty years ago to engraft some church dogmas upon this society, claiming this book for authority, it led me to examine, and compare text with the content. In so doing I became so much interested that I scarcely noted the passage of time. Even to this day, when I open this volume, so familiar is almost every chapter that I can sometimes scarcely lay it aside from the interest I feel in its beautiful pages. But I should be recreant to principle, did I not say, the great error in Christendom is, in regarding these scriptures taken as a whole as the plenary inspiration of God, and their authority as supreme. I consider this as Elias Hicks did one of the greatest drawbacks, one of the greatest barriers to human progress that there is in the religious world, for while this volume is held as it is, and, by a resort to it, war, and slavery, wine drinking, and other cruel, oppressive and degrading evils are sustained, pleading the example of the ancients as authority it serves as a check to human progress, as an obstacle in the way of these great and glorious reformers that are now upon the field. Well did that servant of God, Elias Hicks, warn the people against an undue veneration of the Bible, or of any human authority, any written record or outward testimony. The tendency of his ministry was to lead the mind to the divine teacher, the sublime ruler, that all would find within themselves, which was above men's teaching, human records, or outward authorities. Highly as he valued these ancient testimonies, they were not to take the place of the higher law inwardly revealed, which was and should be, the governing principle of our lives. One of our early friends, Richard Davies, attended a meeting of the independents, and heard the preacher express the sentiment that the time would come when Christians would have no more need of the Bible than of any other book. He remarked on this saying of the preacher, "Hast thou not experienced that time already come." Does not this imply, or may we not infer from this, that our worthy friend has experienced that time already come; was it a greater heresy, than that uttered by the apostle Paul, when he declared that those who had known a birth into the gospel, had no more need of the law? that they were under a higher dispensation than were they who were bound by their statutes and ceremonies? Let us also not hesitate to declare it, and to speak the truth plainly as it is in Jesus, that we believe the time is come when this undue adherence to outward authorities, or to any forms of baptism or of communion of church or sabbath worship, should give place to more practical goodness among men, more love manifested one unto another in our every day life, doing good and ministering to the wants and interests of our fellow beings the world over. If we fully believe this, should we be most honest, did we so far seek to please men, more than to please God, as to fail to utter in our meetings, and whenever we feel called upon to do so in our conversation, in our writings, and to exhibit by example, by a life of non-conformity, in accordance with these views, that we have faith and confidence in our convictions? It needs, my friends, in this day that one should go forth saying neither baptism profiteth anything nor non-baptism, but faith which worketh by love, neither the ordinance of the communion table profiteth anything, nor the absence from the same, but faith which worketh by love. These things should never be regarded as the test of the worshipper. Neither your sabbath observance profiteth any thing, nor the non-observance of the day, but faith which worketh by love. Let all these subjects be held up in their true light. Let them be plainly spoken of—and let our lives be in accordance with our convictions of right, each striving to carry out our principles. Then obscure though we may be, lost sight of almost, in the great and pompous religious associations of the day, we yet shall have our influence and it will be felt. Why do we wish it to be felt? Because we believe it is the testimony of truth, and our duty to spread it far and wide. Because the healthful growth of the people requires that they should come away from their vain oblations, and settle upon the ground of obedience to the requirings of truth.

I desire to speak so as to be understood, and trust there are among you, ears blessed that they hear, and that these principles will be received as the Gospel of the blessed son of God. Happy shall they be, who by observing these, shall come to be divested of the traditions and superstitions which have been clinging to them, leading them to erect an altar "to the unknown God."

In the place of this shall an altar be raised where on may be oblations of

God's own preparing. Thus may these approach our Father in Heaven and hold communion with him—entering his courts with thanksgiving, and his gates with praise, even though there may be no oral expression. He may unite in prayer and in praise, which will ascend as sweet incense, and the blessing will come which we can scarcely contain.

Hannah Whitall Smith,
The Open Secret
(1875)

Hannah Whitall Smith (1832–1911)

Born Hannah Whitall in Philadelphia, she was raised in a strict Quaker home and faith. She married Robert Smith in 1851, and they began a life of religious and spiritual inquiry together. After her husband experienced a baptism of the Holy Spirit at a Methodist camp meeting, Smith began to seek a similar experience but found she was "a dry old stick." Finally in 1867 she had such an experience, and found she was a gifted speaker and writer, able to communicate her powerful experiences and insights to lay audiences. Smith and her husband traveled widely in the United States and England, providing leadership during the latter years of the nineteenth century for the growing holiness movement. Smith was well loved, but her husband fell into disrepute over charges of antinomianism. She maintained her popular speaking and writing, publishing her best-seller, *The Christian's Secret of a Happy Life,* in 1875.

The Open Secret

For Hannah Whitall Smith, the path of personal holiness was not one of austere solemnity, but one of joy and happiness. In this work she recounts the joy the soul experiences when recreated by the sanctifying work of the Holy Spirit. The interest that the holiness movement had in "the higher Christian life" took a variety of forms at the end of the nineteenth century. Smith's characteristic expansiveness expresses her focus on the nature of

God and of salvation in the Christian life. Also included here is her description of God as Mother, a description that is tied, as are all her arguments, to specific scriptural passages.

THE OPEN SECRET, OR, THE BIBLE EXPLAINING ITSELF

BIBLE READINGS.

II. SUBJECT—GOD IS LOVE.

FOUNDATION TEXT.—He that loveth not knoweth not God; for God is love.—I John 4:8.

Notice that it does not say merely that God is loving, but that God is love. That is, it is His very nature, or essence. It is not merely one of His attributes, but it is Himself. Therefore, all that He does is from the root of love; and we must believe this, no matter how it may look, because it could not, in the very nature of things, be otherwise.

"Behold, what manner of love the Father hath bestowed upon us, that we should be called the sons of God; therefore the world knoweth us not, because it knew Him not."—I John 3:1.

We are to behold the "manner of love;" that is, the sort or kind of love. A few questions will help us to do this.

   I. When did God begin to love us?

  II. Why does He love us?

 III. What manner of love is it?

 IV. How much does He love us?

  V. How can we know that He loves us?

 VI. What return can we render for His love?

We will consider these questions one by one. . . .

 III. What manner of love is it? That is, how or in what way does God love us?

  1. As a Creator.

  2. As a Redeemer.

  3. As a Father.

  4. As a Mother.

  5. As a Friend.

  6. As a Brother.

7. As a Shepherd.
8. As a Bridegroom.
9. As He loves Himself.
10. As a Creator.

"But now, thus saith the Lord that created thee, O Jacob, and He that formed thee, O Israel, Fear not; for I have redeemed thee, I have called thee by thy name; thou art mine. When thou passeth through the waters, I will be with thee; and through the rivers, they shall not overflow thee; when thou walkest through the fire, thou shalt not be burned; neither shall the flame kindle upon thee."—Isa. 43:1, 2.

"Remember these, O Jacob and Israel; for thou art my servant: I have formed thee; thou art my servant; O Israel, thou shalt not be forgotten of me. I have blotted out, as a thick cloud, thy transgressions, and, as a cloud thy sins; return unto me; for I have redeemed thee."—Isa. 44:21, 22.

We all know how much we delight in anything we create; how we like to show it to our friends, and to look at it ourselves; how tender we are of its safety, and how jealous we are of any criticisms upon it. And this joy of ours in creation and ownership will help us to understand and believe in the love of our Creator for us who are "the work of His hands."

2. He loves us as our Redeemer.

"I will mention the loving-kindnesses of the Lord, and the praises of the Lord, according to all that the Lord hath bestowed on us, and the great goodness towards the house of Israel, which He hath bestowed on them according to His mercies, and according to the multitude of His loving kindnesses. For He said, Surely they are my people, children that will not lie; so He was their Savior. In all their affliction He was afflicted, and the angel of His presence saved them: in His love and in His pity He redeemed them; and He bare them, and carried them all the days of old."—Isa. 63:7-9.

"For I the Lord thy God will hold thy right hand, saying unto thee, Fear not; I will help thee. Fear not, thou worm Jacob, and ye men of Israel; I will help thee, saith the Lord, and thy Redeemer, the Holy One of Israel."—Isa. 41:13, 14.

"Into Thine hand I commit my spirit; Thou hast redeemed me, O Lord God of truth."—Ps. 31:5

"Hear the word of the Lord, O ye nations, and declare it in the isles afar off, and say: He that scattered Israel will gather him, and keep him, as a shepherd doth his flock. For the Lord hath redeemed Jacob, and ransomed him from the hand of Him that was stronger than he."—Jer. 31:10, 11.

3. He loves us as a Father.

   "He shall cry unto me, Thou art my father, my God, and the rock of my salvation."—Ps. 89:26.

"And His name shall be called . . . the everlasting Father."—Isa. 9:6.

"They shall come with weeping, and with supplications will I lead them: I will cause them to walk by the rivers of waters in a straight way, wherein they shall not stumble; for I am a father to Israel, and Ephraim is my first-born."—Jer. 31:9.

"Like as a Father pitieth His children, so the Lord pitieth them that fear Him."—Ps. 103:13.

"And he arose and came to his father. But when he was yet a great way off, his father saw him, and had compassion, and ran, and fell on his neck, and kissed him. And the son said unto him, Father, I have sinned against heaven, and in thy sight, and am no more worthy to be called thy son. But the father said to his servants, Bring forth the best robe, and put it on him; and put a ring on his hand, and shoes on his feet; and bring hither the fatted calf, and kill it; and let us eat, and be merry: for this my son was dead, and is alive again; he was lost, and is found. And they began to be merry."—Luke 15:20-24.

Our Lord gave this last divine picture of what a father is, in reply to the Pharisees and Scribes, who murmured, saying, "This man receiveth sinners, and eateth with them." And in this reply He silenced forever every unbelieving thought that could make God out to be less tender than the human fathers He has made.

4. God loves us as a Mother.

   "As one whom his mother comforteth, so will I comfort you; and ye shall be comforted in Jerusalem."—Isa. 66:13.

"Sing, O heavens; and be joyful, O earth; and break forth into singing, O mountains; for the Lord hath comforted His people, and will have mercy upon His afflicted. But Zion said, The Lord hath forsaken me, and my Lord hath forgotten me. Can a woman forget her sucking child, that she should not have compassion on the son of her womb? yea, they may forget, yet will I not forget thee. Behold, I have graven thee upon the palms of my hands; thy walls are continually before me."—Isa. 49:13-16.

5. God loves us as a Friend.

"Greater love hath no man than this, that a man lay down his life for his friends. Ye are my friends, if ye do whatsoever I command you. Henceforth I call you not servants; for the servant knoweth not what his Lord doeth, but I have called you friends, for all things that I have heard of my Father I have made known unto you."—John 15:13-15.

"And the Lord spake unto Moses face to face, as a man speaketh unto his friend."—Exod. 33:11.

"But thou, Israel, art my servant, Jacob whom I have chosen, the seed of Abraham my friend."—Isa. 41:8

"And the scripture was fulfilled which saith, Abraham believed God, and it was imputed unto him for righteousness; and he was called the friend of God."—James 2:23

"A man that hath friends must show himself friendly; and there is a friend that sticketh closer than a brother."—Prov. 18:24.

All that our highest ideal of friendship implies, must be ours in a friendship with God. . . .

BIBLE READINGS

IV. SUBJECT—ASSURANCE OF FAITH.

FOUNDATION TEXT.—"Let us draw near with a true heart in full assurance of faith, having our hearts sprinkled from an evil conscience, and our bodies washed with pure water."——Heb. 10:22.

By the assurance of faith is meant a clear and definite knowledge of the forgiveness of sins, of reconciliation with God, and of our relationship with Him as our Father.

About these vital matters we must be able to say "I know." Not "I hope so," or "I wish so," but firmly and unhesitatingly, "I know."

"Blessed is the people that know the joyful sound: they shall walk, O Lord, in the light of thy countenance. In thy name shall they rejoice all the day: and in thy righteousness shall they be exalted."—Ps. 89:15, 16.

"Thou shall know that I the Lord am thy Saviour and thy Redeemer, the Mighty One of Jacob."—Isa. 60:16.

"At that day ye shall know that I am in my Father, and ye in me, and I in you."—John 14:20.

This assurance is necessary for all right living. It ought to be the first step in the Christian life. In the absence of this assurance, lies the secret of much of the failure of Christians. They present the strange anomaly of children who doubt their parentage, of heirs who are afraid to take possession of their inheritance, of a bride who is not sure she has been really married.

What could we expect from such doubts in earthly relationships, but indifference, fear, anxiety, unkindness, sorrow and rebellion?

And are not these the very things that are found far too often in the hearts of God's children, in reference to their relationships to Him?

> "Because thou servedst not the Lord thy God with joyfulness, and with gladness of heart, for the abundance of all things; therefore shalt thou serve thine enemies, which the Lord shall send against thee, in hunger, and in thirst, and in nakedness, and in want of all things: and He shall put a yoke of iron upon thy neck, until He have destroyed thee."—Deut. 28:47, 48.

No soul can serve the Lord with joyfulness who is in doubt as to the reality or the stability of its relations with Him. All human comfort is destroyed in such a case, as affecting earthy relations; and but little divine comfort is, as we all know, to be found in doubtful spiritual relations. . . .

What are we to do then in order to get the assurance of faith?

> "Then said they unto him, What shall we do, that we might work the works of God? Jesus answered and said unto them, This is the word of God, that ye believe on him whom He hath sent."—John 6:28, 29.

We must believe two things. First, what God says concerning Christ. Second, what He says concerning us.

It is not really believing a person if we only believe half he says; and yet many who would consider it the worst of sins to disbelieve God's testimony concerning Christ, consider it no sin at all, but in fact rather virtuous humility, to doubt His testimony concerning themselves. They dare not doubt that Jesus is the Christ, but find no difficulty in doubting whether they are themselves "born of God." And yet God joins the two inseparably together.

> "Whosoever believeth that Jesus is the Christ, is born of God."—I John 5:1.

Here is a plain and simple statement. "Whosoever believeth, *is* born," not will be, but is, now in the present moment; for no one can believe who is not born of God. . . .

BIBLE READINGS

IX. SUBJECT—GOD AS OUR MOTHER.

> "Love divine, of such great loving,
> Only mothers know the cost;
> Cost of love, that, all love passing,
> Gave itself to save the lost!"

FOUNDATION TEXT.—"As one whom his mother comforteth, so will I comfort you; and ye shall be comforted in Jerusalem."—Isa. 66:13.

We all know how a mother comforts her children, and have most of us tasted the sweetness of this comforting. Notice then, the "as" and "so" in this declaration, and accept the Divine Comforter and the heavenly comfort.

> "Sing, O heavens; and be joyful, O earth; and break forth into singing, O mountains: for the Lord hath comforted His people, and will have mercy on His afflicted."—Isa. 49:13.

"I, even I, am he that comforteth you: who art thou, that thou shouldest be afraid of a man that shall die, and of the son of man which shall be made as grass."—Isa. 51:12.

"For the Lord shall comfort Zion; He will comfort all her waste places; and He will make all her wilderness like Eden, and her desert like the garden of the Lord; joy and gladness shall be found therein, thanksgiving, and the voice of melody."—Isa. 51:3.

"Break forth into joy, sing together, ye waste places of Jerusalem: for the Lord hath comforted His people, He hath redeemed Jerusalem."—Isa. 52:9.

God is called the "God of all comfort."

> "Blessed be God, even the Father of our Lord Jesus Christ, the Father of mercies, and the God of all comfort; who comforteth us in all our tribulation, that we may be able to comfort them which are in any trouble by the comfort, wherewith we ourselves are comforted of God."—2 Cor. 1:3-4.

The Holy Spirit is called the Comforter.

> "But the Comforter, which is the Holy Ghost, whom the Father will send in my name; He shall teach you all things, and bring all things to your remembrance, whatsoever I have said unto you."—John 14:26.

Christ, when He was leaving His disciples, provided for their comfort when He should be gone.

> "And I will pray the Father, and He shall give you another Comforter, that He may abide with you for ever. * * * I will not leave you comfortless: I will come to you."—John 14:16-18.

But some will say, if God is like a mother, and comforts as mothers comfort, why is it that they are not comforted?

Have you never seen a little child sitting up stiff in his mother's lap, and refusing to be comforted, in spite of all her coaxing? And do we not often act in very much the same way?

> "O Jerusalem, Jerusalem, thou that killest the prophets, and stonest them which are sent unto thee, how often would I have gathered thy children together, even as a hen gathereth her chickens under her wings, and ye would not!"—Matt. 23:37.

"In the day of my trouble I sought the Lord: my sore ran in the night, and ceased not, my soul refused to be comforted."—Ps. 77:2.

Even a mother's love and tenderness cannot comfort a child that "refuses to be comforted;" and neither can God's. But no sorrow can be too great for His comfort to reach, if we will only take it.

> "Yea, though I walk through the valley of the shadow of death, I will fear no evil; for thou art with me; thy rod and thy staff they comfort me."—Ps. 23:4.

"Then shall the virgin rejoice in the dance, both young men and old together: for I will turn their mourning into joy, and will comfort them, and make them rejoice from their sorrow."—Jer. 31:15.

If we will only listen believingly to His loving words: "Daughter be of good comfort;" we shall surely be comforted.

There are many other ways in which God is like a mother, and a comparison of these points will, I trust, open our eyes to see some truths concerning Him, which have been hitherto hidden from our gaze.

I. The mother runs when the child cries, and listens to the story of its sorrows and its needs, and relieves them.

And just so God.

306

"Then shalt thou call, and the Lord shalt answer; thou shalt cry, and he shalt say, Here I am."—Isa. 58:9.

The "Here I am" of the mother never fails to respond to the child's cry of "Mother, mother, where are you?" And neither does God's.

"I cried unto the Lord with my voice, and He heard me out of His holy hill. I laid me down and slept; I awakened; for the Lord sustained me."—Ps. 3:4, 5.

How alert is the ear of the mother to the feeblest cry of her baby in the night. Let her be sleeping ever so soundly, and she will still hear the tiny cry. And how comforted and quieted the little one is when it realizes the mother's presence and can go to sleep in her care.

"In the day when I cried thou answeredest me, and strengthenedst me with strength in my soul."—Ps. 38:3.

"I cried unto God with my voice, even unto God with my voice; and He gave ear unto me."—Ps. 77:1.

We are sometimes tempted to think that the Lord does not hear our prayers. But let the mother teach us. Could she possibly let the cry of her child go unheeded? And is the earthly mother more tender of her children, than the Heavenly Father is of His? . . .

What, then, is the summing up of the whole matter? Simply this: If God is only as good as the mothers He has made, where can there be any room left for a thought of care or of fear? And if He is as much truer to the ideal of motherhood than an earthly mother can be, as His infiniteness is above hers, then what oceans and continents of bliss are ours for the taking!

Shall we not take it?

> "Learn of this mother to be no more beguiled,
> For, mindful of the mother heart which I have given;
> She in my goodness hath abiding faith:
> And whatso'er of Me another saith,
> Although the words my seem to come from Heaven;
> She ponders well, and tries it by the test,
> Of that which in her own heart she finds best."

CHAPTER THIRTY - THREE

Amanda Berry Smith, An Autobiography (1893)

Amanda Berry Smith (1837–1915)

Smith was born a slave in a family of slaves in Maryland. Her father was determined to see his family reach freedom, and through his perseverance, most of the family made it to Pennsylvania. In her autobiography, Smith describes her conversion when she was nineteen, a young wife in an unhappy marriage. Her account of her own strong-mindedness and God's revelation to her is marked by constant doubts and reaffirmations. Still, Smith attributes her strength to endure two difficult marriages and hard manual labor to the blessing of entire sanctification, which she received in 1868. This was a turning point in her life, and she set out on a new path as preacher and evangelist. Popular throughout New York City, her efforts quickly spread to camp meetings across the United States and Britain, and ultimately included missions to India and West Africa. Never ordained, Smith was a well-known spokeswoman for the holiness movement, gaining an international reputation. She founded the Amanda Smith Orphan's Home for Colored Children in Chicago in 1895, and spent much of the rest of her life working for the welfare of African American children.

An Autobiography

This text was published in 1893 under the complete title, *An Autobiography: The Story of the Lord's Dealings with Amanda Smith the Colored Evangelist, Containing an Account of Her Life Work of Faith, and Her*

Travels in America, England, Ireland, Scotland, India and Africa, as an Independent Missionary. The portions included here recount Smith's experience of sanctification, a blessing that she had desperately desired, thinking of it as something she could "get" and "keep." When she heard at Green Street Church that it was not her work, but God working in her that constituted sanctification, she was relieved and released. Her preaching emphasized the witness of the Spirit in justification and sanctification and the danger of relying on works for either.

AN AUTOBIOGRAPHY

CHAPTER VII. THE BLESSING—ABOUT SEEKING SANCTIFICATION BY WORKS.

I always got up as early on Sunday mornings as on other mornings. I got my breakfast and cleaned up my house, and at nine o'clock my little Mazie went to Sunday School. While she was gone I would cook all my dinner and get everything ready. I did not have time to cook much through the week, as I had often to dry my clothes in the house and I could not have the smell of cooking, so Sunday was the only day I would have a real good dinner, but I never stayed home from church to cook—so I gave my baby his bath and laid him in his cradle, then I got down on my knees and prayed the Lord to keep Will asleep till I went to Green Street Church, and to keep James in a good humor so he would not scold me, for I hated to be scolded, in the worst way. James was peculiar. If he came and I happened to be out, even though I went to carry clothes, he would be vexed. So after Mazie came I said, "Now you read your library book and be a good girl, I am going to Green Street Church this morning; it lets out before our church does, so I will be home in time. You can tell your pa, if he comes before I get back. If Will cries, don't take him up; Just rock him. ". . .

. . . When I reached the steps I shall never forget the thrill of joy that ran through my heart when I heard Brother Inskip pray. . . . When Brother Inskip had finished his prayer he rose and made his announcements; the last hymn was sung, then came the text:—Ephesians, 4th Chapter 24th Verse,— "And that ye put on the new man, which after God is created in righteousness and true holiness." He said, "In preaching from this text this morning the brethren will observe I shall have to make some reference to a sermon that I preached a few Sabbaths ago on sanctification."

. . . "There are a great many persons who are troubled about the blessing of sanctification; how they can keep it if they get it."

"Oh!" I said, "he means me, for that is just what I have said. With my trials and peculiar temperament and all that I have to contend with, if I could get the blessing how could I keep it? Now, some one has told him, for he is looking right at me and I know he means me." And I tried to hide behind the post, and he seemed to look around there. Then I said, "Well, he means me, and I will just take what he says." He used this illustration: "When you work hard all day and are very tired,—"Yes," I said, and in a moment my mind went through my washing and ironing all night,—"When you go to bed at night you don't fix any way for yourself to breathe,"—"No," I said, "I never think about it,"—"You go to bed, you breathe all night, you have nothing to do with your breathing, you awake in the morning, you had nothing to do with it."

"Yes, yes, I see it."

He continued: "You don't need to fix any way for God to live in you; get God in you in all His fullness and He will live Himself."

"Oh!" I said, "I see it." And somehow I seemed to sink down out of sight of myself, and then rise; it was all in a moment. I seemed to go two ways at once, down and up. Just then such a wave came over me, and such a welling up in my heart, and these words rang through me like a bell: "God in you, God in you," and I thought doing what? Ruling every ambition and desire, and bringing every thought unto captivity and obedience to His will. How I have lived through it I cannot tell, but the blessedness of the love and the peace and power I can never describe. O, what glory filled my soul! The great vacuum in my soul began to fill up; it was like a pleasant draught of cool water, and I felt it. I wanted to shout Glory to Jesus! but Satan said, "Now, if you make a noise they will put you out."

I was the only colored person there and I had a very keen sense of propriety; I had been taught so, and Satan knew it. I wonder how he ever did know all these little points in me, but in spite of all my Jesus came out best. As we colored folks used to sing in the gone by years:

> "Jesus is a mighty captain
> Jesus is a mighty captain
> Jesus is a mighty captain
> Soldier of the cross."

"Jesus never lost a battle,
Jesus never lost a battle,
Jesus never lost a battle,
Soldier of the cross."

Hallelujah! Hallelujah! Amen.

I did not shout, and by-and-by Brother Inskip came to another illustration. He said, speaking on faith: "Now, this blessing of purity like pardon is received by faith, and if by faith why not now?"

"Yes," I said.

"It is instantaneous," he continued. "To illustrate, how long is a dark room dark when you take a lighted lamp into it?"

"O," I said "I see it!" And again a great wave of glory swept over my soul—another cooling draught of water—I seemed to swallow it, and then the welling up at my heart seemed to come still a little fuller. Praise the Lord forever, for that day!

Speaking of God's power, he went on still with another illustration. He said: "If God in the twinkling of an eye can change these vile bodies of ours and make them look like his own most glorious body, how long will it take God to sanctify a soul?"

"God can do it," I said, "in the twinkling of an eye," and as quick as the spark from smitten steel I felt the touch of God from the crown of my head to the soles of my feet, and the welling up came, and I felt I must shout: but Satan still resisted me like he did Joshua. . . .

And when they sang these words, "Whose blood now cleanseth," O what a wave of glory swept over my soul! I shouted glory to Jesus. Brother Inskip answered, "Amen, Glory to God." O, what a triumph for our King Emmanuel. I don't know just how I looked, but I felt so wonderfully strange, yet I felt glorious. One of the good official brethren at the door said, as I was passing out, "Well, auntie, how did you like that sermon?" but I could not speak; if I had, I should have shouted, but I simply nodded my head. Just as I put my foot on the top step I seemed to feel a hand, the touch of which I cannot describe. It seemed to press me gently on the top of my head, and I felt something part and roll down and cover me like a great cloak! I felt it distinctly; it was done in a moment, and O what a mighty peace and power took possession of me! . . .

Many times since then my faith has been tried sorely, and I have had much to contend with, and the fiery darts of Satan at times have been sore, but he has never, from that day, had the impudence to tell me that God had not done this blessed work. Hallelujah! what a Saviour!

Everybody does not have direct witness to their sanctification nor to their justification in that way, but it is their privilege to have the clear, distinct witness of the Spirit to both justification and sanctification, and, as a rule, persons who do not get this distinct witness are unsettled in their Christian life, often waver and falter, and are more easily turned aside to new isms and doctrines: but, thank God, He has kept me in perfect peace while my mind has been stayed on Him and I have trusted in Him. Praise His name forever!

James did not come home for two weeks. When he came I sat down on his lap and put my arms around his neck and told him all about it. He listened patiently. When I got through he began his old argument. I said, "Now, my dear, you know I can't argue."

"O well," he said, "If you have got something you can't talk about, I don't believe in it."

"Well," I said, "I have told you all I can and I cannot argue." O, how he tantalized me in every way, but God kept me so still in my soul, and my poor husband was so annoyed because I would not argue. I knew what it meant, but praise God He saved me. I could only weep and pray.

Shortly after I was converted, I was deeply convicted for the blessing of heart purity; and if I had had any one to instruct me, I can see how I might have entered into the blessed experience. But not having proper teaching, like Israel of old, I wandered in the wilderness of doubts and fears, and ups and downs, for twelve years: and but for the Rev. John S. Inskip's having the experience himself, and preaching that memorable Sunday morning, September, 1868, in the old Green Street Church, New York, in all probability I might never have got into the blessed light of full salvation. . . .

After a year or two I went to Philadelphia. There I was married to my second husband, James Smith. Then I had given up seeking the blessing definitely, and so went on. Several years later on, we moved to New York: and, after many more trials, that I have already referred to, I was deeply convicted again for the need of heart purity. And again I began to seek it by works. I read in the Bible, "If I, your Lord and Master, wash your feet, ye ought also to wash one another's feet," John, 13:15. There were four of us sisters who had united in a band to pray for mutual help to each other; Sister Scott, Sister Bangs, Sister Brown, and myself. I told them what the Bible said about it, and they all agreed. I did not tell them I was seeking the blessing of holiness. I was afraid they might say something to turn me aside, and I was so hungry. So I got ready, and I thought as there were only four of us, and we were trying to help each other, that it would be right for all four of us to be together at this time. But now I praise the Lord that He did not allow this to come to pass, though I did not know then that He was hindering them, as I do now. I was the only one that had a small baby. Sister Bangs and Sister Brown had no families, and Sister Scott's children were all grown. So I had them come and meet at my house every Monday afternoon. Sister Scott always came. Sister Bangs would be there one afternoon, and Sister Brown would not be there. Then when Sister Brown was there, Sister Bangs wouldn't be there. So they were never all there at once. Still I held on and thought it was best not to have this feet-washing done unless we were all together. So I told the sisters and they agreed with me that the four, ought to be together. We did not try to get up a society of this kind, but just we four united for our own mutual help. After three or four weeks went on, and we were defeated every time, I decided not to do it. I prayed about it, and it seemed to come to me that I was not to do it. So that is how the Lord saved me from the mistake of seeking salvation by works. How I ever praise Him for His loving kindness, and for His tender mercy, and for His great patience and forbearance with me. I see now that if I had not been hindered as I was, that I should have gone about teaching that immersion, and the washing of feet, were necessary in order to be sanctified, which would have been a great mistake, but the Lord saved me from it. Praise His name. Amen.

Elizabeth Cady Stanton, *The Woman's Bible* (1895–98)

Elizabeth Cady Stanton (1815–1902)

Born in New York City, Elizabeth Cady married Henry Stanton and enjoyed many happy years of marriage, raising seven children. She and her husband were active in anti-slavery conventions, but Stanton quickly realized that in the anti-slavery camp women were less than equal. Disappointment at the injustice among friends whom she expected would be more "enlightened" was a lightning-rod experience, helping transform her concerns about women's rights into a public campaign. She became good friends with Lucretia Mott, and together they organized the woman's rights convention at Seneca Falls in 1848. Among the many legal injustices women faced, Stanton believed the right to vote to be the most basic obstacle to equality, and she was a vocal activist for this struggle throughout her life.

The Woman's Bible

Although she had been raised Presbyterian, as an adult Stanton shed much of what she had been taught, particularly notions of special revelation and providence. Instead, she believed in a beneficent God and a rational and ordered universe. She saw organized religion as the very root of women's oppression. The Bible had been twisted to men's advantage and intentionally misunderstood to impose women's slavery. To remedy this misuse of Scripture, Stanton published *The Woman's Bible* with commentaries written by a panel of educated women to address points particularly crucial to women in the biblical text. *The Woman's Bible* provides an intentionally feminist reading of the Bible, and it gives insight into the range of biblical criticism of the nineteenth century. Stanton served as editor of the project over several years, publishing the first volume in 1895 and the second in 1898. Here her introduction to the book gives her rationale that the Bible be used to liberate, rather than to enslave, women.

THE WOMAN'S BIBLE

INTRODUCTION.

From the inauguration of the movement for woman's emancipation the Bible has been used to hold her in the "divinely ordained sphere," prescribed in the Old and New Testaments.

The canon and civil law; church and state; priests and legislators; all political parties and religious denominations have alike taught that woman was made after man, of man, and for man, an inferior being, subject to man. Creeds, codes, Scriptures and statutes, are all based on this idea. The fashions, forms, ceremonies and customs of society, church ordinances and discipline all grow out of this idea.

Of the old English common law, responsible for woman's civil and political status, Lord Brougham said, "it is a disgrace to the civilization and Christianity of the Nineteenth Century." Of the canon law, which is responsible for woman's status in the church, Charles Kingsley said, "this will never be a good world for women until the last remnant of the canon law is swept from the face of the earth."

The Bible teaches that woman brought sin and death into the world, that she precipitated the fall of the race, that she was arraigned before the judgment seat of Heaven, tried, condemned and sentenced. Marriage for her was to be a condition of bondage, maternity a period of suffering and anguish, and in silence and subjection, she was to play the role of a dependent on man's bounty for all her material wants, and for all the information she might desire on the vital questions of the hour, she was commanded to ask her husband at home. Here is the Bible position of woman briefly summed up.

Those who have the divine insight to translate, transpose and transfigure this mournful object of pity into an exalted, dignified personage, worthy our worship as the mother of the race, are to be congratulated as having a share of the occult mystic power of the eastern Mahatmas.

The plain English to the ordinary mind admits of no such liberal interpretation. The unvarnished texts speak for themselves. The canon law, church ordinances and Scriptures, are homogeneous, and all reflect the same spirit and sentiments.

These familiar texts are quoted by clergymen in their pulpits, by statesmen in the halls of legislation, by lawyers in the courts, and are echoed by the press of all civilized nations, and accepted by woman herself as "The Word of God." So perverted is the religious element in her nature, that with faith and works she is the chief support of the church and clergy; the very powers that make her emancipation impossible. When, in the early part of the Nineteenth Century, women began to protest against their civil and political degradation, they were referred to the Bible for an answer. When they protested against their unequal position in the church, they were referred to the Bible for an answer.

This led to a general and critical study of the Scriptures. Some, having made a fetish of these books and believing them to be the veritable "Word of God," with liberal translations, interpretations, allegories and symbols, glossed over the most objectionable features of the various books and clung to them as divinely inspired. Others, seeing the family resemblance between the Mosaic code, the canon law, and the old English common law, came to the conclusion that all alike emanated from the same source; wholly human in their origin and inspired by the natural love of domination in the historians. Others, bewildered with their doubts and fears, came to no conclusion. While their clergymen told them on the one hand, that they owed all the blessings and freedom they enjoyed to the Bible, on the other, they said it clearly marked out their circumscribed sphere of action: that the demands for political and civil rights were irreligious, dangerous to the stability of the home, the state and the church. Clerical appeals were circulated from time to time conjuring members of their churches to take no part in the anti-slavery or woman suffrage movements, as they were infidel in their tendencies, undermining the very foundations of society. No wonder the majority of women stood still, and with bowed heads, accepted the situation.

Listening to the varied opinions of women, I have long thought it would be interesting and profitable to get them clearly stated in book form. To this end six years ago I proposed to a committee of women to issue a Woman's Bible, that we might have women's commentaries on women's position in

316

the Old and New Testaments. It was agreed on by several leading women in England and America and the work was begun, but from various causes it has been delayed, until now the idea is received with renewed enthusiasm, and a large committee has been formed, and we hope to complete the work within a year.

Those who have undertaken the labor are desirous to have some Hebrew and Greek scholars, versed in Biblical criticism, to gild our pages with their learning. Several distinguished women have been urged to do so, but they are afraid that their high reputation and scholarly attainments might be compromised by taking part in an enterprise that for a time may prove very unpopular. Hence we may not be able to get help from that class.

Others fear that they might compromise their evangelical faith by affili-ating with those of more liberal views, who do not regard the Bible as the "Word of God," but like any other book, to be judged by its merits. If the Bible teaches the equality of Woman, why does the church refuse to ordain women to preach the gospel, to fill the offices of deacons and elders, and to administer the Sacraments, or to admit them as delegates to the Synods, General Assemblies and Conferences of the different denominations? They have never yet invited a woman to join one of their Revising Committees, nor tried to mitigate the sentence pronounced on her by changing one count in the indictment served on her in Paradise.

The large number of letters received, highly appreciative of the under-taking, is very encouraging to those who have inaugurated the movement, and indicate a growing self-respect and self-assertion in the women of this generation. But we have the usual array of objectors to meet and answer. One correspondent conjures us to suspend the work, as it is "ridiculous" for "women to attempt the revision of the Scriptures." I wonder if any man wrote to the late revising committee of Divines to stop their work on the ground that it was ridiculous for men to revise the Bible. Why is it more ridiculous for women to protest against her present status in the Old and New Testament, in the ordinances and discipline of the church, than in the statutes and constitution of the state? Why is it more ridiculous to arraign ecclesiastics for their false teaching and acts of injustice to women, than members of Congress and the House of Commons? Why is it more auda-cious to review Moses than Blackstone, the Jewish code of laws, than the English system of jurisprudence? Women have compelled their legislators in every state in this Union to so modify their statutes for women that the old common law is now almost a dead letter. Why not compel Bishops and Revising Committees to modify their creeds and dogmas? Forty years ago it seemed as ridiculous to timid, time-serving and retrograde folk for women to demand an expurgated edition of the laws, as it now does to demand an expurgated edition of the Liturgies and the Scriptures. Come, come, my conservative friend, wipe the dew off your spectacles, and see that the world is moving. Whatever your views may be as to the importance of the proposed work, your political and social degradation are but an outgrowth of your status in the Bible. When you express your aversion, based on a blind feeling of reverence in which reason has no control, to the revision of the Scriptures, you do but echo Cowper, who, when asked to read Paine's "Rights of Man," exclaimed, "No man shall convince me that I am improperly governed while I *feel* the contrary."

Others say it is not *politic* to rouse religious opposition. This much-lauded policy is but another word for *cowardice*. How can woman's position be changed from that of a subordinate to an equal, without opposition, without the broadest discussion of all the questions involved in her present degradation? For so far-reaching and momentous a reform as her complete independence, an entire revolution in all existing institutions is inevitable.

Let us remember that all reforms are interdependent, and that whatever is done to establish one principle on a solid basis, strengthens all. Reformers who are always compromising, have not yet grasped the idea that truth is the only safe ground to stand upon. The object of an individual life is not to carry one fragmentary measure in human progress, but to utter the highest truth clearly seen in all directions, and thus to round out and perfect a well balanced character. Was not the sum of influence exerted by John Stuart Mill on political, religious and social questions far greater than that of any statesman or reformer who has sedulously limited his sympathies and activities to carrying one specific measure? We have many women abundantly endowed with capabilities to understand and revise what men have thus far written. But they are all suffering from inherited ideas of their inferiority; they do not perceive it, yet such is the true explanation of their solicitude, lest they should seem to be too self-asserting.

Again there are some who write us that our work is a useless expenditure of force over a book that has lost its hold on the human mind. Most intelligent women, they say, regard it simply as the history of a rude people in a barbarous age, and have no more reverence for the Scriptures than any other work. So long as tens of thousands of Bibles are printed every year, and circulated over the whole habitable globe, and the masses in all English-speaking nations revere it as the word of God, it is vain to belittle its influence. The sentimental feelings we all have for those things we were educated to believe sacred, do not readily yield to pure reason. I distinctly remember the shudder that passed over me on seeing a mother take our family Bible to make a high seat for her child at table. It seemed such a desecration. I was tempted to protest against its use for such a purpose, and this, too, long after my reason had repudiated its divine authority.

To women still believing in the plenary inspiration of the Scriptures, we say give us by all means your exegesis in the light of the higher criticism learned men are now making, and illumine the Woman's Bible, with your inspiration.

Bible historians claim special inspiration for the Old and New Testaments containing most contradictory records of the same events, of miracles opposed to all known laws, of customs that degrade the female sex of all human and animal life, stated in most questionable language that could not be read in a promiscuous assembly, and call all this "The Word of God."

The only points in which I differ from all ecclesiastical teaching is that I do not believe that any man ever saw or talked with God, I do not believe that God inspired the Mosaic code, or told the historians what they say he did about woman, for all the religions on the face of the earth degrade her, and so long as woman accepts the position that they assign her, her emancipation is impossible. Whatever the Bible may be made to do in Hebrew or Greek, in plain English it does not exalt and dignify woman. My standpoint for criticism is the revised edition of 1888. I will so far honor the revising committee of nine men who have given us the best exegesis they can according to their ability, although Disraeli said the last one before he died, contained 150,000 blunders in the Hebrew, and 7,000 in the Greek.

But the verbal criticism in regard to woman's position amounts to little. The spirit is the same in all periods and languages, hostile to her as an equal.

There are some general principles in the holy books of all religions that teach love, charity, liberty, justice and equality for all the human family, there are many grand and beautiful passages, the golden rule has been echoed and re-echoed around the world. There are lofty examples of good and true men and women, all worthy our acceptance and example whose lustre cannot be dimmed by the false sentiments and vicious characters bound up in the same volume. The Bible cannot be accepted or rejected as a whole, its teachings are varied and its lessons differ widely from each other. In criticising the peccadilloes of Sarah, Rebecca and Rachel, we would not shadow the virtues of Deborah, Huldah and Vashti. In criticising the Mosaic code we would not question the wisdom of the golden rule and the fifth Commandment. Again the church claims special consecration for its cathedrals and priesthood, parts of these aristocratic churches are too holy for women to enter, boys were early introduced into the choirs for this reason, woman singing in an obscure corner closely veiled. A few of the more democratic denominations accord women some privileges, but invidious discriminations of sex are found in all religious organizations, and the most bitter outspoken enemies of woman are found among clergymen and bishops of the Protestant religion.

The canon law, the Scriptures, the creeds and codes and church discipline of the leading religions bear the impress of fallible man, and not of our ideal great first cause, "the Spirit of all Good," that set the universe of matter and mind in motion, and by immutable law holds the land, the sea, the planets, revolving round the great centre of light and heat, each in its own elliptic, with millions of stars in harmony all singing together, the glory of creation forever and ever.

Pandita Ramabai,
A Testimony
(1907)

Pandita Ramabai (1858–1922)

Born in India, Pandita Ramabai was the daughter of orthodox Hindu parents. When she was eight, her mother, who had been taught to read the sacred Puranic literature by Ramabai's father, began to teach her, providing a grounding in reading and literature that allowed her to continue in self-education as a young adult. There were no schools for girls or women, and training in the sacred literature was forbidden. That Ramabai was not only an educated woman but a woman who knew Hindu scripture was certainly exceptional. After her family suffered during an extreme famine, Ramabai and her brother journeyed to Calcutta in 1878 in hopes of a better life. In 1881, at age twenty-two, she married a man of Shudra caste who died of cholera less than two years later, leaving her with an infant. In 1883 she left for England to study and "fit myself for lifework." There she was taken under the wing of the Sisters of Wantage. She was baptized and found in their rescue work with prostitutes an impressive example of Christian witness. After returning to India, she established in 1889 a similar ministry, the Mukti Mission, to provide education and opportunities for women and girls of India. She remained a champion of reform and of the education of women until her death in 1922.

A Testimony

Written and published by Ramabai in 1907, this autobiography provides both historical and theological accounting of this extraordinary woman's development. Beginning as a devout student of Hindu literature, she found happiness in study. However, as she pursued further sacred studies while in Calcutta, Ramabai was asked to speak to the Pardah women concerning their duties as women according to the Shastras. Through her study, Ramabai came to believe that the Hindu religion enslaved women, teaching that women were "very bad, worse than demons," were to worship their husbands "with whole-hearted devotion as the only god" and were denied attainment of Moksha, or liberation from Karma, unless they achieved, through some meritorious religious act, reincarnation as a high caste man. During this same time she was introduced to Christianity and was baptized into the Church of England in 1883. In Christianity, Ramabai says she found freedom from caste and sex. "No caste, no sex, no work, and no man was to be depended upon to get salvation, this everlasting life, but God gave it freely to any one and every one who believed on His Son Whom He sent to be the 'propitiation for our sins.' " This report offers a fascinating view of the encounter of Indian culture and Christianity.

A TESTIMONY

An Honorable Heritage

My father, though a very orthodox Hindu and strictly adhering to caste and other religious rules, was yet a reformer in his own way. He could not see why women and people of Shudra caste should not learn to read and write the Sanskrit language and learn sacred literature other than the Vedas.

He thought it better to try the experiment at home instead of preaching to others. He found an apt pupil in my mother, who fell in line with his plan, and became an excellent Sanskrit scholar. . . .

A Unique Education

When I was about eight years old, my mother began to teach me and continued to do so until I was about fifteen years of age. During these years she succeeded in training my mind so that I might be able to carry on my own education with very little aid from others. I did not know of any schools for girls and women existing then, where higher education was to be obtained.

Moreover, my parents did not like us children to come in contact with the outside world. They wanted us to be strictly religious and adhere to their old faith. Learning any other language except Sanskrit was out of the question. Secular education of any kind was looked upon as leading people to worldliness which would prevent them from getting into the way of Moksha, or liberation from everlasting trouble of reincarnation, in millions and millions of animal species, and undergoing the pains of suffering countless millions of diseases, and deaths. . . .

Calcutta—Deeper Hindu Studies and Scepticism

While staying in Calcutta we became acquainted with many learned Pandits. Some of them requested me to lecture to the Pardah women on the duties of women according to the Shastras. I had to study the subject well before I could lecture on it; so I bought the books of the Hindu law published in Calcutta. Besides reading them I read other books which would help me in my work. While reading the Dharma Shastras I came to know many things which I never knew before. There were contradictory statements about almost everything. What one book said was most righteous, the other book declared as being unrighteous. While reading the Mahabharata I found the following, "The Vedas differ from each other; Smrities, that is, books of sacred laws, do not agree with one another; the secret of religion is in some hidden place: the only way is that which is followed by great men."

This I found true of about everything, but there were two things on which all those books, the Dharma Shastras, the sacred epics, the Puranas and modern poets, the popular preachers of the present day and orthodox high-caste men, were agreed, that women of high and low caste, as a class were bad, very bad, worse than demons, as unholy as untruth; and that they could not get Moksha as men. The only hope of their getting this much-desired liberation from Karma and its results, that is, countless millions of births and deaths and untold suffering, was the worship of their husbands. The husband is said to be the woman's god; there is no other god for her. This god may be the worst sinner and a great criminal; still HE IS HER GOD, and she must worship him. She can have no hope of getting admission into Svarga, the abode of the gods without his pleasure, and if she pleases him in all things, she will have the privilege of going to Svarga as his slave, there to serve him and be one of his wives among the thousands of the Svarga harlots who are presented to him by the gods in exchange for his wife's merit.

The woman is allowed to go into higher existence thus far but to attain Moksha or liberation, she must perform such great religious acts as will obtain for her the merit by which she will be reincarnated as a high caste man, in order to study Vedas and the Vedanta, and thereby get the knowledge of the true Brahma and be amalgamated in it. The extraordinary religious acts which help a woman to get into the way of getting Moksha are utter abandonment of her will to that of her husband. She is to worship him with whole-hearted devotion as the only god; to know and see no other pleasure in life except in the most degraded slavery to him. The woman has no right to study the Vedas and Vedanta, and without knowing them, no one can know the Brahma; without knowing Brahma no one can get liberation, therefore no woman as a woman can get liberation, that is, Moksha. . . .

. . . My eyes were being gradually opened; I was waking up to my own hopeless condition as a woman, and it was becoming clearer and clearer to me that I had no place anywhere as far as religious consolation was concerned. I became quite dissatisfied with myself. I wanted something more than the Shastras could give me, but I did not know what it was that I wanted. . . .

Finding Christ

. . . I do not know if any one of my readers has ever had the experience of being shut up in a room where there was nothing but thick darkness and then groping in it to find something of which he or she was in dire need. I can think of no one but the blind man, whose story is given in St. John chapter nine. He was born blind and remained so for forty years of his life; and then suddenly he found the Mighty One, Who could give him eyesight. Who could have described his joy at seeing the daylight, when there had not been a particle of hope of his ever seeing it? Even the inspired evangelist has not attempted to do it. I can give only a faint idea of what I felt when my mental eyes were opened, and when I, who was "sitting in darkness saw Great Light," and when I felt sure that to me, who but a few moments ago "sat in the region and shadow of death, Light *had* sprung up." I was very like the man who was told, "In the name of Jesus Christ of Nazareth rise up and walk. . . . And he leaping up stood, and walked, and entered with them into the temple, walking and leaping and praising God."

I looked to the blessed Son of God who was lifted up on the cross and there suffered death, even the death of the cross, in my stead, that I might be made free from the bondage of sin, and from the fear of death, and I received life. O the love, the unspeakable love of the Father for me, a lost sinner, which gave His only Son to die for me! I had not merited this love, but that was the very reason why He showed it to me.

How very different the truth of God was from the false idea that I had entertained from my earliest childhood. That was that I must have merit to earn present or future happiness, the pleasure of Svarga, or face the utterly inconceivable loss of Moksha or leberation. This I could never hope for, since a woman, as a woman, has no hope of Moksha according to Hindu religion. The Brahman priests have tried to deceive the women and the Shudras and other low-caste people into the belief that they have some hope. But when we study for ourselves the books of the religious law and enquire from the higher authorities we find that there is nothing, no nothing whatever for us.

They say that women and Shudras and other low-caste people can gain Svarga by serving the husband and the Brahman. But the happiness of Svarga does not last long. The final blessed state to which the Brahman is entitled is not for women and low-caste people. But here this blessed Book, the Christians' Bible says:—

"When we were yet without strength, in due time Christ died for the ungodly. For scarcely for a righteous man will one die: yet peradventure for a good man some would even dare to die. But God commendeth His love toward us, in that, while we were yet sinners Christ died for us. . . . For . . . when we were enemies, we were reconciled to God by the death of His Son." Romans 5:6-10.

"In this was manifested the love of God toward us, because that God sent His only begotten Son into the world, that we might live through Him. Herein is love, not that we loved God, but that He loved us, and sent His Son to be the propitiation for our sins." I John 4:9, 10.

How good, how indescribably good! What good news for me a woman, a woman born in India, among Brahmans who hold out no hope for me and the like of me! The Bible declares that Christ did not reserve this great salvation for a particular caste or sex.

"But as many as received Him, to them gave He power to become the sons of God, even to them that believe on His name: which were born, not of blood, nor of the will of the flesh, nor of the will of man, but of God." John 1:12, 13. "For the grace of God that bringeth salvation hath appeared to all men." Titus 2:11. "The kindness and love of God our Saviour toward man appeared, not by works of righteousness which we have done, but according to His mercy He saved us." Titus 3:4.

No caste, no sex, no work, and no man was to be depended upon to get salvation, this everlasting life, but God gave it freely to any one and every one who believed on His Son Whom He sent to be the "propitiation for our sins." And there was not a particle of doubt left as to whether this salvation was a present one or not. I had not to wait till after undergoing births and deaths for countless millions of times, when I should become a Brahman man, in order to get to know the Brahma. And then, was there any joy and happiness to be hoped for? No, there is nothing but to be amalgamated into Nothingness-Shunya, Brahma.

The Son of God says, "Verily, verily, I say unto you He that heareth my word, and believeth on Him that sent me hath everlasting life, and shall not come into condemnation but is passed from death unto life." John 5:24.

"If we receive the witness of men, the witness of God is greater; for this is the witness of God which He hath testified of His Son. He that believeth on the Son of God hath the witness in himself: he that believeth not God, hath made Him a liar: because he believeth not the record that God gave of His Son. And this is the record, that GOD HATH GIVEN TO US ETERNAL LIFE, AND HIS LIFE IS IN HIS SON. He that hath the Son hath life; and he that hath not the Son of God hath not life. These things have I written unto you that believe on the name of the Son of God; that ye may know that *ye have eternal life* and that ye may believe on the name of the Son of God." 1 John 5:9-13.

The Holy Spirit made it clear to me from the Word of God, that the salvation which God gives through Christ is present, and not something future. I believed it, I received it, and I was filled with joy. . . .

At the end of 1896 when the great famine came on this country, I was led by the Lord to step forward and start new work, trusting Him for both temporal and spiritual blessings . . .

Bombay—Founding of Mukti Mission—Home of Salvation

. . . There were only two day-pupils in my school, when it was started a little more than eighteen years ago. No one was urged to become a Christian, nor was any one compelled to study the Bible. But the Book was placed in the library along with other religious books. The daily testimony to the goodness of the True God awakened new thoughts in many a heart.

After the first ten years of our existence as a school, our constitution was changed slightly. Since then, every pupil admitted in the school has been receiving religious instruction, retaining perfect liberty of conscience.

Many hundreds of the girls and young women who have come to my Home ever since its doors were opened for them have found Christ as I

326

have. They are capable of thinking for themselves. They have had their eyes opened by reading the Word of God, and many of them have been truly converted and saved, to the praise and glory of God. I thank God for letting me see several hundred of my sisters, the children of my love and prayer, gloriously saved. All this was done by God in answer to the prayers of faith of thousands of His faithful servants in all lands, who are constantly praying for us all. . . .

Georgia Harkness, *Understanding the Christian Faith* (1947)

Georgia Harkness (1891–1974)

Born in Harkness, New York, Georgia Harkness was raised in the Methodist Episcopal Church and found her spiritual and ecclesial home there all her life. She completed her Ph.D. at Boston University in 1923, entering the field of theological studies in which she taught for nearly forty years. While she was a woman of keen mind and rigorous scholarship, her writing interests were always focused on the lay reader and on providing resources for the devotional and evangelical life. Harkness was noted for her own spiritual life—uncommon among twentieth-century theologians—although it was marked by periods of profound despair as well as renewal. As Professor of Applied Theology at Garrett Seminary and then at Pacific School of Religion, Harkness wrote prolifically on classical theological doctrines, devotional practices, and social issues. She was active in the affairs of the General Conference of the Methodist Church and in the World Council of Churches throughout her life, working toward institutional justice for women and laypeople. She worked passionately against the injustices of segregation, violence, and the use of atomic weapons. After her retirement in 1961, she continued to be active in publishing and religious affairs until her death in 1974.

Understanding the Christian Faith

Harkness published thirty-five books, reflecting her constant concern with educating lay Christians in the basics of Christian faith and life. In the introduction to this volume, *Understanding the Christian Faith,* Harkness uses the modern analogy of consumer goods to claim that "it is the layman, not the theologian in the seminary or even the minister" who is ultimately the target "consumer" for Christianity's "product." Even so, it is rare to find "any clear understanding of what the Christian faith is or what it means." This book is an attempt to remedy the church's failure to ground lay Christians in a deep understanding of faith. In these excerpts we read Harkness's explication of what faith is and is not, of the nature of human beings, and of the nature and content of salvation.

UNDERSTANDING THE CHRISTIAN FAITH

Chapter I

THE MEANING OF FAITH

1. What faith is not

It often happens that wrong ideas as to what faith involves create confusion and lead to false expectations. In order to go forward without obstruction, let us clear away the underbrush by asking first what faith is not.

To have faith does not mean to be gullible. Faith is not believing on inadequate evidence or with the evidence pointing in the opposite direction. In religion, as in other things, if one tries to believe something "by main strength and awkwardness," the believer's position is awkward but not strong. No intelligent person would believe everything he reads in the newspapers, including the claims of the patent medicine advertisements to cure all ailments! So in religion one must use discretion, not supposing that the demands of faith require him to believe everything that may be set forth in pious words.

The assumption that what we take on faith we take with closed minds, as if we had blinders on to shut out whatever light might creep in from other sources, lies at the root of the quarrel between religion and science. . . .

In the second place, though faith is related to belief, faith is never wholly a matter of intellectual assent to the truth of a statement. One can believe in God with a very complete set of arguments, yet not have any faith that makes a difference in living. On the other hand, with a minimum of intellectual foundations—though always with *some*—one may have a powerful faith. One's belief ought to be as near right as hard thinking and inquiry will make it, for otherwise faith though strong is apt to be inflexible and misdirected. But it is a mistake to suppose that when we discover we must alter some belief, our faith will collapse. . . .

And in the third place, faith is not identical with mystery—a deep, dark reservoir into which to dump anything that seems unexplainable. The danger of this view lies in the fact that on this basis the more knowledge we get, the more our faith recedes. . . .

2. What faith is

Faith, then, does not mean belief without any basis, or intellectual assent to certain ideas, or a leap from solid footing into a chasm of mystery. But what does it mean?

It means, first, *positive trust* in somebody or something, the willingness to commend one's life to another's keeping or to act on some conviction believed to be true. The familiar definition, "Faith is *assurance* of things hoped for, a *conviction* of things not seen," brings out this meaning. Go through all the biblical statements quoted above, and there is not one of them that does not emphasize this active, positive aspect, both in the exercise of faith and in its fruits.

Some analogies on the human level will make clearer what religious faith entails. One does not eat his dinner or lie down on his bed at night without faith that the food will nourish and not poison him, that the bed will support and not suffocate him. One does not usually go to a doctor unless he has faith that the doctor will help him get well. One does not—or ought not—to marry without faith that the other person will co-operate to form a home. In all these instances suspicion can undermine faith, and it ought to undermine it if there are valid grounds for mistrust. Otherwise one is credulous rather than trusting. But if we distrust where we ought to have faith, we not only make ourselves and others unhappy but we cut ourselves off from bodily health and enrichment of spirit. Life could not go on fruitfully without a large-scale exercise of faith in our everyday social relations.

Transfer this principle to our relation to God, and what do we find? The basic atheism is not intellectual rejection of belief in God's existence. If one cares enough to question about God, there is far more hope for him than if he is indifferent. As Tennyson put it:

> There lives more faith in honest doubt,
> Believe me, than in half the creeds.

The basic atheism is unwillingness to commit our lives to God's keeping, callousness to God's demands, the ordering of life as if God did not exist.

This is the "sin of unbelief," a lack of faith so widespread in our time that society has been honeycombed by it and engulfed in world-wide destruction. To have faith in God is not merely to assert that God exists (which few people dispute) but to do the much harder thing of putting our trust in God and his way as the basis for individual and social living. . . .

This suggests a second meaning, that of *courageous adventure*. Indeed courage is presupposed in faith as trust and commitment, for while there are some things to which to commit ourselves without incurring risk, this is not true of many things of importance. To get married, or choose a vocation, or give oneself to a cause is to act on faith—not blindly, but with full awareness that difficulties as well as delights are in store. We must count the cost and be willing to pay it before we can go ahead. To "walk by faith and not by sight" does not mean to stumble around in the dark, but with many of the details hidden to go forward boldly by the light we have. . . .

But what does it mean to be "saved by faith"? Part of it is man's trusting and obedient response to God, of which we have been speaking. But before we can respond, God must have acted. So a third meaning of faith appears.

Saving faith means *saving help*—an experience in which one feels that light and strength and the joy of victory over temptation flow into his life from God. . . .

Faith then means confident trust, courageous adventure, and an inflowing of God-given power. But has it nothing to do with truth? It has a great deal. This leads us to a fourth meaning, which we might call *illumined belief*.

It is faith that enables us to have eyes to see and ears to hear. It is faith as "insight" that quickens the mind to truer "sight." As one learns the truth about science only when his eyes are opened by an eagerness that drives him to learn, as one really sees great art or listens to great music only when his soul is sensitive to it, as one finds depths of richness in a friend only through an outgoingness of spirit that opens new channels, so one learns the truth about God only when he "stands in faith." One may get a detached sort of knowledge, which is true enough as far as it goes, by a weighing of arguments and canvassing of evidence as to the existence and nature of God. One does not really get to Christian faith until he lets God capture his spirit. . . .

Faith is the union of trusting confidence and courageous action with response to God's leading, and of all these with the insight that lights the way toward truth. It is this combination that makes Christian faith such a powerful force. Our world, far from having outgrown it, desperately needs more. Faith is not all there is of religion, but without it we shall have neither saving hope nor conquering love. . . .

Chapter VII

WHAT IS MAN?

. . . The reason why it is not easy to say clearly just what man is, is the fact that when one begins to describe one aspect of man's nature, another apparently contradictory but equally real aspect presents itself. Then unless both sides are included, the description becomes not only fragmentary but false. The Christian understanding of man can best be stated in four of these paradoxes:

1. Man is both nature and spirit.
2. Man is both free and bound.
3. Man is both child of God and sinner.
4. Man is both transient and eternal.

We shall attempt in this chapter to suggest the meaning of the first three, leaving the fourth until we come to a special chapter on immortality.

1. *Man as nature and spirit*

To say that man is nature is simply to say what few people have ever denied—that we each have a body. This body is composed of physical and chemical elements, very intricately related. It has much in common with the bodies of the higher animals, and has a long biological past. Each human body is marvelously equipped with organs of sensation, muscular movement, digestion, circulation, respiration, reproduction, self-repair of injury, and other functions that we seldom think about unless they get out of order. The human body takes longer to mature than the bodies of most of the lower animals, and it will endure an amazing amount of strain, but it wears out in seventy or eighty years.

If we ask whether our bodies are the product of nature or of God, it is a false alternative, for everything in nature is the handiwork of God. That God has been fashioning the human organism through billions of years of creative labor should not make us think less, but more, highly of it. . . .

But is the body all? Christian faith affirms vigorously that it is not. In the majestic epic of creation with which Genesis begins, there are three key sentences: "In the beginning God created . . . And God saw that it was good . . . And God created man in his own image, in the image of God created he him." This conviction that man is a living soul made in the divine image is central to our understanding of ourselves and our fellow man. Let us add to this witness from the Old Testament, Jesus' unvarying estimate of the worth of every human soul as a child of God—however weak, sinful, or outcast by men one might be—and we have the foundations of the Christian view of man and his destiny.

The term "soul" has gone out of fashion in many quarters, particularly among psychologists. This is not wholly loss, for it is inaccurate to speak of the soul as a third thing about us that is not mind or body—a mysterious something that cannot be discovered or defined. Nevertheless, when the soul is understood as spirit, or as mind or consciousness in the broadest sense, it means something very real. Perhaps the best way to get at what it means is to think of the difference between the human spirit and all lower forms of animal life. A man can weigh moral issues and make moral decisions, can strive after truth and beauty, can learn from the past experience of the human race and project his aspirations into the long future, can form fellowships with other men for mutual enrichment, can worship God and come into fellowship with him. These capacities make of man a "living soul" in a sense not shared by any other creature, and justify us in assuming with the author of Genesis that man is God's supreme creation made in the divine image.

2. *Man as free and bound*

If we undertake to select one attribute which above all distinguishes human personality from animal life and from the world of physical nature, it is man's freedom. If we glance again at the characteristics named above which make him a soul, we see it is only because man has some freedom of choice that he can decide between good and evil, employ his intelligence to discover truth, become sensitive to beauty, appropriate meanings from the past or project them as goals into the future, increase the values in a society, or come into conscious fellowship with God. God might have chosen to make us automatic puppets or mechanically determined robots, but he chose to make us men with freedom to achieve or mar our destinies. . . .

Nevertheless, we are never wholly free, and it is as serious a mistake to overlook our limitations as to deny the fact of our freedom. Our heredity, our social environment, and our own previous experience have set for us certain paths that are easier to follow than others, though in normal persons the grooves are seldom so fixed that we cannot possibly get out of them. Our bodies, useful servants that they are, are subject to fatigue and disease; they have to be fed and clothed; they will not do all that in our more ambitious moments we ask of them. We live in a physical world which in its basic order cannot be changed, and which in the arrangement of its parts is subject—but never wholly so—to control by human wills. We live in a society of which many aspects—but not every aspect at once—can be altered. On any project we work at, whether it is getting a meal, reading a book, driving a car, controlling the use of atomic energy, or making world peace, human freedom can be exercised effectively only when our limitations, as well as the possibilities open to us, are taken into account.

Some of these limiting factors are established by God in the creation of the world. Such things as gravitation in the physical world, the eventual death of a living organism, the inevitable collapse of a society built on hate and greed, are elements in the way things are made. We had better accept them, for protest will not change them. Others, such as preventable disease, ignorance, poverty, strife, and all manner of social evils, are manmade limitations and by a right use of human freedom can be removed. A large part of what is meant by the coming of God's Kingdom on earth is the lifting of such limitations so that all men, as God's sons, may be free.

3. Man as child of God

. . . It is essential that we keep a right balance in our judgment of man's nature. Religious humanism and the more extreme forms of liberalism have sometimes made so much of man's power and self-sufficiency that God almost vanished from the picture. Or, if God did not disappear, the difference between God and man became so slight that humility about our status tended to disappear. In contrast with this assumption of the divineness of human nature, the new orthodoxy puts its emphasis on the difference between God and man, and on the sinfulness which always and everywhere corrupts human nature. There is truth in both these positions, and error in both if carried to extremes. We must never forget that it is God who has made us, and not we ourselves; that our lives are in his keeping; that the only appropriate attitude for the Christian is humble worship of God and dependence on our Creator.

Sinners we are, and sinners we remain save for the unmerited, forgiving mercy of God. Nevertheless, we are children of God, and *all* men are his children—made in his image with the stamp of divinity upon their souls.

To hold this belief about man is vital to our Christian outlook and action. Upon it hinge many issues. Take, for example, democracy. Whatever the political system, there can be no real democracy except that which is founded on the conviction that all human beings, of whatever race, or color, or class, or sex, are of supreme worth in God's sight and ought therefore to

334

be treated as persons. This conviction is the only real leverage by which to combat race prejudice, economic exploitation, mass unemployment, forced labor, or other forms of slavery. Only on the basis of the equality and inherent worth of men and women, adults and children, old persons and young, can family fellowship exist. Not until this principle is extended to include the persons of all nations in the family of God, great nations and small, white and colored, victor and vanquished, shall we have an international order founded on the ideal of justice for all—and without this foundation we shall not have peace. . . .

If this is true of our basic human relations, what man thinks of himself is equally important to personal living. The undermining of a sense of meaning and destiny for one's life is one of the most serious aspects of our contemporary scene. From it has come much cynicism, despair, and loss of nerve. Whatever happens, one ought to live with courage, dignity, and hope. One can so live if he thinks of himself as a child of God and, in spite of tragic sin and folly, knows himself to be the object of God's continuing love and care. Lacking this conviction, one is apt to find his stamina slipping and inner resources crumbling before the avalanche of misery that has engulfed our time. Only the union of humility with an awareness of human dignity that is not of our own making but the gift of God, can enable us to transform confusion and chaos into "a time for greatness."

4. Man as sinner

But not only is it necessary to preserve a sense of man's dignity as God's child; it is equally, and perhaps even more, necessary to see all men including ourselves as sinners. What, then, do we mean by sin? . . .

In the first place, any act or attitude that is sinful runs counter to the nature of God and the righteous will of God. This is the truth that lies in the often distorted doctrine of human depravity. When we measure even our best acts and aspirations by the standard of God's holy will as revealed in Christ, we all have sinned and come short of the glory of God. The eclipse of the concept of sin during the brief ascendancy of humanistic liberalism was a direct outgrowth of our failure to take seriously God's holiness and the rigor of his moral demands. When man becomes the measure of all things, we talk of "cultural lags" and "antisocial behavior." When God is restored to his rightful place of primacy in human thought, sin, our ancient enemy, again is seen to be our ever-present and most malignant foe.

In the second place, any sin, whether of overt act or inner attitude, presupposes freedom to do or to be otherwise. To the extent that a person really does what he must do or is what he must be, *and cannot help himself,* to that extent he is victim and not sinner. As nobody is wholly free, so nobody is wholly depraved. But the other side of this comforting truth is that one rarely, if ever, is wholly helpless and therefore free from guilt. In almost every situation there is freedom enough left to do better than one does. . . .

In the third place, sin presupposes a knowledge of good and evil adequate to form a basis of choice. . . .

And in the fourth place, sin, according to the Christian frame of thought, involves at the same time relation to our neighbor and to God. As the Christian requirement of love links love of God and love of neighbor in a twofold Great Commandment from which neither element can be dropped, so sin against neighbor through lack of human love is sin against God. . . .

. . . There is born in all of us, not "original sin" as a hereditary corruption passed on from Adam's guilt, but a biological tendency to self-centeredness. This is as natural and unsinful in little children as is the impulse to eat or sleep or cry from discomfort. It is a useful endowment, not only for self-preservation, but for the growth of personality through the relating of all experience to the self. But such self-centeredness, though very necessary, is very dangerous, and in adult life easily passes over into willful selfishness. If uncurbed, it becomes the self-love which is the root of all other sins and of most of our unhappiness.

The forms such self-love takes, in the ordinary events of living, are manifold. It shows itself in desire to have our own way regardless of the wishes or rights or needs of others; in the narrowing of interests to what immediately touches us; in thirst for personal recognition, compliments, and applause; in eagerness in conversation or action always to occupy the center of the stage; in jealousy of others who secure recognition or privileges or goods we want; in self-pity; in peevishness and petty complaint when things do not go as we would have them. These are, at best, unlovely traits when we see them in others. As indications that we love ourselves more than we love our neighbor or our Lord, they are evidences of sin so life strangling that God alone can give release. . . .

Chapter VIII

SALVATION

. . . Even among many people otherwise favorable to religion, the idea of salvation is in poor standing. This is chiefly for two reasons. First, the term is not well understood. From revival sermons of an earlier day it has come to mean a sharp separation of the saved from the damned, with the saved going to the bliss of heaven while sinners forever burn in hell. This seems so inconsistent with the God of love revealed in Christ that this idea of salvation has been widely given up, but with nothing to put in its place. In the second place, those who see a more appropriate meaning in terms of the peace, joy, and spiritual victory of the Christian are often still at a loss to know how to lay hold upon it for themselves. . . .

What, then, are we saved *by?* This can be said in a sentence but requires a lifetime for its understanding. We are saved by the grace of God—by the free, gracious, outpouring of God's love upon us and his forgiveness when we repent of our sin and turn to him for cleansing and strength. We do not save ourselves; it is God that saves us. But this does not mean that it costs nothing on our part. God can save us only as we meet his conditions and open our lives to receive his power. . . .

REFERENCES

1. Gospel of Mary

Grant, Robert. *Gnosticism: A Sourcebook of Heretical Writings from the Early Christian Period.* New York: Harper & Row, 1961.

2. Thecla

Roberts, Alexander, and James Donaldson, eds. *The Acts of Paul and Thecla.* In *The Ante-Nicene Fathers,* vol. VIII. New York: The Christian Literature Company, 1885; reprint, Grand Rapids: Eerdmans, 1972.

3. Perpetua

Wilson-Kastner, Patricia, et al., eds. *A Lost Tradition: Women Writers of the Early Church.* Lanham, Mass.: University Press of America, 1981.

4. Acts of the Martyrs

Musurillo, Herbert. *The Acts of the Christian Martyrs.* Oxford, Eng.: Clarendon Press, 1972.

5. Macrina

Schaff, Philip, and Henry Wace, eds. *The Soul and the Resurrection.* In *Nicene and Post-Nicene Fathers,* Second Series, vol. V. New York: The Christian Literature Company, 1893; reprint, Grand Rapids: Eerdmans, 1972.

6. Paula

Schaff, Philip, and Henry Wace, eds. *Letter to Eustochium.* In *Nicene and Post-Nicene Fathers,* Second Series, vol. VI. New York: The Christian Literature Company, 1893; reprint, Grand Rapids: Eerdmans, 1972.

REFERENCES

7. Egeria

Wilson-Kastner, Patricia, et al., eds. *A Lost Tradition: Women Writers of the Early Church.* Lanham, Mass.: University Press of America, 1981.

8. Leoba

Talbot, C. H., ed. and trans. *The Anglo-Saxon Missionaries in Germany.* New York: Sheed and Ward, 1954.

9. Dhuoda

Wilson, Katharina M. *Medieval Woman Writers.* Athens: University of Georgia Press, 1984.

10. Hrotsvit of Gandersheim

Wilson, Katharina M. *Medieval Woman Writers.* Athens: University of Georgia Press, 1984.

11. Hildegard of Bingen

Steele, Francisca Maria, ed. and trans. *The Life and Visions of St. Hildegarde.* London: Heath, Cranton and Ousely, 1914.

12. Hadewijch of Brabant

Sijthoff, A. W. *Mediaeval Netherlands Religious Literature.* Translated and introduced by Eric Colledge. New York: London House and Maxwell, 1965.

13. Beatrice of Nazareth

Brunn, Emilie Zum, and Georgette Epiney-Burgard. *Women Mystics in Medieval Europe.* Translated by Sheila Hughes. New York: Paragon House,1989.

14. Clare of Assisi

Armstrong, Regis J., O.F.M., and Ignatius C. Brady, O.F.M., trans. *Francis and Clare: The Complete Works.* Classics of Western Spirituality Series. New York: Paulist Press, 1982.

15. Mechthild of Magdeburg

Menzies, Lucy, trans. *The Revelations of Mechthild of Magdeburg, or the Flowing Light of the Godhead.* London: Longmans, Green and Co., 1953.

16. Angela de Foligno

Steegman, Mary G., trans. *The Book of Divine Consolation of the Blessed Angela of Foligno.* New York: Cooper Square Publishers, Inc., 1966.

17. Marguerite Porete

Wilson, Katharina M. *Medieval Women Writers.* Athens: University of Georgia Press, 1984.

18. Birgitta of Sweden

Harris, Marguerite Tjader, ed. *Birgitta of Sweden: Life and Selected Revelations.* Translated by Albert R. Kezel. Classics of Western Spirituality Series. New York: Paulist Press, 1990.

19. Julian of Norwich

Julian of Norwich. *Revelations of Divine Love.* Translated by Clifton Wolters. New York: Scholars Press, 1986.

20. Catherine of Siena

Noffke, Suzanne, O.P., trans. *Catherine of Siena: The Dialogue.* Classics of Western Spirituality Series. New York: Paulist Press, 1980.

21. Catherine of Genoa

Hughes, Serge, trans. *Catherine of Genoa: Purgation and Purgatory, The Spiritual Dialogue.* Classics of Western Spirituality Series. New York: Paulist Press, 1979.

22. Vittoria Colonna

Bainton, Roland. *Women of the Reformation in Germany and Italy.* Minneapolis: Augsburg, 1971.

23. Teresa of Avila

Kavanaugh, Kieran, O.C.D., and Otilio Rodriguez, O.C.D. *Teresa of Avila: The Interior Castle.* Classics of Western Spirituality Series. New York: Paulist Press, 1979.

24. Jane de Chantal

Thibert, Peronne Marie, V.H.M. *Francis de Sales, Jane de Chantal: Letters of Spiritual Direction.* Classics of Western Spirituality Series. New York: Paulist Press, 1988.

25. Juana Inés de la Cruz

Trueblood, Alan S., trans. *A Sor Juana Anthology.* Cambridge, Mass.: Harvard University Press, 1988.

26. Madame Jeanne Guyon

Guyon, J.M.B. de la Mothe. *Spiritual Torrents.* Translated by A. W. Marston. London: H.R. Allenson, Ltd., 1908.

27. Susanna Wesley

Clark, Adam. *Memoirs of the Wesley Family; collected Principally from Original Documents.* New York: The Methodist Episcopal Church at the Conference Office, 1832.

28. Ann Lee

United Society. *Testimonies concerning the Character and Ministry of Mother Ann Lee and the First Witnesses of the Gospel of Christ's Second Appearing; Given by Some of the Aged Brethren and Sisters of the United Society, including a Few Sketches of Their Own Religious Experiences: Approved by the Church.* Albany, N.Y.: Packard & Van Benthuysen, 1827.

29. Jarena Lee

Andrews, William L. *Sisters of the Spirit: Three Black Women's Autobiographies of the Nineteenth Century.* Bloomington: Indiana University Press, 1986.

30. Phoebe Palmer

Oden, Thomas C. *Phoebe Palmer: Selected Writings.* Sources of American Spirituality Series. New York: Paulist Press, 1988.

31. Lucretia Mott

Greene, Dana, ed. *Lucretia Mott: Her Complete Speeches and Sermons.* New York: The Edwin Mellen Press, 1980.

32. Hannah Whitall Smith

Smith, Hannah Whitall. *The Open Secret; or, the Bible Explaining Itself.* New York: Fleming Revell Company, 1885.

33. Amanda Berry Smith

Smith, Amanda Berry. *An Autobiography: The Story of the Lord's Dealings with Mrs. Amanda Smith, The Colored Lady Evangelist.* Chicago: Meyer & Brother, Publishers, 1893; reprint New York: Garland Publishing, Inc., 1987.

34. Elizabeth Cady Stanton

Stanton, Elizabeth Cady. *The Woman's Bible.* Salem, N.H.: Ayer Company Publishers, 1972.

35. Pandita Ramabai

Ramabai, Pandita. *A Testimony.* 9th ed. Kedgaon, Poona Dist., India: Ramabai Mukti Mission, 1968.

36. Georgia Harkness

Harkness, Georgia. *Understanding the Christian Faith.* Nashville: Abingdon Press, 1947.

BIBLIOGRAPHY OF PRIMARY SOURCES

General Sources

Clark, Elizabeth, and Herbert Richardson, eds. *Women and Religion: A Feminist Sourcebook of Christian Thought*. New York: Harper & Row, 1977.

Conn, Joann Wolski. *Women's Spirituality: Resources for Christian Development*. New York: Paulist Press, 1991.

Deen, Edith. *Great Women of the Christian Faith*. New York: Harper and Bros., 1959.

Hardesty, Nancy. *Great Women of Faith: The Strength and Influence of Christian Women*. Grand Rapids: Baker Book House, 1980.

Ruether, Rosemary Radford, and Rosemary Skinner Keller, eds., *Women and Religion in America*. 3 vols. San Francisco: Harper & Row, 1983.

Sources Organized by Periods

I. Up to 1200 C.E.

Brock, Sebastian P., and Susan Ashbrook Harvey, trans. *Holy Women of the Syrian Orient*. Berkeley: University of California Press, 1987.

Brunn, Emilie Zum, and Georgette Epiney-Burgard. *Women Mystics in Medieval Europe*. Translated by Sheila Hughes. New York: Paragon House, 1989.

Callahan, Virginia Woods, trans. "The Life of Macrina," *Ascetical Works*. In *The Fathers of the Church, a New Translation*, Vol. 58. Washington, D.C.: Catholic University of America Press, 1947.

Clark, Elizabeth A., trans. *The Life of Melania the Younger*. Volume 14, *Studies in Women and Religion*. New York: The Edwin Mellen Press, 1984.

Dronke, Peter. *Women Writers of the Middle Ages: A Critical Study of Texts from Perpetua († 203) to Marguerite Porete († 1310)*. Cambridge, Eng.: Cambridge University Press, 1984.

Grant, Barbara L., trans. "Five Liturgical Songs by Hildegard von Bingen (1098–1179)." *Signs: Journal of Women in Culture and Society* 5, 3 (1980) : 557-67.

BIBLIOGRAPHY OF PRIMARY SOURCES

Grant, Robert. *Gnosticism: A Sourcebook of Heretical Writings from the Early Christian Period.* New York: Harper & Row, 1961.

Hanning, Robert, and Joan Ferrante, trans. *The Lais of Marie de France.* New York: E.P. Dutton, 1978.

Hart, Mother Columba, O.S.B., and Jane Bishop, trans. *Hildegard of Bingen: Scivias.* Classics of Western Spirituality Series. New York: Paulist Press, 1990.

Hroswitha. *Hroswitha of Gandersheim: Her Life, Times and Works.* Athens: University of Georgia Press, 1977.

Layton, Bentley. *The Gnostic Scriptures.* Garden City, N.Y.: Doubleday, 1987.

Lesko, Barbara S., ed. *Women's Earliest Records: From Ancient Egypt and Western Asia.* Brown University, Providence Rhode Island: Proceedings of the Conference on Women in the Ancient Near East, November 5-7, 1987. Atlanta, Georgia: Scholars Press, 1989.

Musurillo, Herbert. *The Acts of the Christian Martyrs.* Oxford, Eng.: Clarendon Press, 1972.

Petroff, Elizabeth Alvida. *Medieval Women's Visionary Literature.* Oxford, Eng.: Oxford University Press, 1986.

Radice, Betty, trans. *The Letters of Abelard and Heloise.* Baltimore and London: Penguin, 1974.

Roberts, Alexander, and James Donaldson, eds. *The Acts of Paul and Thecla.* In *The Ante-Nicene Fathers,* Volume VIII. New York: The Christian Literature Company, 1885; reprint, Grand Rapids: Eerdmans, 1972.

Robinson, James M., ed. *The Nag Hammadi Library in English.* San Francisco: Harper & Row, 1988.

Schaff, Philip, and Henry Wace, eds. *Letter to Eustochium.* In *Nicene and Post-Nicene Fathers,* Second Series, Volume VI. New York: The Christian Literature Company, 1893; reprint, Grand Rapids: Eerdmans, 1972.

_____. *The Soul and the Resurrection.* In *Nicene and Post-Nicene Fathers,* Second Series, Volume V. New York: The Christian Literature Company, 1893; reprint, Grand Rapids: Eerdmans, 1972.

Schneemelcher, W., ed. *New Testament Apocrypha.* 2 vols. Introduction by E. Hennecke. Philadelphia: Westminster Press, 1965.

Steele, Francisca Maria, ed. and trans. *The Life and Visions of St. Hildegarde.* London: Heath, Cranton and Ousely, 1914.

Talbot, C. H., ed. and trans. *The Anglo-Saxon Missionaries in Germany.* New York: Sheed and Ward, 1954.

_____. *The Life of Christina of Markyate, A Twelfth Century Recluse.* Oxford: Clarendon Press, 1959.

Wilson, Katharina M. *Medieval Women Writers.* Athens: University of Georgia Press, 1984.

_____, trans. *The Dramas of Hrotsvit of Gandersheim.* Matrologia Latina. Saskatoon, Saskatchewan: Peregina Publishing Co., 1985.

Wilson-Kastner, Patricia et al., eds. *A Lost Tradition: Women Writers of the Early Church.* Lanham, Mass.: University Press of America, 1981.

II. 1200–1500 C.E.

Armstrong, Regis J., O.F.M., and Ignatius C. Brady, O.F.M., trans. *Francis and Clare: The Complete Works*. Classics of Western Spirituality Series. New York: Paulist Press, 1982.

Bogin, Meg. *The Women Troubadours*. New York and London: Paddington Press, 1976.

Brunn, Emilie Zum, and Georgette Epiney-Burgard. *Women Mystics in Medieval Europe*. Translated by Sheila Hughes. New York: Paragon House, 1989.

Canton, William. *The Story of Saint Elizabeth of Hungary*. London: Herbert and Daniel, 1912.

Christine de Pizan. *The Book of the City of Ladies*. Translated by Earl Jeffrey Richards. New York: Persea Books, 1982.

Colledge, Edmund, O.S.A., and James Walsh, S.J., trans. *Julian of Norwich: Showings*. Classics of Western Spirituality Series. New York: Paulist Press, 1978.

Dronke, Peter. *Women Writers of the Middle Ages: A Critical Study of Texts from Perpetua (t 203) to Marguerite Porete (t 1310)*. Cambridge: Cambridge University Press, 1984.

Gardner, Edmund. *The Cell of Knowledge: Seven Early English Mystical Treatises*. London: Duffield, 1910; reprint, New York: Cooper Square, 1966.

Gertrude of Helfta. *The Exercises of Saint Gertrude*. Translated by a Benedictine nun of Regina Laudis. Westminster, Md.: Newman Press, 1956.

Greenspan, Karen. "Erklaerung des Vaterunsers: A Critical Edition of a Fifteenth Century Mystical Treatise by Magdalena Beutler of Freiburg." Ph.D. thesis, University of Massachusetts at Amherst, 1984.

Halligan, Theresa A., ed. *The Booke of Gostlye Grace of Mechtild of Hackeborn*. Toronto: Pontifical Institute of Medieval Studies, 1979.

Harris, Marguerite Tjader, ed. *Birgitta of Sweden: Life and Selected Revelations*. Classics of Western Spirituality Series. New York: Paulist Press, 1990.

Hart, Mother Columba, O.S.B., trans. *Hadewijch: The Complete Works*. Classics of Western Spirituality Series. New York: Paulist Press, 1980.

Hughes, Serge, trans. *Catherine of Genoa: Purgation and Purgatory, The Spiritual Dialogue*. Classics of Western Spirituality Series. New York: Paulist Press, 1979.

Julian of Norwich. *Revelations of Divine Love*. Translated by Clifton Wolters. New York: Scholars Press, 1986.

Kempe, Margery. *The Book of Margery Kempe*. Edited by Sanford Brown Meech. London: Oxford University Press, 1940.

Lachance, Paul. *The Spiritual Journey of the Blessed Angela of Foligno According to the Memorial of Frater A. Studia Antoniana* 29. Rome: Pontificum Athenaeum Antonianum, 1984.

May, William Harold. "The Confession of Prous Boneta Heretic and Heresiarch." In *Essays in Medieval life and Thought*. Edited by John H. Mundy, Richard W. Emery, and Benjamin N. Nelson. New York: Biblo and Tannen, 1965.

Menzies, Lucy, trans. *The Revelations of Mechthild of Magdeburg, or the Flowing Light of the Godhead*. London: Longman Green and Co., 1953.

Noffke, Suzanne, O.P., trans. *Catherine of Siena: The Dialogue*. Classics of Western Spirituality Series. New York: Paulist Press, 1980.

Petroff, Elizabeth Alvida. *Medieval Women's Visionary Literature*. Oxford: Oxford University Press, 1986.

Sijthoff, A. W. *Medieval Netherlands Religious Literature*. Translated and introduced by Eric Colledge. New York: London House and Maxwell, 1965.

Steegman, Mary G., trans. *The Book of Divine Consolation of the Blessed Angela of Foligno*. New York: Cooper Square Publishers, Inc., 1966.

Wilson, Katharina M. *Medieval Women Writers*. Athens: University of Georgia Press, 1984.

III. 1500–1800 C.E.

Bainton, Roland. *Women of the Reformation in Germany and Italy*. Minneapolis: Augsburg, 1971.

_____. *Women of the Reformation in France and England*. Minneapolis: Augsburg, 1973.

_____. *Women of the Reformation from Spain to Scandinavia*. Minneapolis: Augsburg, 1977.

Clark, Adam. *Memoirs of the Wesley Family; Collected Principally from Original Documents*. New York: The Methodist Episcopal Church at the Conference Office, 1832.

Fletcher, Mary Bosanquet. *The Journal of Mary Bosanquet Fletcher*. In *The Life of Mrs. Mary Fletcher* by Henry Moore. 3rd edition. London: Methodist Conference Office, 1818.

Guyon, J. M. B. de la Mothe. *Spiritual Torrents*. Translated by A. W. Marston. London: H. R. Allenson, Limited, 1908.

Hasting, Selina, Countess of Huntingdon. *The Life and Times of Selina, Countess of Huntingdon*. 2 vols. London: William Edward Painter, 1844.

Hill, Bridget. *Eighteenth-Century Women: An Anthology*. London: George Allen & Unwin, 1984.

Johnson, Dale A. *Women in English Religion 1700–1925*. Volume 10, Studies in Women and Religion. New York: The Edwin Mellen Press, 1983.

Kavanaugh, Kieran, O.C.D., and Otilio Rodrigues, O.C.D. *Teresa of Avila: The Interior Castle*. Classics of Western Spirituality Series. New York: Paulist Press, 1979.

Thibert, Peronne Marie, V.H.M. *Francis de Sales, Jane de Chantal: Letters of Spiritual Direction*. Classics of Western Spirituality Series. New York: Paulist Press, 1988.

Trueblood, Alan S., trans. *A Sor Juana Anthology*. Cambridge, Mass.: Harvard University Press, 1988.

United Society. *Testimonies concerning the Character and Ministry of Mother Ann Lee and the First Witnesses of the Gospel of Christ's Second Appearing; Given by Some of the Aged Brethren and Sisters of the United Society, including a Few Sketches of Their Own Religious Experience: Approved by the Church*. Albany: Packard & Van Benthuysen, 1827.

V. 1800 C.E.

Andrews, William L. *Sisters of the Spirit: Three Black Women's Autobiographies of the Nineteenth Century*. Bloomington: Indiana University Press, 1986.

Booth, Catherine. *Life and Death, Being Reports of Addresses Delivered in London.* London: Salvation Army, 1883.

_____. *Papers on Aggressive Christianity.* London: Partridge, 1980.

DuBois, Ellen Carol. *Elizabeth Cady Stanton, Susan B. Anthony: Correspondence, Writings, Speeches.* Studies in the Life of Women Series. New York: Schocken Books, 1987.

Greene, Dana. *Lucretia Mott: Her Complete Speeches and Sermons.* New York: The Edwin Mellen Press, 1980.

Harkness, Georgia. *The Dark Night of the Soul.* New York: Abingdon-Cokesbury Press, 1945.

_____. *Understanding the Christian Faith.* Nashville: Abingdon Press, 1947.

_____. *Foundations of Christian Knowledge.* Nashville: Abingdon Press, 1955.

Johnson, Dale A. *Women in English Religion 1700–1925.* Volume 10, Studies in Women and Religion. New York: The Edwin Mellen Press, 1983.

Kelly, Elin M., ed. *Elizabeth Seton: Selected Writings.* Volume 5, Sources of American Spirituality Series. New York: Paulist Press, 1986.

Oden, Thomas C. *Phoebe Palmer: Selected Writings.* Sources of American Spirituality Series. New York: Paulist Press, 1988.

Palmer, Phoebe. *Promise of the Father: Or, A Neglected Specialty of the Last Days.* Boston: Segen, 1859.

Ramabai, Pandita. *A Testimony.* 9th ed. Kedgaon, Poona Dist., India: Ramabai Mukti Mission, 1968.

Rogal, Samuel J. *Sisters of Sacred Song: A Selected Listing of Women Hymnodists in Great Britain and America.* New York: Garland Publishing, 1981.

Smith, Amanda Berry. *An Autobiography: The Story of the Lord's Dealings with Mrs. Amanda Smith, The Colored Lady Evangelist.* Chicago: Meyer & Brother, Publishers, 1893; reprint, New York: Garland Publishing, Inc., 1987.

Smith, Hannah Whitall. *The Open Secret; or, the Bible Explaining Itself.* Tarrytown, N.Y.: Fleming Revell Company, 1885.

Stanton, Elizabeth Cady. *The Woman's Bible.* Salem, N.H.: Ayer Company Publishers, 1972.

Willard, Francis. *Woman in the Pulpit.* Boston: Lothrop, 1888.